THE SILENT AND THE DAMNED

THE SILENT AND THE DAMNED

The Murder of Mary Phagan and the Lynching of Leo Frank

ROBERT SEITZ FREY
AND
NANCY THOMPSON-FREY

Foreword by
JOHN SEIGENTHALER

MADISON BOOKS
Lanham • New York • London

Copyright © 1988 by

Robert Seitz Frey & Nancy Thompson-Frey

Madison Books

4720 Boston Way
Lanham, MD 20706

3 Henrietta Street
London WC2E 8LU England

Printed in the United States of America

British Cataloging in Publication Information Available

Library of Congress Cataloging-in-Publication Data

Frey, Robert Seitz, 1955-
The silent and the damned.

Bibliography: p.
Includes index.
1. Murder—Georgia—Atlanta—Case studies.
2. Phagan, Mary, d. 1913.   3. Frank, Leo, 1884-1915.
I. Thompson-Frey, Nancy, 1955-   . II. Title.
HV6534.A7F74   1987   364.1'523'09758231   87-24758
ISBN 0-8191-6491-7

Madison
★ BOOKS ★

To Becky, Joshua, and Jeremy
for being, and being ours

CONTENTS

LIST OF ILLUSTRATIONS

ACKNOWLEDGMENTS

This is to express appreciation to Dr. George L. Berlin of Baltimore Hebrew College for his assistance in developing the primary thematic contours of this work.

We owe a debt of gratitude to Gary S. Hauk, Reference Librarian at Pitts Theology Library of Emory University in Atlanta. Mr. Hauk went far beyond the call in answering the request for information on the Frank case.

We also would like to thank William R. Glass of Emory University, Professor Stanley N. Rosenbaum of Dickinson College, Ms Pat Olson of the *Christian Century*, Ms Joy K. Floden of the Central Congregational Church in Atlanta, and Dr. Joseph Troutman of the Atlanta University Center.

Much appreciated were the efforts of Granville Meader, Ph.D., in reading this manuscript in its early stages and providing words of support throughout the writing effort.

Special thanks go to the staff members of the Atlanta Historical Society, the Georgia Department of Archives and History, the Special Collections Department of Emory University, the Atlanta Office of the Anti-Defamation League, and the Harvard Law School Library. People at each of these institutions and offices were very helpful in facilitating our research efforts. Michael Winograd of ADL in Atlanta and Dale Schwartz, an attorney with Troutman, Sanders, Lockerman & Ashmore in Atlanta, gave personal attention to our questions as did Virginia Shadron of the

Georgia Department of Archives and History and Judith Mellins of Harvard Law School. John L. Seigenthaler, president and publisher of the *Nashville Tennessean*, was extremely generous in sharing his time and insight into the Frank case with us. Beverly Burnett of the *Tennessean* was also very helpful.

We would like to acknowledge the interest and enthusiasm brought to this project by Charles A. Lean, managing editor of Madison Books. Lastly, we thank Roy Hoopes for adding his editorial polish and personal interest and knowledge to our manuscript.

FOREWORD

By John Seigenthaler

It was a dramatic murder trial that marked a sad moment of history in the annals of the American system of justice; a controversy that would make and break careers of public figures; an event that would stir the smoldering coals of anti-Semitism in Atlanta, ruin the cultural reputation of a great city for a decade and subvert the administration of justice in the state of Georgia for more than 70 years. Finally, a book can record the last chapter: truth exposed, injustice branded, wrong righted.

Imagine the circumstances: a 13-year-old girl murdered, her mauled body found hidden in the basement of the pencil factory where she worked and had come one day to claim her paycheck.

The physical evidence indicated that she was strangled, that she was not raped, and that she was robbed of the pittance of her paycheck. Two barely legible, hardly literate handwritten notes were located by police near the body.

Overnight, little Mary Phagan, the victim of brutal murder, became a national heroine. And within a fortnight Leo Frank, the Jewish manager of the factory accused as her murderer, became a national villain.

Tension in the community began to grow from the night the body was discovered until the morning the trial of Leo Frank began. At the time the crucial testimony was given,

crowds mobbed the streets outside the courthouse scream-
ing for the conviction and execution of "the Jew."

The chief witness against Leo Frank was Jim Conley, a
drunken janitor who was, himself, a suspect when the police
arrested him. Lies poured out of him. He had not been at
the factory that day, he said. He could not read or write
and could not have written the notes found near the body.
Five separate stories he told police as they grilled him over
several days—until, finally, with the help of the prosecutors,
he crafted a tale that was strong enough to win an indictment against Frank, his employer.

Frank, said Conley, had committed the murder and he
had enticed him, with promise of money, to help him hide
the body in the basement. Frank had dictated to him the
notes found near the body, Conley swore.

The government found witnesses to swear—falsely, it
later turned out—that Frank was a sexual deviant. It was an
attempt to make it appear that Frank had not raped the
little girl because his sexual preferences were not "normal."

His defense was strong; the evidence, with the exception
of Conley's perjury, was absurdly circumstantial; but the
mob atmosphere that surrounded the courtroom was real
and threatening.

On the morning that the guilty verdict was rendered the
trial judge, so certain that Frank would be cleared and so
fearful that the angry mob would try to lynch him, ordered
that he not enter the courtroom but be held in custody
away from the scene.

The frightened jury's verdict of "guilty" appeased the
mob's lust for the blood of "the Jew."

Almost unnoticed in the heat of the trial testimony and
clearly forgotten with the verdict, had been the brief,
virtually meaningless testimony of little Lonnie Mann, a
stuttering office boy who had worked for Leo Frank and
had been in the factory that day Mary Phagan lost her life.

The lad had been instructed by his parents not to tell

what he had seen that day and it was almost 70 years before his crucial evidence was revealed.

So Frank was sentenced to hang. The governor of Georgia conducted his own inquiry into the facts and, convinced that Frank was not guilty, commuted the sentence to life imprisonment.

Once more, mob rule exploded. The residence of the governor had to be protected by a ring of security guards. The governor left the state and vacationed in California to evade the mob. His decision robbed the scaffold briefly—but permanently robbed the governor of a brilliant political future.

The mob was to be heard from one more time in the Frank case. Shortly after he entered prison, Leo Frank was the victim of a brutal assault by a convict who sought to "avenge" Mary Phagan. Frank survived the knife wound to his throat. But later a mob broke into prison, kidnapped him, drove him to a field opposite Mary Phagan's home and lynched him.

It was a case with historic consequences. As the career of Gov. John Marshall Slaton ended with his efforts to save Leo Frank's life, the career of Tom Watson, the populist race-baiter and anti-Semite, was made. He was washed into the U. S. Senate on the wave of hate rhetoric he spewed in the aftermath of the deaths of Mary Phagan and Leo Frank. Many leading Jewish families deserted Atlanta in the wake of the murder trial and subsequent lynching. And the Anti-Defamation League of B'nai B'rith was born in reaction to the outrageous flood of anti-Semitic propaganda that surrounded the Frank case.

This is but a brief, admittedly judgmental synopsis of a tragic miscarriage of justice. But the full story is told with calm, careful deliberation by Robert Seitz Frey and Nancy Thompson-Frey, authors who have thoroughly researched and faithfully related events that rocked the state of Georgia and shocked the nation more than seven decades ago.

It is a story that has previously attracted the interest of

authors. Books by Harry Golden and Leonard Dinnerstein published in the mid-1960s called attention to the then almost-forgotten case.

But this work by Robert and Nancy Frey is the first book published since Alonzo Mann, the former office boy, came forward with his long-held secret.

And this volume also is the first to analyze the mostly indolent, ignorant and, at times, cowardly response of the Christian church media when its influence might have pointed to injustice and saved a human life.

A word of caution about the account. It gives far too much credit to this writer for the journalistic development of the Alonzo Mann story that led to the posthumous pardon of Leo Frank. A team of journalists who are my colleagues at *The Tennessean* deserve the lion's share of the credit. The leader of that team was Jerry Thompson whose reporter's instincts led him unerringly to Alonzo Mann. He was supported in his investigation by Robert Sherborne, Sandra Roberts and Nancy Rhoda. The team's work was coordinated by Frank Ritter, our paper's deputy managing editor. Alonzo Mann's courage and determination to tell his story before his death was, of course, the vital link in making the pardon possible. Two Nashville lawyers, Bill Willis, counsel for *The Tennessean* who advised the team of journalists, and John Jay Hooker Jr., who at our request and at his own expense, took Alonzo Mann before the Georgia pardoning authorities, also contributed to our work. We were aided by many others who knew of the injustice that had occurred and were anxious to have it righted. They include, most significantly, Bill Gralnick of the American Jewish Committee and Randall Falk, Rabbi, of The Temple Ohabai Sholom in Nashville. And all of us who worked on the journalistic enterprise admired the perseverance and dedication of Dale Schwartz and Charles Wittenstein, the Atlanta lawyers who never gave up hope of winning a pardon for Leo Frank.

I dwell on these debts not out of any sense of false

modesty, and certainly not in ingratitude to the authors of this fine book, but to give a brief, perhaps, unimportant dimension and a slightly different perspective to one small aspect of their work.

Leo Frank was, as the authors state, the American Dreyfus. We must live with the smear of his unjust death. And this book will help us recall that our potential for evil is imminent when racist or anti-Semitic poisons bubble from beneath the surfaces of our national psyche. Thankfully, at long last, this book can be written recording that the state of Georgia finally recognized and wiped out the stain of mob rule. As slow and as grudging and as guarded as the pardon was in coming, it reminds us all that injustice will never be secure so long as good men and women pursue justice.

INTRODUCTION

On March 11, 1986, the State of Georgia pardoned Leo Frank. Seventy-three years earlier, on August 25, 1913, Frank had been found guilty of murdering thirteen-year-old Mary Phagan. And it was, to say the least, an unusual trial. It took place in Atlanta only forty-eight years after the end of the Civil War in an atmosphere of mob hostility and violence. During the entire month of the trial, the angry citizens in the street and the courtroom demanded a verdict of guilty. The jury was scared, the judge was scared, and the prosecutors were scared.

The Ku Klux Klan had been officially disbanded by Imperial Wizard Nathan Bedford Forest in 1869, but its spirit still lived in the South. In fact, the K.K.K. would be officially revived two years after the trial, and the Mary Phagan murder played a part in the formation of one of its Georgia chapters. The Klan mentality permeated the atmosphere that dominated the Frank trial. It might have been thought a black man was on trial for raping a white girl. The fact is, the charge of rape was never brought. Leo Frank was white and the man who gave the highly suspect and contradictory testimony that doomed the white man was black. There has never been a trial quite like it in the United States, and it is hoped there never will be another.

What made this hideous stain on our legal system possible was the same thing that made the Dreyfus Affair possible in late nineteenth century France: Leo Frank was a Jew, and in pre-World War I Atlanta, the curse of racial and class prejudice was not directed solely at blacks. Kikes, Wops, Micks, Niggers, the White Trash: they were the enemies. And from the end of the Civil War until well into the twentieth century, the southern Establishment knew its enemies and it knew how to hate. Blacks were to be feared and hated the most, of course, but they at least knew their place and rarely caused trouble. But the Jews! Many of them were smarter and could make money more readily than the Gentiles, even marry Establishment sons and daughters. Maybe they were the real enemy—the ones to really hate.

And it all seemed to boil to a head in the summer of 1913. The fact that Frank was convicted by a black man, who, by his own confession to a friend, had had too much corn liquor the day he said he witnessed Frank's seemingly guilty actions, made no difference. Every effort to appeal the verdict—even two petitions to the Supreme Court—failed. It was not until 1986 that the State of Georgia admitted its error. But by then, most of the principals in the case were dead. Even Alonzo Mann—who was a very frightened fourteen-year-old boy on the day of the crime and too scared to tell the truth at the trial—was dead. It was his testimony, brought to the surface in 1982 by the then-publisher of the *Nashville Tennessean* and present editorial director of *USA Today*, John Seigenthaler, that made it impossible for the Georgia Board of Pardons and Paroles not to reconsider the Frank case. But Mann died in 1985, at the age of eighty-seven, unaware that the man who all his life he had known was innocent was finally pardoned.

To show how deep the emotions from the original crime still run, when Mary Phagan's great-niece was asked after the pardon who she felt killed her great-aunt in 1913, she said quite simply that the evidence shows the murderer was Leo M. Frank.

As for Frank, what Mary Phagan's relatives thought or the Georgia parole board decided made little difference. He had been dead seventy-one years, the only Jew ever lynched in America.

Despite all the evidence suggesting his innocence, Leo Frank seemed destined to die to atone for the death of pretty little Mary Phagan. But what really happened at the pencil factory in Atlanta on that Saturday morning in April 1913?

Chapter 1

THE MURDER

Nightwatchman Newt Lee made his way down the ladder into the dreary basement of the National Pencil Factory in the early hours of Sunday morning. His step was faulty, and he missed the last rung. The small gas jet which burned at the bottom of the ladder had been turned down very low. Lee did not usually go all the way down into the basement, but this night he had to use the "colored" toilet.

Gripping his lantern, he peered about the large room, expecting nothing. Cinders from the furnace crunched under his shoes as the old man made his way around in the gloomy dampness. The night had been quiet.

After coming out of the toilet, his eyes fell upon a frightening sight. Holding the lantern a bit higher so as to get the most light from the soot-blackened globe, Newt Lee saw a body lying face up in the sawdust. Lee was terribly frightened. It was about 3:20 A.M., Sunday, April 27, 1913, when he called the Atlanta police station and told Call Officer Anderson that there was the body of a young white woman at the National Pencil Factory.

Three Atlanta policemen, an ex-county policeman, and a newspaper correspondent from the *Atlanta Constitution* hurried to the building on Forsyth Street. Sergeant Dobbs later testified that Newt Lee, a black man who had worked about three weeks at the factory, was not frightened or trembling when the officers arrived. Atlanta newspaper accounts tell another story: Lee was said to display a wild and excited manner and to have had trouble finding the body once the police arrived. When the police lanterns finally picked up the body in their lights, it was not a pretty sight. It was lying face down and when Sergeant Brown looked more closely, he exclaimed: "This is nothing but a child."

The child was cold. Unable to tell whether the body was black or white, Sergeant Brown took some wood shavings from the floor and rubbed the girl's face with them. But he still could not be positive; so he rolled the girl's stocking down from her right knee: the skin was white.

The body was extremely dirty. Dirt was inside the dead girl's mouth, and her tongue was swollen and protruding from between her teeth. She had been strangled to death. A piece of heavy twine was tied around her neck, and a strip from her underskirt was tied around her neck, too. Her hands were folded beneath her body, but they were not tied. Her clothing had been torn and several pieces were missing. On the back of her head at the left was a wound, and there were cuts on her face and forehead.

A pink parasol was found near the trap door over by the ladder, though some sources say the parasol was discovered in the elevator shaft. One shoe and a man's bloody handkerchief were discovered in a trash pile by the furnace in the basement. Two handwritten notes were found near the body, one about three feet away and the other some distance further. On the girl's left wrist was a gold bracelet, now bent. A signet ring with the letter "W" was still on the little finger of her right hand.

Miss Grace Hicks, an employee of the pencil company, was brought to the factory to identify the body. When she saw the corpse she fainted. But after being revived she identified it as Mary Phagan, who had worked at the same machine with her in the "metal" room. Efforts to contact the factory's superintendent, Leo Frank, were unsuccessful until a few hours later in the morning. While still in the factory basement, the police forced Newt Lee to panto-mime exactly how he had discovered the body. Despite a thorough search of the basement by police that morning Mary's silver mesh handbag, which held a few dollars, was missing and never found.

It was noted that the rear door leading from the basement to a generally unfrequented alleyway had been forced open from the inside. The staple, which held the lock in place, had been pried off with an iron bar and there were several bloody fingermarks that had been made in pushing the sliding door back. After an investigation at the murder scene by members of Coroner Paul Donehoo's staff, the body was removed to P. J. Bloomfield's undertaker establish-ment on South Pryor Street.

This apparent murder was not the first tragedy that had taken place inside the dark walls of the ancient Venable Building, then occupied by the National Pencil Factory. Older citizens of Atlanta recalled a serious fire there, when the building had been used as a livery stable. A gentleman by the name of Pettigrew and one of his rescuers died from their burns, and Pettigrew's money had been stolen, pre-sumably during the rescue attempt. Besides the fire, at least a half dozen fatal shootings had occurred within fifty yards of the building.

Later there was some newspaper speculation that this murder might join the ranks of Atlanta's unsolved crimes. For example, the dead body of Miss Sophie Kloecker "was found floating in the lake at Lakewood park on May 24, 1904. . . . So mystifying was the affair that the coroner held two inquests with two separate juries, a thing that had never been done before" in Atlanta. Another unsolved case was that of Mrs. Mary Lilly, who had been strangled to death with a pair of tongs on May 12, 1906.

*
**

Saturday, April 26, 1913, was overcast and gloomy, but the weather did not dampen the holiday atmosphere in Atlanta. It was Confederate Memorial Day, a holiday tradition that began in 1866, and almost everybody went to the parades downtown. And there was also an opera and the baseball game between the Atlanta Crackers and the Birmingham Barons of the Southern League. Throughout the South, Memorial Day commemorated the War Between the States and the veterans of Robert E. Lee. A festive spirit ran high. School children in Atlanta marched in the big parade along with the Seventeenth Regiment and its band. Proud, battle-scarred veterans of Lee's army marched too.

The Atlanta Crackers ball club, organized in 1901, was headed by three well-known Atlantans, including a lawyer and a manufacturer. In 1907 and 1909, William A. "Billy" Smith had managed the fledgling club to Southern League pennants; and at the beginning of the 1913 baseball season, the league imposed a limit of $300 per month on players' salaries and strongly encouraged managers to develop the younger players.

The spirit of the War Between the States was very much alive in the hearts of many Atlantans. It still is, in the South. Georgia had been the fourth state to secede from the Union on January 19, 1861. Lincoln had been burned in effigy in Atlanta the December before. The Gate City served as the major supply and distribution center for the Confederacy of Jefferson Davis. On November 14 and 15, 1864, the Union army of General William Tecumseh Sherman set fire to Atlanta as it left for its "march to the sea." The devastation was so complete that only four hundred structures remained standing when Sherman's troops left. In the decades that followed, Atlanta built itself from the ashes of indignation and defeat to become the flower of the South. A new city seal, "Resurgens Atlanta," was adopted in 1887. It depicts a phoenix rising from the flames of Sherman's destruction. In July 1898, General John B. Gordon led a reunion of thirty thousand Confederate veterans in the "Gate City of the South."

On that Saturday morning in 1913, Mary Phagan, wearing a lavender dress with white lace trim and a fine blue hat with flowers, took a streetcar into town from her home in the Bellwood (Bankhead) suburb of the city. She was on her way to the National Pencil Factory to collect her pay and then to watch the Memorial Day parade. Mary, who was about one month away from her fourteenth birthday, worked in the "metal" room on the second floor of the factory. She was among the hundred or so young girls and women who worked for the pencil company. Her job was to put erasers into the metal holders on the pencils. The National Pencil Factory manufactured lead pencils known as "Magnolias" and "Jeffersons."

That same day, a meeting of fifteen hundred sociological workers was held in the Auditorium in Atlanta. The agenda of this Southern Sociological Congress[1] included an attack on child labor. The Phagan girl worked for about twelve cents an hour at the National Pencil Factory. This was not unusual: many factories in the South and all over America employed children at low wages in the early years of this century.

The English Avenue streetcar picked Mary up near her house at 146 Lindsay Street at about 11:50 that Saturday morning. Factory employees were usually paid at noon on Saturdays, but this Saturday, being a holiday, notices had been posted that pay envelopes would be available on Friday evening. Mary did not know that her pay of $1.20 had been ready on Friday. She had not been able to work for several days because the shipment of metal to be used for the pencil tips had not arrived.

Leo Frank, the superintendent of the National Pencil Company, was at the factory that Saturday preparing the weekly financial report. He had planned to go to the Cracker ballgame in the afternoon, but the threat of rain kept him inside. When Mary Phagan entered Mr. Frank's office on the second floor of the factory at around noon, she asked him for her pay envelope. Neither knowing her name nor asking for it, Frank simply requested her employee number. He went to the cash box and handed the envelope to the girl. Mary asked Mr. Frank if the metal for the pencils had come in yet. He told her "no."

Although many claimed to have thought they saw her, no one ever testified to seeing Mary Phagan alive after she left Leo Frank's office that Saturday.

When Mary did not return home that Saturday evening, her mother and stepfather became worried. She had never been known to stay away at night. Police headquarters were notified and a lookout notice was put on the bulletin board. At daybreak on Sunday morning, a messenger came to the Coleman house to let them know that Mary had been found dead in the pencil factory. Fannie Coleman, the girl's mother, fainted and did not recover for about an hour. Then she required constant attention by a physician.

Mary Phagan was born on June 1, 1900, in Marietta, Georgia, to John and Frances Phagan—at least that is the date that appears on the girl's tombstone. However, her mother testified that she was one month away from her fourteenth birthday. This would put the year of her birth at 1899. The family later moved from Marietta to Bellwood, near Atlanta, and John and the children worked for the Bellwood Mill. John Phagan died in 1911. Within one year, Mrs. Phagan married another millworker named J. William Coleman, and by May of 1913 he was working for the Sanitary Department for the City of Atlanta. The family included two girls, Mary and Ollie, and three boys, Ben, Joshua, and Charlie. Ollie Mae Phagan was eighteen when her sister died. She worked as a salesgirl at Rich Brothers store. Ben Phagan was a sailor onboard the *U.S.S. Franklin* at the time of his sister's death.

Mary was considered the prettiest girl in the neighborhood and was liked by everyone who knew her. She had been cast as "Sleeping Beauty" on the Christmas Eve before her death in a play put on by her church, the First Christian Church, near Atlanta. She was also a member of Pastor L. O. Bricker's Bible School. As far as her parents knew, Mary was not in love with anyone. They did not allow her to have sweethearts or to receive male callers at the house. She was said to be a "model girl"—bright, eager, and cheerful.

With the discovery of Mary Phagan's body that Sunday morning in April, a public delirium began in Atlanta that continued for more than two years. Almost six thousand people, including family, friends, and curious spectators, visited Bloomfield's to see the murdered girl's corpse. Police said it was the largest crowd ever to view a murder victim's body in the City of Atlanta.

W. J. Phagan, Mary's grandfather, declared that "the living God will see to it that the brute is found and punished according to his sin." Grandfather Phagan was terribly disturbed by Mary's death and there was some concern that his health would not permit his attending the funeral. W. J. Phagan died the following year at the age of sixty.

Four men were under arrest by Monday evening. One was Newt Lee, the nightwatchman. The other three men arrested were John M. Gantt, Arthur Mullinax, and Gordon Bailey. Gantt was a former timekeeper and chief clerk at the National Pencil Company. A cash shortage had been discovered which Gantt was unwilling to make right and he was discharged on April 7. Gantt later testified that he knew Mary Phagan prior to her employment at the factory. Mullinax was a streetcar conductor in Atlanta; Bailey, a black man, was an elevator operator at the pencil factory.

Following his arrest as he stepped off a streetcar in Marietta, Gantt admitted that he knew the murdered girl and was in the factory on Saturday to collect a pair of shoes he had left behind when he had been discharged. Superintendent Leo Frank corroborated Gantt's story about going to the factory about 6:00 P.M. to retrieve his shoes.

Detectives had evidence that Mullinax, who worked as a substitute conductor on the English Avenue streetcar, was well acquainted with Mary Phagan. They were often seen talking to one another on the girl's ride from home to the pencil factory. Mullinax was twenty-eight years old.

Leo Frank was also questioned by police on the Monday morning after the murder, but not placed under arrest. He returned home at noon. Attorneys Luther Z. Rosser Sr. and Herbert Haas represented Frank during the questioning. (The name *Haas* is a very old Jewish name in Atlanta, appearing in records as early as 1847.)

Because of the unrest among the female employees at the pencil factory, the company was closed for business that Monday. The same day, a jury impaneled by the coroner and accompanied by three or four policemen, searched the dark basement of the pencil factory for incriminating evidence. The machine room on the second floor was also examined. Several strands of blond hair were found clinging to a lathe and there were tiny blood stains on the floor. The machine room was close to the office of Leo Frank.

City detectives were puzzled by the two notes written in lead pencil found near the Phagan girl's body. One note read: "He said he wood love me land down like the night witch did it but that long tall black negro did buy his slef." The other said: "mam that negro hire down here did this i went to make water and he push me down that hole a long tall negro black that hoo it wase long sleam tall negro i wright while play with me."

On Monday evening Leo Frank hired the Pinkerton Detective Agency in Atlanta to assist the police in solving the murder at his factory. That same night John Gantt was put through a grueling third-degree interrogation at the police station in an attempt to wring a confession from his lips. But Gantt maintained he was innocent.

Tuesday morning's *Atlanta Constitution* carried the announcement of a reward on page one. One thousand dollars was to be paid to those people providing information justifying the arrest and leading to the conviction of the murderer or murderers of Mary Phagan. That same morning, Mary Phagan's funeral party arrived at the Citizens' Cemetery in Marietta. Hundreds of men and women and boys and girls followed the train of carriages with the white coffin to the Second Baptist Church. The choir sang "Rock of Ages," which was frequently interspersed with the sobs of Fannie Coleman. Reverend Linkous prayed for the police of Atlanta. He asked the gatherers not to hold too much rancor in their hearts for the "imp of satan" who had killed the little girl. Mary's aunt, Miss Lizzie Phagan, fainted and had to be carried from the small country church.

When Dr. Linkous finished, the casket was opened one last time. One of the members of the congregation, a sunburned farmer, growled that "the nigger [Newt Lee] knows all about it." "If we had that scoundrel in Marietta, we'd know how to get him to talk. We'd make him be polite."

When the first shovelful of earth was thrown into the grave, Mrs. Coleman broke down completely. "She was taken away when the spring was coming—the spring that was so like her. Oh and she wanted to see the spring. She loved it—it loved her."

"Goodby, Mary, . . . Goodby. It's too big a hole to put you in, though. It's so big—b-i-g, and you were so little— my own little Mary!"

At least, that was the way the *Atlanta Constitution* reported the funeral on April 30th. The front page had a photograph of the flower-strewn gravesite. A cross had been *drawn* along the bottom edge of the picture. Later, the Marietta Camp No. 763 of the United Confederate Veterans erected a marker at the head of the little girl's final resting place.

Citizens' Cemetery in Marietta lies adjacent to Confederate Cemetery. Mary's grave is now surrounded by other members of the Phagan family—her sister Ollie (who died at the age of sixty-eight in 1963), her aunt Lizzie (who died at the age of sixty-three in 1949), her mother (who died at the age of seventy-three in 1947), and her grandfather. Mrs. Coleman's tombstone is engraved with the words "Mother of Mary Phagan." Mary's stepfather is buried in College Park, Georgia.

A marble slab about six feet long covers Mary's grave. On it are inscribed these haunting words:

IN THIS DAY OF FADING IDEALS AND DISAPPEARING LAND MARKS, LITTLE MARY PHAGAN'S HEROISM IS AN HEIRLOOM THAN WHICH THERE IS NOTHING MORE PRECIOUS AMONG THE OLD RED HILLS OF GEORGIA.

SLEEP, LITTLE GIRL; SLEEP IN YOUR HUMBLE GRAVE BUT IF THE ANGELS ARE GOOD TO YOU IN THE REALMS BEYOND THE TROUBLE [sic] SUNSET AND THE CLOUDED STARS, THEY WILL LET YOU KNOW THAT MANY AN ACHING HEART IN GEORGIA BEATS FOR YOU, AND MANY A TEAR, FROM EYES UNUSED TO WEEP, HAS PAID YOU A TRIBUTE TOO SACRED FOR WORDS.

While Marietta mourned the loss of the beloved child, the police investigation continued. Every lead was followed, including the possibility that Mary Phagan had been the victim of white slave traders. New evidence emerged against nightwatchman Newt Lee. During each night of his duty at the pencil factory, he was supposed to punch the timepiece every thirty minutes. On the Saturday night of the murder, Lee had punched the clock every half-hour up until 9:32 P.M. Then, between 9:30 that evening and 3:00 A.M. Sunday, there were three irregularities in the punch tape of the timeclock, which showed that Lee did not punch in every half-hour as he was supposed to have done. Of special interest was the fact that Lee failed to punch the timepiece between two and three o'clock Sunday morning, the immediate time before which Mary Phagan's body was reportedly discovered. In addition, police found a blood-soaked shirt at Newt Lee's home on Hendrix Avenue in Atlanta. The watchman claimed not to have seen that shirt for two years.

Around noon on Tuesday, April 29, Leo Frank was working in the offices of the pencil company. Obviously the murder of an employee in the factory weighed heavily in his thoughts. Suddenly, Detectives Starnes and Black of the Atlanta police department appeared at his office and arrested Frank. He submitted to the officers willingly—and it would be the last day he would ever work at the factory. He could hardly have imagined the whirlwind of events soon to unfold.

That same afternoon, Frank and Lee were given the third degree at police headquarters by various officials, including Chief Newport Lanford, Chief James Beavers, and Pinkerton Detective Scott. They were interrogated at the same time in the same room on the third floor of the station, and at one point, they were left alone in the hope that Frank would be able to extract more information from Lee. He failed.

Chief Beavers had a checkered career with the Atlanta police department. He assumed the position of police chief on August 11, 1911, but resigned four years later rather than be demoted for official incompetence. In November 1917, he was reinstated as police chief after charges against him were dropped. In 1923, he was suspended from the force by the Atlanta mayor, only to return triumphantly to power in early 1927.

During questioning, Leo Frank admitted that he had been alone in the factory between 4:00 and 6:00 P.M. on Saturday, working on the office books and reports. However, throughout that Memorial Day several people were in and out of the factory. Two mechanics, Harry Denham and John Arthur White, were working on the fourth floor of the building until about four o'clock that afternoon. The daytime watchman was there, in addition to N. V. Darley, an assistant superintendent, and Hattie Hall, a stenographer who had helped Frank with paperwork in the morning. Mr. Darley was manager of the Georgia Cedar Company, a branch of the National Pencil Company. Another person who came to the factory that Memorial Day was Mrs. J. A. White. She brought her husband's lunch.

Questioning further revealed that Newt Lee arrived for work around 4:00 P.M. that Saturday, but because Frank had decided not to go to the ballgame and because it was a holiday, Lee was given permission to leave until 6:00 P.M. At six o'clock, Lee came back to the factory and John Gantt arrived at about the same time to pick up his shoes. Frank allowed Gantt to enter the factory but referred him to the nightwatchman.

Frank said he went directly home, arriving at about 6:30 P.M. He stayed there until he was called by Detective Starnes at six o'clock Sunday morning, when he was informed of the murder at the factory. The detective picked Frank up from the home of his in-laws at 68 East Georgia Avenue, where he and his wife resided, and then drove to the pencil company building at 37–41 South Forsyth Street.

During Frank's examination, his attorney, Luther Rosser, attempted to gain entrance to the interrogation room on the third floor of the police station. Access was denied. The stairway to the third floor was guarded by one Officer West. Later, Rosser and Chief Beavers argued heatedly about the lawyer's not being allowed into the room with his client.

By Tuesday evening, the day of the funeral, a charge of suspicion of murder was entered against Leo Frank.

Endnotes

1. Many local delegates to this Congress were Jewish. In a major address to the convention the president of Furman University (Greenville, South Carolina) launched a vituperative attack against Jews and Catholics, claiming Jews had failed in their stewardship.

Chapter 2

THE INDICTMENT

A major piece in the Mary Phagan puzzle was the question of whether the young girl ever left the pencil factory after she received her pay on Memorial Day. One man, Edgar Sentell, insisted that he had seen the girl at about midnight Saturday in the company of a man who looked like Arthur Mullinax. Police were not convinced of Sentell's story.

The two illiterate notes discovered beside Mary Phagan's battered body also remained a mystery. Police asked all the suspects, including Leo Frank, to write the same words that were on the two notes. One thing was certain—Mary Phagan had not written the notes. First, her penmanship and punctuation were proper. Second, even if she had been alive in the basement of the factory, it was almost pitch dark and therefore impossible to find paper and pencil and scratch out two notes, though to be sure there were pencil stubs lying all around the basement. It was, after all, a factory that manufactured lead pencils. Finally, the notes were written on *two* different types of pencil-company paper. Three handwriting experts commissioned by the *Atlanta Journal* were of the opinion that Newt Lee had written the notes.

The *Journal*, the only one of the three big Atlanta daily

papers that did not sensationalize the case, tried to steer a middle-of-the-road course in its reporting of the crime and the ensuing trial. In late April 1913, Atlanta businessmen protested the many sensational "extras" issued by the city's newspapers. The merchants felt the unwarranted sensational reporting was hurting business and that the community was being aroused to a dangerous degree.

It seemed everyone in and around Atlanta and Marietta had an opinion about the murder. The police responded to hundreds of calls and "tips." Family members also had their theories: J. W. Coleman, the dead girl's stepfather, believed that Newt Lee had killed her. According to his theory, Mary had been bound and gagged from about noon on Saturday until such time as Lee could assault and murder her when no one was at the factory.

The coroner's inquest began shortly after nine o'clock on Wednesday, April 30th. The panel hearing the testimony consisted of H. Ashford, Glenn Dewberry, J. Hood, C. Langford, John Miller, and C. Sheats. The testimony of the witnesses was less than conclusive. In this first closed-door session, Newt Lee testified that he found the body face up in the basement. The police who answered the call that Sunday morning had found the girl's body face down. When Lee called the police station to report the murder, he said he had discovered a young white woman's body in the basement. The police, on the other hand, had had great difficulty telling whether the dead girl was black or white. The differences in these stories were perplexing.

Lee also said Leo Frank called him on the telephone between 7:00 and 8:00 P.M. that Saturday night to ask if everything was all right. According to the nightwatchman, Frank had never called him from home before, which was probably not significant because Newt Lee had only worked at the pencil factory for three weeks and would have had no adequate knowledge of what normal procedure really was. W. F. Anderson, the officer who had taken Lee's call on

Sunday morning, testified before the panel that the cord around Mary Phagan's neck was six or seven feet long.

The night before the coroner's inquest, a young white man named Walter Graham smuggled a derringer revolver into a cell next to Newt Lee's at police headquarters. Tuesday night the weapon was fired and Lee was said to be very frightened for his life. Detectives questioned him about the Phagan murder shortly after the incident, but he did not change his story.

On the same day of the inquest, the City Council of Atlanta appropriated one thousand dollars for information leading to the arrest of the murderer or murderers.

One theory was that Mary had actually been drugged and the cord around her neck was a decoy. Another theory, pursued by the police, was that the murderer had planned to burn his victim in the factory furnace on Sunday morning. And Coroner Paul Donehoo decided to exhume the body of Mary Phagan to examine the contents of her stomach. Nine days after burial, her body was lifted from the grave and undigested cabbage and bread were removed from her stomach.

At two o'clock Thursday afternoon, a sixth arrest was made in the Phagan case. James Conley, a black sweeper at the National Pencil Factory, was seen washing out a shirt at a faucet behind that building. Police detectives were summoned because there were marks on the shirt resembling blood. Conley claimed they were rust stains, but the police held him until a chemical analysis could be made to determine whether the stains were in fact blood.

Late that same afternoon, Leo Frank and Newt Lee were transferred to the Fulton County jail from police headquarters on the basis of coroner's warrants; J. M. Gantt and Arthur Mullinax were released from police custody. The city detectives, the coroner, and Solicitor Dorsey all focused on building evidence to support their contention that Mary Phagan never left the pencil factory the Saturday she was killed.

At this point, Leo Frank was not a prime suspect in the case. The police detained him chiefly because they felt that he could supply valuable information leading to the killer.

Saturday, May 3rd, was a pretty day in Atlanta. The first hot spell of the year was forcing an early appearance of the straw hat and peek-a-boo waist. Famed bandmaster John Philip Sousa was in town for the Brookhaven Gun Club shoot. Sousa had one of the finest collections of guns in the world. During an interview the bandmaster was asked by a reporter what his idea of heaven was. "A horse, a dog, a gun, and a girl!", Sousa replied. As to why the girl was named last, he said that "they don't take to you like the horse or the dog."

Although Frank had not been charged with anything, support for the young Atlanta Jew was already beginning to build. The men of Gate City Lodge 144 of B'nai B'rith in Atlanta honored their fellow lodge member with the prestigious rank of president. In a letter published in the *Atlanta Journal*, Milton Klein offered strong evidence in support of Mr. Frank's character and good works. Frank, said Klein, was "the most polished of gentlemen, with the kindest of heart and the broadest of sympathy." Mr. Klein, also a member of the same B'nai B'rith lodge, pointed to Frank's great work with the employees of his factory.

Meanwhile, if the Mary Phagan murder went unsolved, it would not be for lack of effort. Moses Frank, Leo Frank's uncle, returned to Atlanta the first week in May to help establish the innocence of his nephew. Leo's uncle had been about to leave on a trip for Europe, but he changed his plans on his nephew's behalf. Solicitor General Hugh M. Dorsey of the Atlanta Circuit, the man who would later serve as prosecutor in the Frank trial, began an independent probe of the Phagan murder in early May. This was in addition to the ongoing investigations of the Atlanta city detectives and the Pinkertons employed by the National Pencil Company. And a number of private citizens who lived near the Coleman residence employed the well-known

Atlanta attorney Colonel Thomas B. Felder, who would provide assistance to the prosecution in the case.

On May 5, a young man was arrested in Houston, Texas, on suspicion of murder in the Phagan killing. Paul Beniston Bowen checked into the St. Jean Hotel on Sunday evening, May 4th, and occupied a room adjacent to Mrs. A. Blanchett. The woman told the police that Bowen's action had aroused her suspicions. She claimed she heard him say, "Why did I do it? If I could just live it over again I would not do it."

In Bowen's belongings police found letters with Atlanta postmarks and signed "Mary" or "M. P." There were also a blood-stained woman's vest, copies of Atlanta newspapers, and photographs identified as that of the murdered girl. In all, pictures of more than fifty girls were discovered in the young man's trunk. Two days later, Bowen was released for lack of evidence.

The body of Mary Phagan, which had been exhumed once under the direction of Coroner Donehoo, was removed from the grave yet a second time. The principal reason for the second exhumation was to cut some hair from the girl's head to compare with the hair found on the lathe in the "metal room" of the pencil factory.

A notable protest was lodged by the consul of Greece in Atlanta. Demetre Vafiada called the *Journal* to object to the insinuation that the cord around Mary Phagan's neck had been tied by a Greek simply because it had been fashioned in a particular way. About a hundred Atlanta Greeks had gathered the night before on Whitehall Street to protest the newspaper's headline, which linked a Greek to the murder on the basis of the knot tied around the girl's neck.

The Phagan inquest was resumed on Thursday, May 8. Testimony was heard from "Boots" Rogers, a former county policeman, who had gone with the Atlanta police in response to Newt Lee's call. It was Rogers' relative, Miss Grace Hicks, who identified the body.

Miss Corinthia Hall, an employee of the pencil factory,

declared that Mr. Frank's conduct toward the female employees was irreproachable.

"You never saw him display any undue familiarity toward any of them, did you?"

"No, sir."

"Did you ever see him chuck any of them under the chin, or try to kiss them?"

"No, sir!"

City bacteriologist and chemist Dr. Claude Smith reported the stains on Newt Lee's shirt were "probably human blood". The state-of-the art for forensic medicine in 1913 was obviously still developing. Today's analytical techniques could not only determine that a substance was human blood but what the blood type was. Also, the hair found in the second floor "metal room" where police suspected the murder had occurred could have been positively identified by today's methods. But the best testimony by friends and co-workers of the dead girl was that the hair discovered "looked like" Mary Phagan's hair.

The coroner questioned Lemmie A. Quinn, Mary Phagan's foreman in the metal department at the factory. Quinn had gone to the factory that Saturday to see Mr. Schiff to talk baseball with him. Quinn testified that he had spoken with Mr. Frank between 12:20 and 12:30 that afternoon.

Leo Frank, Newt Lee, some of the detectives, and several character witnesses were also called before the coroner on this final day of the inquest. At 6:30 Thursday evening, May 8, the Mary Phagan murder inquest drew to a close. Deputy Plennie Minor carried the news of the coroner's jury's verdict to Frank and Newt Lee. Leo Frank was in the hallway of the Tower, reading an afternoon newspaper. The deputy approached him and said the jury had ordered that he and Lee be held for an investigation by the grand jury! Newt Lee hung his head dejectedly when he heard the verdict. Leo Frank replied that it was no more than he expected.

Who was Leo Frank; and what was the nature of Atlanta's Jewish community in 1913? Generally Atlantans did not know him at all. He was not a politician or a social trendsetter. As a result, numerous rumors were circulated about his character, which the average man on the street could neither prove nor disprove. One rumor, persistently passed in various forms, was that Frank had been married to a woman in Brooklyn, New York. At the request of the *Atlanta Journal*, the *Brooklyn Eagle* investigated the rumor and found it to be untrue. No record in Brooklyn showed that Frank had ever married there.

Leo Max Frank was born in Cuero, Texas, on April 17, 1884. The little town (also called Paris) lies within a hundred miles of San Antonio. He was the son of Rae and Rudolph Frank. When Leo was several months old, the family moved to Brooklyn. His father, who was 67 in 1913, was a traveling salesman. Leo attended the public schools and Pratt Institute in Brooklyn. Dr. Luther Halsey Gulick was principal of the Pratt Institute when Leo was a student there and Miss Annie Carroll Moore was the librarian. She wrote to *The New York Times* in 1914 describing the good impression young Leo had made upon her while under her observation. Mrs. Elizabeth H. Spalding, Frank's English teacher at Pratt Institute, also wrote to the *Times*, lauding his "rare thoughtfulness, good judgment, and straightforward manliness."

Leo entered Cornell University in Ithaca, New York, in the fall semester of 1902. During his academic career there, he was a member of the Cornell Congress and participated in the H. Morse Stephens debate. Frank, who was a mechanical engineering major, played basketball for four years on his class team. The 1906 yearbook also said that he was a member of the Cornell Society of Mechanical Engineering (CSME).

Leo Frank was a thin young man who wore thick,

wire-rimmed glasses. He weighed only between 125 and 130 pounds and in many photographs he looked frightened, nervous, and frail. He had the habit of smoking cigars and enjoyed the game of bridge.

Following his graduation from Cornell in June 1906, he accepted a position as a draftsman with B. F. Sturtevant [Sturdivant] Company of High Park, Massachusetts. Six months later he became a testing engineer and draftsman for the National Meter Company of Brooklyn. Beginning in December 1907, Frank spent nine months in Europe in apprenticeship under the renowned German manufacturer Eberhard Faber, whose name appears to this day on pencils, pens, and erasers. It was Faber who built the first U.S. pencil factory in 1861. He was the last in a family of lead pencil manufacturers dating back to Kasper Faber, who died in 1784.

When Leo returned to America in August 1908, he went to Atlanta to learn and supervise the Frank family's pencil business there. In October, 1910, he married Miss Lucille Selig, daughter of a prominent Jewish family in Atlanta. Emil Selig, Lucille's father, was a salesman. He and his wife Josephine had three daughters. Rabbi David Marx's Temple and the Standard Club in Atlanta counted Leo Frank among their members.

Despite the fact that he was born in Texas, Leo Frank was perceived as a northerner, a Yankee Jewish industrialist. It may be conjectured that Mary Phagan was the latest victim of Yankee "blue-bellied" aggression, which could explain the Confederate marker on her grave.

The original group of Jews who came to North America had, of course, met opposition, namely, from the authorities of Dutch New Amsterdam. Arriving from Dutch Recife in 1654, following capture of that town by the Portuguese, this small band of Jews was allowed to stay in New Amsterdam only after it petitioned the Dutch East India Company in Holland. The first group of Jews to arrive in the southern colonies landed in Georgia in 1733. They, too, met opposition, although Governor James Oglethorpe granted them privilege to stay.

The first Jews came to the rough railroading town of Marthasville (later called Atlanta), Georgia, in the mid–1840s. Two Jewish men were known to be among the contributors to a Christian religious school established there in 1847. The land on which Atlanta now stands was once Creek and Cherokee Indian territory. Atlanta's first permanent white settler was a man named Hardy Ivy, who built his homestead there in the spring of 1833. Within ten years, the tiny town of Terminus was officially designated the southeastern end of the Western and Atlantic Railroad tracks. Terminus had thirty people and six buildings then. The first business firm was Johnson & Thrasher.

Terminus began to be called Marthasville in the early 1840s, in honor of the daughter of the governor of Georgia. By the end of 1843, Terminus was renamed Marthasville. In a little over a year, the townspeople began to call it Atlanta, and that became the official name in December 1845. Five years later, the city's population was estimated to be twenty-five hundred strong with nearly five hundred slaves. Atlanta became the seat of newly established Fulton County in late 1853. Gas lamps lit the streets of the town by the middle of the decade.

The "Gate City of the South," as Atlanta became known in the latter 1850s, heard Stephen A. Douglas speak there just before the start of the war. Douglas defended the integrity of the Union. By that time, Atlanta had over ninety-five hundred inhabitants. After General Lee's surrender at Appomattox, the population of Atlanta has been described as primarily Confederate war widows.

Following the carnage of the Civil War, the State of Georgia actively sought foreign settlers to bolster its labor supply. This official recruitment program, spurred by the emancipation of blacks from slavery, was not supported by most native Georgians. Jews started to enter the South in large numbers only after the end of the Civil War in 1865, and by 1875, the Jewish community in Atlanta numbered about six hundred people.

Despite Georgia's call for foreign labor and the influx of Jews and other groups into the state, the South in general had fewer immigrants than other regions of the country. The majority of the native whites of the South during the early decades of the twentieth century were of Scotch-Irish descent, whose forebears came to America in two great waves during the 1700s. The main sources of the population of Georgia were England, Scotland, and Ireland. Conformity to tradition and local mores was held in high esteem in the southern consciousness, in contrast to that of the cities of the North and the western frontiers, where differences were commonplace due to the ethnic mixtures.

The majority of Jews who came to Georgia before 1880 were of German origin. They did not experience the full impact of the native American culture because of their relatively small numbers, cultural orientation, and tendency to assimilate into the general southern way of life. The German Jewish community in Atlanta worked extremely hard to create an atmosphere of good will with the rest of the city's inhabitants. Professional partnerships frequently included Jews as well as Gentiles. Arthur Heyman, a Jewish attorney, was a partner in the law firm of Dorsey, Brewster, Howell and Heyman. The prosecutor in Frank's trial was the "Dorsey." In addition, twelve Jews were elected or appointed to office in Atlanta between 1873 and 1911. This was significant political representation for a group that never was more than three per cent of the total population. Even after the Frank case had played to its tragic climax, Victor Kriegshaber, a German Jew, was elected president of the Atlanta Chamber of Commerce, in 1916.

By 1913, the Atlanta Jewish community was the largest in the South, with slightly more than five thousand Jews when the city had a total population of around 175,000. The cornerstone of the house of worship for Rabbi David Marx's Hebrew Benevolent Congregation (later Temple) had been laid in place on May 14, 1875. Dedication of the building came two years later. The Congregation itself had been organized in June 1867.

Social and political conditions in Russia from 1881–1917 were to have profound effects upon Rabbi Marx's small German Jewish community in Atlanta. During the reigns of Alexander III through Nicholas II, there was a dramatic shift in czarist Jewish policy away from amalgamation and "Russification" to a program of physical violence (pogroms) and severe economic restrictions. The infamous May Laws of 1882, the expulsion of the Jews of Moscow in 1891, the savage and devastating Kishinev (Bessarabia) pogroms of 1903–05, and the Beilis affair stand within the broad sweep of government-sanctioned anti-Jewish action of those thirty-six years.

As a result of these and other pressures, the Jews of Russia and Eastern Europe emigrated to the United States in large numbers beginning in the 1880s and continuing through the First World War. This, of course, was prior to the legislation restricting immigration into the United States, which was enacted during the first five years of the 1920s.

By 1910, the 1,200 East European Jews of Atlanta were the largest foreign-born group in the city. These Russian Jews ghettoized themselves near the center of Atlanta and were very visible to the general public. Anti-Jewish social discrimination in Atlanta coincided with the arrival of the Russian Jews; and the exclusion of the West European leadership from the elite clubs was the first significant instance of discrimination.

From time to time in Atlanta's history, the prohibition of liquor was a very heated political issue, particularly during the mayoral race of 1888. Twenty years later prohibition went into effect in the city following a statewide referendum. A sizable percentage of the city's saloons were owned by Russian Jews and saloons, vice, and crime were all deplored alike in the public mind. As a result, the

Russian saloonkeepers were held in contempt by large segments of Atlanta's population.

Although the public originally distinguished between the new Russian immigrants and the established West European Jews, after 1900 the differentiation nearly vanished in popular thought. A Jew was, in effect, a Jew. There seems to have been a direct correlation between discrimination and the degree to which the Jewish community disturbed the existing social structure in Atlanta.

Atlanta's Jews were very civic-minded. The Hebrew Orphan's Home, for example, was established in 1889 to care for the Jewish orphans of the southeastern states. Jewish involvement in the general life of the city included work with the Robert E. Lee Fire Co. No. 4, the erection and repair of several local churches (Christians responded in kind), participation in a program to help the poor at Christmastime, and contribution to the construction of a juvenile reformatory in 1894. Money was raised during the Spanish-American War to aid wounded soldiers hospitalized near Atlanta and support was given to build a Presbyterian university in the city. Rabbi Marx campaigned for free kindergartens and playgrounds. Jews supported the YMCA and Boys Club too, but the greatest monument to their public philanthropy was the Henry Grady Memorial Hospital.

It is noteworthy, however, that fraternal lodges such as the Elks, the Shrine, and the Free and Accepted Masons provided the "only sphere of local associational life in which large numbers of Jews and Gentiles could mix comfortably." The points of contact between the Jewish and Gentile communities of Atlanta were primarily between the elite of both communities.

The general Jewish experience in America through the end of the nineteenth century was marked to a large degree by tolerance, at least officially and publicly. To be sure, there had been the occasional exception: General Grant's Order Number 11, the denial of accommodations to Jewish banker Joseph Seligman at the Grand Union Hotel in Saratoga, New York, and the pamphlet entitled *The Jew at Home* written by Joseph Pennell. General Grant's Order, issued in December, 1862, during the Civil War, is a rare instance in American Jewish experience of official anti-Semitism sponsored by an arm of the United States government. The Order called for the evacuation of all Jews living in the Tennessee Department. Behind this Order was the severe cotton shortage in the North along with a critical lack of certain medical goods. At the same time there was a surplus of raw cotton in the South and Jews were viewed as reaping a benefit trading between the North and the South. They were ordered to evacuate the area in which this trading could occur.

Another incidence of anti-Jewish action in America took place in Thomasville, Georgia, in August 1862, during a time of fear and economic pressure. A group of prominent citizens "passed a series of resolutions by which the resident Jews were given ten days' notice of expulsion, Jewish peddlers were prohibited from entering Thomas County, and a Committee of Public Safety was appointed with the responsibility of enforcing the resolutions." The proceedings of the meeting which produced these resolutions were published in the *Thomasville Weekly Times*, evoking protests from Jews in other parts of Georgia. The role of Confederate Jewish soldiers in protesting the attempted expulsion was particularly conspicuous. Historian Louis Schmeir notes that "Though the controversy died out quickly as the Confederate government took steps against the counterfeiters and provided for the defense of South Georgia, the town of Thomasville would continue to bear the stigma of anti-Semitism well into the twentieth century."

"Leo M. Frank did murder, in that in the county aforesaid (Fulton), state of Georgia, on the 26th of April, in the year of our Lord 1913, with force of arms he did unlawfully and with malice aforethought kill and murder one Mary Phagan by then and there choking her, said Mary Phagan, with a cord that he placed around her neck."

Such was the true bill issued by the grand jury in the Phagan murder case on Friday, May 23, 1913. Leo Frank would have to stand trial for the girl's murder. He had become the prime suspect, although Newt Lee was still held at the Tower on a suspicion warrant for the grand jury.

That Saturday morning Jim Conley, the black sweeper jailed as a material witness for the state, claimed in an affidavit that Leo Frank had him write the two notes found near Mary Phagan's body. Conley maintained Frank had directed him to write the notes the Friday before the murder.

Jim Conley could write. Notes to his girlfriend Annie Maud Carter are still preserved in the Georgia Department of Archives and History in Atlanta. Conley's letters, frequently addressed to "Baby doll" or "My dear little girl," contain vulgar and intimate language. Originally, however, Conley had declared that he could not write.

Chapter 3

THE TRIAL

The disrepute of the Atlanta police department was a significant issue in the Phagan murder case. There was pressure on the department to salvage its image as guardian of law and order (severely undercut by the unsolved murders of thirteen black women in the city), as widespread charges of police inefficiency and corruption were circulating throughout Fulton County. Atlanta's crime rate soared following the turn of the century with the rapid increase in population: between 1900 and 1910, the number of city residents increased from 90,000 to nearly 155,000.

Now, a little white girl had been murdered and there had to be a conviction. The department needed to come out on top on this one. Before Leo Frank was ever indicted by the grand jury, three of Atlanta's detectives had resigned their positions. Apparently they did not want to be involved in a situation which demanded that they concentrate on gathering evidence to convict Frank and ignore anything which might clear him.

Leo Frank's decision to hire the Pinkerton Detective Agency on behalf of the National Pencil Company proved to be an unfortunate move on two counts. First, Solicitor General Dorsey insisted that Frank had employed the Pinkertons to cover up his own guilt. Part of the trial testimony focused on the question of whether Frank or his attorneys requested the Pinkertons to suppress evidence in the case. Second, an ordinance in the City of Atlanta made all private detectives subject to police supervision and control. No private agency could operate in the city without the consent of the Board of Police Commissioners. Harry Scott, the assistant superintendent of the Pinkertons in Atlanta, was quoted as saying, "unless the Jew is convicted the Pinkerton Detective Agency will have to get out of Atlanta." This statement would be recalled under oath by L. P. Whitfield, a Pinkerton detective who worked on the Phagan investigation.

At the same time, Colonel Thomas B. Felder, who had been hired by a committee of citizens living in the vicinity of the Phagan girl's family, charged Chief Lanford with endeavoring to shield the Phagan murder suspects. In a statement issued on May 24, 1913, Felder said: "I would have the good people of this community know that from the day and hour of the arrest of Lee and Frank, charged with the murder of little Mary Phagan, Newport Lanford and his co-conspirators have left 'no stone unturned' in their efforts to shield and protect these suspects."

Felder was associated with the mayor in fighting police graft and he was upset that a hidden dictograph had been used when he was interviewed by Chief Lanford. According to the dictograph report, Felder attempted to bribe Chief Lanford to turn over to him an affidavit by J. W. Coleman. In anger, Felder accused the police and the Pinkertons of shielding both Frank and Lee. This might, some people thought, have encouraged the police to convict Frank, thereby repudiating Felder and preventing the graft investigation.

The Sunday before the Mary Phagan murder trial, the *Atlanta Constitution* devoted a full page to a discussion of the legal forces on both sides of the case. Leo Frank was described as having friends and relatives of wealth and influence and was reported to have employed legal talent of the highest order: Luther Z. Rosser, Herbert Haas, Rueben Arnold, and Morris Brandon would serve as defense counsel. Rosser, then fifty-four, was a native of Gordon County, Georgia, and a member of the local bar association since 1883. In his thirty years of Atlanta legal practice, "Mr. Rosser had gained renown both as a criminal and civil advocate." He had the reputation of an expert examiner of witnesses.

Hugh M. Dorsey, the Solicitor General of the Fulton County Superior Court, was the principal counsel representing the State. Dorsey, forty-two, was assisted by Frank A. Hooper, Sr. and Assistant Solicitor General E. A. Stephens. Mr. Hooper was a native of Floyd County, Georgia. That Sunday morning the *Constitution* also wrote that "A trial is necessarily a public affair, in order that decency and fairness may be guaranteed."

The trial would be held on the first floor of the old city hall building. The Fulton County courthouse was then under construction. Judge Leonard S. Roan, the trial judge, expressed some concern about the frightful weather because a large crowd was anticipated.

The trial was scheduled to begin Monday morning, July 28, and the weather prophecy called for temperatures around 90 degrees. Leo Frank had not been out of the Tower since May 8th, when he was confined there by the coroner's jury. Most of the citizens of Atlanta had never even seen him, much less knew anything about him. When the ten o'clock hour arrived, Pryor Street in front of the temporary courthouse was filled with a mob of curious onlookers. All day, through the blazing heat, the crowd hugged the hot walls of the city hall building like "lethargic leeches," gazing intently at the open windows of the courtroom. A few minutes after ten, Leo Frank was led into the courtroom by a deputy. Dressed with scrupulous neatness, Mr. Frank wore a distinctive looking gray suit. As he entered the courtroom, he smiled cordially to several friends and spoke briefly with a woman employee of the pencil factory.

When Judge Roan called the court to order, all took their seats. Members of the jury sat to the right of the judge's bench. Leo Frank was flanked by his wife and mother at the defense table. Mrs. Lucille Frank wore a thin China silk shirtwaist, a black skirt and black hat, and white kid gloves.

Chief Lanford, Detective Campbell, Attorney Hooper, and Hugh Dorsey sat at the prosecution's table. More than a score of reporters were at the press table taking notes. Behind the participants, there were seats for spectators, separated only by a railing from the drama which unfolded. Detective Waggoner was assigned to preserve order at the trial.

By 1:30 P.M., a jury had been selected from the 144 veniremen. Once the twelve were sworn in, Judge Roan adjourned until three o'clock. During the recess, Frank and his wife and mother ate dinner together in the anteroom.

A claim agent with the Atlanta and West Point Railroad named Fred Winburn was foreman of the jury. All the jurors (see below) were white men; eleven were married and their average age was thirty-five. Kimball House Hotel served as quarters for the jury during the course of the trial and each juror received two dollars a day. When the Kimball House Hotel opened its doors in October 1870, it was billed as "the finest in the South." It burned down thirteen years later, but reopened in 1885. Those fifteen years saw the readmission of the State of Georgia to the Union, a cordial return visit by General Sherman to the city he once burned, and the founding of the *Atlanta Journal*. Woodrow Wilson made his residence in Atlanta in 1882 when he practiced law there. Joel C. Harris published *Uncle Remus*, and John S. Pemberton made the first "ideal brain tonic." Pemberton's tonic became world famous as Coca-Cola, "Georgia Champagne."

Jury Selected to Try Frank

C. J. BASEHART, age 26, single, pressman; 216 Bryan Street. Nicknamed "Burtuss Dalton" after the state's witness who described Daisy Hopkins as a "peach." Daisy Hopkins was a prostitute alleged to use the National Pencil Factory for assignations.

A. H. HENSLEE, age 36, married, head salesman at Franklin Buggy Company of Barnesville; 47 Oak Street. Nicknamed "Big Newt."

J. F. HIGDON, age 42, married, building contractor; 108 Ormewood Avenue. Nicknamed "Luther Rosser."

W. M. JEFFRIES, age 33, married, real estate; Bolton, Ga. Nicknamed "Judge Roan" and "Holloway," the witness whom Hugh Dorsey accused of trapping him.

MARCELLUS JOEHENNING, age 46, married, shipping clerk; 161 Jones Street. Nicknamed "Daisy Hopkins."

W. F. MEDCALF, age 36, married, mailer; 136 Kirkwood Avenue. Nicknamed "Albert McKnight" after the disowned husband of Minola, cook for the Selig family.

J. T. OZBURN, age 36, married, optician; 30 Ashby Street. Nicknamed "Christopher Columbus Barrett" after the employee who had discovered the blood spots.

FREDERICK VAN L. SMITH, age 37, married, electrical manufacturing agent; 481 Cherokee Avenue. Nicknamed "Rabbi."

DEDER TOWNSEND, age 23, married, paying teller; 17 East Linden Street. Nicknamed "Bride," since he had been married only four months.

FRED E. WINBURN, age 39, married, claim agent for the Atlanta and West Point Railroad; 213 Lucille Avenue. Nicknamed "John Black," after the detective who was grilled so fiercely by Luther Rosser.

A. L. WISBEY, age 43, married, cashier; 31 Hood Street. Nicknamed "John Starnes" after the city detective.

M. S. Woodward, age 34, married, cashier at King Hardware Company; 182 Park Avenue. Nicknamed "Little Newt." He was a running mate and close friend of A. H. Henslee, called "Big Newt."

In the afternoon of July 28, Mrs. J. W. Coleman was called to the stand as the first witness for the State of Georgia. She broke down when she saw her daughter's clothing and cried again during cross-examination. Mrs. Coleman wore a simple black mourning dress and a black hat with heavy veil.

The nightwatchman, Newt Lee, was also called to the stand that first afternoon. He testified that he came to work at about 4:00 P.M. on the Saturday of the murder. Mr. Frank had sent him into town until six o'clock, and then had called him from home around seven o'clock that evening to ask if everything was all right at the factory. When Lee arrived at the factory that Saturday afternoon he found all the doors to the building unlocked, the usual procedure. Lee did say that with the doors to the factory unlocked when he returned at 6:00 P.M., anyone could have entered the building while Mr. Frank was working in the second floor office. The nightwatchman said he was told to check all the rooms of the factory, including the basement, every half-hour. He went to the basement Saturday night for the first time around seven o'clock, but only went to the bottom of the ladder and checked for fire. He went all the way down into the basement about 3:00 A.M. the following morning to use the toilet—the one Mr. Frank had ordered him to use. In the trial transcript, next to Lee's name is the notation "colored."

By day's end, both Hugh Dorsey and Rueben Arnold were pleased with the progress they had made. That night two black men reportedly attempted to burglarize the home of Mr. Frederick Van L. Smith, one of the jurors.

During the second day, Luther Rosser tried to connect Newt Lee with the crime, or at least to show that he knew more about the death of Mary Phagan than he had told. But Lee continued to stick with his original story. Only Lee, Sergeant Dobbs of the police force, and Detective Starnes were called to testify Tuesday. At one point, Solicitor Dorsey claimed Luther Rosser was trying to impeach his witness John Starnes. Tuesday's crowd was considerably larger than on the first day; many people had to stand in order to see the proceedings.

Sergeant Dobbs testified that the girl's body had been dragged from the elevator shaft to the spot where it was found lying. Newt Lee was not nervous when the police first arrived, Dobbs said. But Mr. Frank was very nervous the Sunday morning after the murder, said Detective Starnes. The policeman said he noticed the factory superintendent rubbing his hands. This brought a hail of crossfire from the defense. Starnes went on to say that Lee was, in fact, nervous when the officers arrived.

"Frank's most ordinary movements, such as catching a street car on this corner or that, the lowering of his head, the fashion of his hair, the rubbing of his hands, the tone of his voice, the contour of his lips, were magnified and lifted into glaring light. . . . " Even the way he swallowed was discussed in detail during the trial. "This was for the purpose of showing that Frank was guilty *because he was nervous and Newt Lee wasn't*."[1] Yet, more than two hundred witnesses vouched for Frank's good character.

On Wednesday, Detective John Black's testimony was shot to the ground under the merciless cross-fire of Luther Rosser. Time and again, the detective contradicted himself or confessed he did not remember. Since Black had developed much of the evidence against Frank, the invalidation of his testimony was significant. But Black insisted there were no blood stains discovered on the "metal" room floor on Sunday during the police investigation.

One especially interested spectator at the Thursday afternoon session at the city hall building was Mrs. Callie Scott Appelbaum. Judge Roan had also presided in her murder trial; the jury eventually found her innocent of murdering her husband Jerome.

The wife of mechanic John Arthur White was the first person to take the stand on Thursday, July 31. Maggie White had gone to the factory twice on Memorial Day and had seen Mr. Frank both times. Her husband was one of the men working on the fourth floor; she had brought him some lunch. A black man was standing behind some boxes on the first floor, Mrs. White said. She could not identify the man, but she saw him around one o'clock that Saturday.

New testimony came out Thursday. A machinist employed at the pencil factory declared that he had found what was supposed to be Mary Phagan's pay envelope near her machine in the second floor "metal" room. R. B. Barrett also stated that he had discovered blood stains on the floor by her machine and a strand of hair on the machine itself. The machinist's testimony supported Solicitor Dorsey's contention that the murder was committed on the second floor of the factory and that the body was taken to the basement at a later time.

Harry Scott of the Pinkerton Detective Agency hired by Leo Frank was then put on the stand. Scott testified that he refused a request by Defense Attorney Haas to report his investigative progress to Haas and his client prior to reporting to the Atlanta police. Scott implied that Haas wanted to suppress evidence about the case. Since Leo Frank had employed the Pinkerton Agency, it would seem reasonable to expect that company's agents to report to him or his designated representatives. The request was interpreted by Dorsey and Scott as interference with a police investigation.

After finishing with Harry Scott, the prosecution called E. F. Holloway, day watchman and timekeeper for the National Pencil Company. Despite being a witness for the prosecution, Holloway's testimony was favorable to Frank. On that day in April, Holloway unlocked the elevator motor in order to saw some boards for Denham and White, the mechanics on the fourth floor. The saw and the elevator worked off the same motor. When he finished, Holloway left the elevator unlocked.

Asked about the blood spots, Holloway stated that there were frequently blood stains in the "metal" room. Often, one of the girls would injure a finger on the machinery and bleed on the floor. In addition, the blood spots were only six feet from the ladies' toilet. Sometimes the girls would leave blood on the floor going toward the sink if they cut themselves. Holloway also testified that the cord found around Mary Phagan's neck was not unusual or difficult to find at the factory. Identical cords were lying all over the building because they were wrapped around every bundle of slats and pencils. It was possible for anyone entering the building to find one of the cords and use it.

The manager of the Georgia Cedar Company was next on the stand. N. V. Darley was very familiar with the defendant and the operation of the pencil factory. According to Darley, Frank's slight size would make it difficult to subdue Mary Phagan who, though only 4 feet 11 inches, weighed 125 pounds herself. Darley also characterized Frank as a very nervous type of person. He had often observed Frank wringing his hands, pulling his hands through his hair, and rubbing his hands together, especially when anything went wrong at the factory.

Since he was also in a managerial position, Darley was familiar with the financial report Frank prepared Saturday afternoon. He described how these calculations were done and testified that no one could correctly perform all of the operations involved in the report if very upset: they required clear thinking, and Leo Frank would not have been able to do that if he had just murdered someone.

With regard to the "murder notes," Darley said both types of note pads could be found all over the factory. One kind was used by foremen in making notes or reports. The order forms were also readily available, especially loose sheets strewn around because of misplaced carbons. According to Darley, the timeclock tape of Lee's nightly rounds did not mean much. Anyone who knew how to operate the timeclock could have done an entire night's punches in the space of about ten minutes. Hence, Newt Lee could have been anywhere in the factory or not in the factory at all for long periods of time without its showing up on the timeclock.

The prosecution brought in several witnesses with medical backgrounds to discuss Mary Phagan's physical condition. First was Dr. Claude Smith, the city bacteriologist. Next Dr. J. W. Hurt, the county physician, was sworn in. Hurt's testimony dwelt on the question of the time of death, which could not be placed. Much of the difficulty had to do with stomach contents and an inability to determine how quickly whole cabbage leaves would be digested.

On April 26, Mary Phagan had eaten cabbage and bread for breakfast prior to leaving for the trolley car. When the post-mortem examination was done, there were whole cabbage leaves and bread found undigested in her stomach. Medical analysis could not determine exactly how long after she had eaten the cabbage and bread death occurred—opinion varied from one-half hour to several hours. Exercise in the form of running to catch the trolley would slow the digestive process. Since Mary obviously did not take the time to chew her food, it is probable that she was late leaving to catch the streetcar and ran to make it to her stop before the car pulled away. She certainly did not consume a leisurely breakfast. There was also the possibility that fear and extended unconsciousness disturbed the functions of her digestive system. Cabbage is generally difficult to digest, especially when it is swallowed in almost whole, unchewed leaves as Mary had done. The fact that the bread was likewise undigested would, under normal circumstances, indicate a relatively short time span between ingestion and death. However, the circumstances were hardly normal. Fear and the blow to her head, if it only rendered her unconscious, would have slowed down her digestion.

By nine o'clock Sunday morning, April 27, rigor mortis

had set in completely. That would indicate death had occurred quite a few hours earlier. But again, this was not certain: the speed with which bodies go through rigor mortis varies, and the doctors could give no definite information about time of death.

Dr. Hurt also dealt extensively with the question of rape. Mary Phagan's hymen was not intact when Hurt examined her. He detected no injury to the hymen, implying that it had not been ruptured just prior to death. She was not pregnant. He concluded that Miss Phagan was menstruating at the time of her death. Hurt saw no evidence of vaginal laceration or violence, and concluded there had been no rape.

But there were certain questions unanswered. The cause of death was not determined. Dr. Hurt did not examine Mary's lungs for signs of congestion, which would have occurred if she had died of strangulation, so he could not say for sure if the blow to her head killed her, stunned her, or rendered her unconscious. It is possible that the cord around her neck was placed there after unconsciousness or after death or even while she was still alert.

Dr. H. T. Harris examined the body after exhumation, ten days after burial. There was no spermatazoa in the vaginal tract, he said. While he felt there had been violence done to the vagina, he thought it could have been caused by Dr. Hurt's digital examination of the area.

From the evidence presented by Drs. Hurt and Harris, it seems that rape was not the motive for the attack on Mary Phagan. Further, it seemed unlikely that Leo Frank would attack the girl to steal $1.20. His salary of $150 per month made Mary's pittance a poor reason for murder. Others, however, might have found the sum worth stealing. Attempted theft could have led to murder if there was resistance.

James Conley was the State's major witness. He was a 27-year-old black man who had gone to public school in Atlanta for two years. His police record was extensive, although he had not served long sentences. He had worked for the National Pencil Company for about two years, during which time he had been in prison on three occasions. He had also been in prison about seven or eight times in the previous five years, according to his own testimony.

More than once, Conley had been found drunk in the factory. Many people testified at the trial as to his generally poor character and his lack of credibility under oath. The woman he lived with was never subpoenaed to corroborate his story of his whereabouts on the Saturday night of the murder. Her testimony would have been admissible because she was not his lawful wedded wife. Jim Conley's attorney was William M. Smith.

Conley's testimony suggested that he was in the factory all day on Memorial Day and observed everyone's movements very closely—or perhaps that his story was well rehearsed. He did admit consuming large quantities of alcohol that day, and this fact alone should have cast doubt on his memory. It was also possible that he was the "Negro" Mrs. White saw by the boxes near the elevator that day.

Jim Conley declared that on many previous occasions he had "watched" as a lookout while Leo Frank "visited" with ladies in the factory and that he had acted as lookout on Thanksgiving Day, 1912. (In his earlier affidavits, Conley had stated that his "watching" meant being a watchman for the factory. But this was not possible, since Newt Lee was the first black watchman ever employed at the factory.) Conley described Frank's encounters with the ladies as not being normal. He intimated that Frank had confessed to Conley that he (Frank) "wasn't built like other men". Claiming to have caught glimpses of these encounters, Conley said that he had never known "men what got children" to have done those things. His description of the lady lying on a table with her skirts up and Frank kneeling in front of her may certainly have been seen as a perversion.

Conley stated that on Memorial Day, Mary Phagan went upstairs. He heard a scream, and then Monteen Stover, another employee, went up and came back down. Then Frank called to Conley and asked if he had seen a little girl go upstairs. Conley said he saw two go up but only one come back down. Then, according to Conley, Frank said he tried to have his way with the other one. But she would not cooperate, so he hit her. Conley said Frank told him to go see how she was. When the floorsweeper returned, he told Frank she was dead. Frank then told Conley to wrap the body up and take it down to the basement. Conley's testimony was that Frank had to help him carry the body all the way to the basement. He also said that Leo Frank had to unlock the elevator which they used to transport Mary Phagan's body to the basement.

When they returned to Frank's office, according to Conley, Leo Frank gave him some notepads and a pencil and proceeded to dictate a total of four "murder notes." Frank then told Conley to burn Mary's body in the furnace. He allegedly gave Jim Conley $200, but took it back, promising to return the money later. Frank was said to have been very nervous throughout this entire period of time. He was said to have muttered about having wealthy relatives in New York and, so, why should he hang? Before Conley left Frank's office, his boss told him that if he [Conley] were arrested he [Frank] would put up the bond and send Conley away.

Conley's description of events on that Saturday is full of contradictions and changes. From the time of his arrest, his story changed repeatedly. At least five different versions were given in affidavits. On the stand, he contradicted testimony given by other State's witnesses earlier in the trial. In one affidavit prior to the trial, Conley swore that Leo Frank had dictated the murder notes to him on Friday afternoon. Only when the Atlanta police told Conley that his story would not do because it showed premeditation did he change it to having written the notes on Saturday. Early in the interrogation process Conley refused to admit that he had been in the pencil factory at all on Saturday,

April 26. Even his story in the last affidavit before the trial had changed by the time he ascended the witness stand. He claimed then that he met Frank on the street Saturday, by chance, and went to the factory at his boss's urging. Then at the trial he swore that Frank had made an appointment for Conley to come to the factory on Saturday afternoon.

Until his courtroom testimony, Jim Conley denied ever having seen Monteen Stover or hearing a scream on Memorial Day at the factory. By the time he was under oath, both of these supposed facts had changed.

Harry Scott, the Pinkerton detective, testified once again. He had been present during police interrogations of Jim Conley. The police, according to Scott, dictated changes in the story when they felt what Conley was saying "would not fit" or "would not do." Scott also stated under oath that "anything in his [Conley's] story that looked to be out of place we told him wouldn't do. After he had made his last statements we didn't wish to make any further suggestion to him at that time." If Scott's testimony was true, the Atlanta police changed the story of a key witness in order to bolster their case against the primary suspect!

According to Monteen Stover, she had collected her pay from Leo Frank between 11:55 A.M. and 12:05 P.M. on April 26. Conley claimed he saw Mary Phagan go upstairs before Miss Stover did. But Mary Phagan did not get off the trolley car at Marietta and Hunter streets outside the factory until 12:10 P.M.

After Conley left the stand, Mrs. White was again called. She stated that the Negro she saw was about Conley's size and build, but she could not be certain the man was Conley.

Next, N. V. Darley returned to the stand. He refuted Conley's statement that Darley and Leo Frank were on friendly terms with Jim Conley, and said that they did not engage in friendly banter and back slapping with the floor-sweeper, as Conley had claimed. Darley also gave information about the door leading to an area of the factory building previously used by the Clark Wooden Ware

Company. That door, Darley said, had been nailed shut when the Clark Wooden Ware Company moved out. He also said that the door was found broken down after the murder and that he had it renailed.

E. F. Holloway was recalled and his testimony also refuted Conley's. Conley claimed that he was paid whether he bothered to punch the factory's timeclock or not. But Holloway stated that on numerous occasions he had to find Conley and have him punch the timeclock so Conley could be paid. There were no exchanges of friendliness and joking between Conley and Frank, said Holloway, who insisted that he was always at the factory on Saturdays and that women never came to visit Leo Frank there. Frank always conducted himself like a gentleman with females—employees and others who had business there, such as the wives of employees. According to Holloway, Lucille Frank was at the factory at least one Saturday a month, and sometimes more often. Her visits made it unlikely that her husband would be meeting other women there.

As its first witness, the defense called W. M. Matthews, a motorman for the Georgia Railway and Electric Company. He was operating a trolley on Memorial Day. Matthews stated that Mary Phagan boarded his trolley car on the English Avenue line at Lindsay Street around 11:50 A.M. She left the trolley at 12:10 P.M. at the stop at Broad and Hunter streets. He also testified that George Epps frequently rode on his trolley, but on April 26 was definitely not a passenger. Young Epps had given a statement to police asserting that he had seen and spoken with Mary Phagan on the trolley that day. (Later, the newspapers carried a story in which Epps rescinded his previous statement.) W. T. Hollis, the street car conductor, supported Mr. Matthews' testimony in all respects.

Next, the defense called Mr. Herbert G. Schiff, an assistant superintendent at the pencil factory. He had been employed with the company for about five years. Schiff stated that he earned $80-per-month and that Leo Frank earned $150-per-month. On several occasions he had seen Jim Conley try to borrow money from female employees. He confirmed Holloway's testimony that Lucille Frank was frequently present on Saturdays, often taking dictation from her husband. Schiff said Conley was familiar with the layout of the basement because the Negro employees ate there.

Miss Hattie Hall was sworn in. She was a stenographer employed by the National Pencil Company, although she also worked for Montag Brothers. (Sigmund Montag, a business partner in the pencil company, handled the finances and Miss Hall assisted him.) On Saturday April 26, Leo Frank asked Hattie Hall to come to the pencil factory to take some dictation for him. She stated that Leo Frank did not work on the financial report in the morning. Miss Hall left the factory at 12:02 P.M. by the timeclock, and reported there was no "little girl" coming into the building at that time.

Next on the stand was Corinthia Hall, a forelady in the factory's finishing room. Memorial Day she saw Mr. White, Mr. Denham, and May Barrett and her daughter on the fourth floor.

Magnolia Kennedy testified that on Friday, April 25, Mr. Schiff was handing out pay envelopes, as usual. She was standing behind Helen Ferguson waiting to be paid, but Miss Ferguson did not ask for Mary Phagan's pay envelope. Earlier Helen Ferguson had said that she requested both her own and Mary Phagan's pay envelopes from Leo Frank. But the National Pencil Company had a policy whereby no one was allowed to pick up another person's pay without written permission from that person. Miss Ferguson's earlier story had seemed to imply that Frank purposely did not give Mary Phagan's envelope to Helen Ferguson so that he could meet Miss Phagan and lure her into illicit activities.

Wade Campbell was the next defense witness. He was the brother of Mrs. J. A. White and had been employed at the pencil factory for a year-and-a-half. After Mary Phagan was killed, Campbell saw Jim Conley avidly scanning the newspapers for reports of the murder and progress of the investigation. (Conley had testified that he did not read well enough to read the newspapers.)

According to testimony provided by Lemmie Quinn, R. B. Barrett, the man who found the supposed blood spots in the "metal" room, often spoke to him about collecting the reward money if Leo Frank were convicted of the murder. Mr. Quinn was in Frank's office on April 26 and saw the superintendent at 12:20 P.M.

Harry Denham worked at the factory from 7:00 A.M. to 3:10 P.M. on Memorial Day. The elevator, he said, definitely did not run that day because the noise from the motor would have been heard on the fourth floor. If the car hit bottom in the basement, vibrations would also have been felt throughout the building.

The Selig family's cook also gave her testimony to the court. The Franks lived with the Seligs at the time of the murder. Minola McKnight stated that her husband, Albert, was not in the Seligs' kitchen between 1:00 and 2:00 P.M. on April 26, contrary to his statement. She also asserted that Hugh Dorsey along with her husband and another man tried to force her to say that Leo Frank had been very upset that day. They wanted her to endorse a statement that Mr. Frank asked his wife, Lucille, to get his gun so he could kill himself. Despite the fact that Mrs. McKnight left the Selig home at 8:00 P.M. that night, she was supposed to testify that Leo Frank made it impossible for Lucille to sleep because of his extreme nervousness. Minola McKnight said she refused to be party to what she termed outright lies. She was then placed in jail as a material witness. She finally signed a false statement, because Hugh Dorsey told her that signing the affidavit was the only way she would be released. Mrs. McKnight swore in court that Leo Frank arrived home at about 1:20 P.M. on Saturday for lunch and did not leave home to return to the office until after 2:00 P.M. He ate his usual lunch and was not nervous.

Emil Selig, father of Lucille Frank, was then called. On

Memorial Day, Leo Frank came home and ate his lunch as usual, Selig said. There were no bruises, scratches, or other signs of struggle on Leo's body. His manner was normal at lunch and that evening. Leo greeted several guests who were visiting the Seligs and even related a humorous story he had read in the paper. As to the telephone call to Newt Lee, Mr. Selig testified that Mr. Frank would frequently call the factory at night and speak to the watchman.

Both Miss Helen Kerns and Mrs. A. P. Levy stated that they saw Leo Frank on his way home for lunch between one and two o'clock on April 26.

Rebecca Carson, an employee of the factory, spoke with Jim Conley and another man called "Snowball," after the murder. She said Conley was so upset that he dropped his broom and ran out of the room when he heard that the Negro Mrs. White had seen by the boxes at the foot of the stairs was probably the murderer. When she asked where he had been on the day of the murder, Conley told Miss Carson: "I was so drunk I don't know where I was or what I did."

Alonzo Mann's testimony was fairly short: "I am office boy at the National Pencil Company," he said. "I began working there April 1st, 1913. I sit sometimes in the outer office and stand around in the outer hall. I left the factory at half past eleven on April 26th. When I left there Miss Hall, the stenographer from Montags, was in the office with Mr. Frank. Mr. Frank told me to phone to Mr. Schiff and tell him to come down. I telephoned him, but the girl answered the phone and said he hadn't got up yet. I telephoned once. I worked there two Saturday afternoons of the weeks previous to the murder and stayed there until half past three or four. Frank was always working during that time. I never saw him bring any women into the factory and drink with them. I have never seen Dalton there. On April 26th, I saw Holloway, Irby, McCrary and Darley at the factory. I didn't see Quinn. I don't remember seeing Corinthia Hall, Mrs. Freeman, Mrs. White, Graham, Tillander, or Wade Campbell. I left there 11:30." On cross-examination by the State the fourteen-year-old office boy said, "When Mr. Frank came that morning he went right on into the office and was at work there and stayed there. He went out once. Don't know how long he stayed out."

Mrs. Rae Frank, Leo's mother, also took the stand. She testified that her son had no wealthy relatives in Brooklyn or in New York, at all. Leo's father, Rudolph Frank, had been a traveling salesman. Mr. Frank was in poor health and no longer able to work. The only relative of independent means was Leo's uncle, Moses Frank, who lived in Atlanta.

Leo Frank's brother-in-law, Charles F. Ursanbach, his sister, Mrs. Ursanbach, and his other sister, Mrs. A. E. Marcus, all testified in his behalf. Charles Ursanbach and Leo Frank were supposed to go together to the Atlanta Crackers game on Memorial Day. Because of the overcast weather and his work at the factory, Leo called Mr. Ursanbach and left a message with his cook to cancel the outing.

Frank Payne had been the office boy at the National Pencil Company on Thanksgiving Day 1912. Jim Conley left the factory at 10:20 A.M. that day, Payne said, and both Leo Frank and Herbert Schiff were still working at that time. There were no women with them. Payne's normal duties would have kept him around the office all day, and the defense argued that he was in a better position to observe Frank and Schiff than Conley, who had said Frank was engaged in illicit activities that Thanksgiving Day a year earlier.

The foreman of the varnishing department, Joe Stelker, testified that the supposed blood stains on the "metal" room floor were probably just varnish mixed with pigment. He said there were often spills of pigment and varnish mixed with haskoline in many areas of the factory.

A Pinkerton detective, W. D. McWorth, testified that he found a cut strand of cord which matched the cord discovered around Mary Phagan's neck. This strand was lying near the door to the Clark Wooden Ware Company. There were also some papers dated February 11, 1911, next to the cord. In the same area, McWorth found a pay envelope which had the number "186" and the initials "M. P." written on it.

Quite possibly this was Mary Phagan's last pay envelope. Judging from the area in which it was found, Mary went down the stairway from Frank's office and was accosted by someone waiting near the front hallway. Mrs. White's "Negro" may have confronted the lone young girl and tried to get her pay. If a struggle developed, she could have been hit on the head and lowered down the chute inside the door to the Clark Wooden Ware Company. This chute led to the basement. Mary Phagan's attacker could then have gone down the ladder to the basement and killed the semi-conscious or unconscious girl. Conley's reaction to the statement about the "Negro" probably being the murderer and his avid interest in the newspaper stories seemed to suggest that he had some connection with Miss Phagan's murder.

Conley swore under oath that he defecated in the base-ment inside the elevator shaft on Memorial Day morning. If he and Frank had indeed used the elevator to take Mary's body to the basement, the excrement would have been smashed when the elevator hit bottom. On Sunday morning the police themselves stated that there was a perfectly formed pile of feces in the elevator shaft. It would appear, therefore, that the elevator could not have been used on Saturday afternoon. Fortunately, the first police officers on the scene after Newt Lee's call used the ladder to reach the site of the body. (The excrement was smashed eventually, but not until later in the day on Sunday when the police used the elevator to go down to the basement.)

Mr. A. D. Greenfield was one of the owners of the Venable Building where the National Pencil Company's factory was located. He had owned the building since 1900. Greenfield's testimony concerned primarily the building's history. Originally it was leased to Montag Brothers, who, in turn leased an area to the Clark Wooden Ware Company. When Montag needed more space, it moved to another location nearby and the National Pencil Company, a related firm, moved into the Venable Building. When the Clark Wooden Ware Company moved out of the building, the doorway to their area was nailed up and was not used by the pencil factory. There was no outside entrance into Clark Wooden Ware. Clark employees came into the building through the entrance to the pencil company.

The defense brought in several experts to refute the prosecution's medical evaluations. Professor George Bachman, a professor of physiological chemistry at the Atlanta College of Physicians and Surgeons, testified that cabbage could sit in the stomach for a long time without digestion progressing very far. Digestive processes vary with the individual. The speed with which one person might digest cabbage would probably be different from that of another person. A child's digestion would certainly not be the same as an adult's, and the function and speed of their digestive tract were not usually studied. Professor Bachman also stated that unmasticated cabbage would certainly require a lot of time before it would even begin to be digested.

Dr. Willis Westmoreland also provided medical support for the defense. He dealt with the question of violence to the vaginal area and the possibility of rape. According to Dr. Westmoreland, congestion of the vagina could be due to ongoing or recent menstruation. And a digital examination of the organ, such as the one performed by Dr. Hurt at the initial post-mortem, could definitely strip away epithelial cells. Dr. Harris' examination, which revealed evidence of vaginal violence, was conducted after Dr. Hurt's digital exam, so Dr. Harris could not give a definitive report about when the epithelial stripping had occurred. It was also germane that Dr. Harris conducted the check after the body had been embalmed: the embalming process would have changed many critical aspects of the body's physiology.

Thus, examinations done after Mary Phagan's body had been exhumed would not be accurate.

The law in Georgia specified that the defendant in a criminal case could not give testimony under oath in his or her own behalf but could make an unsworn statement to the jury. A defendant's spouse was not permitted to testify in the trial, neither for nor against the accused. When the defendant did deliver a statement, defense lawyers could not ask him or her any questions. Of course, the prosecuting attorney would not ask questions as he would not want his case demolished by unexpected replies.

Leo Frank took the stand, without benefit of oath, in his own defense. He recounted his early life and progressed to the events of Confederate Memorial Day. Frank stated: "Miss Hall left my office on her way home at this time and to the best of my information there were in the building Arthur White and Harry Denham and Arthur White's wife on the top floor. To the best of my knowledge it must have been from 10 to 15 minutes after Miss Hall left my office, when this little girl, whom I afterwards found to be Mary Phagan, entered my office and asked for her pay envelope. I asked for her number and she told me; I went to the cash box and took her envelope out and handed it to her, identifying the envelope by the number. She left my office and apparently had gotten as far as the door from my office leading to the outer office, when she evidently stopped and asked me if the metal had arrived, and I told her no. She continued on her way out and I heard the sound of her footsteps as she went away. It was a few moments after she asked me this question that I had an impression of a female voice saying something; I don't know which way it came from; just passed away and I had that impression. This little girl had evidently worked in the metal department by her question and had been laid off owing to the fact that some metal that had been ordered had not arrived at the factory; hence, her question. I only recognized this little girl from having seen her around the plant and did not know her name, simply identifying her envelope from her having called her number to me."

Frank also declared: "Gentlemen, I know nothing whatever of the death of little Mary Phagan. I had no part in causing her death nor do I know how she came to her death after she took her money and left my office. I never even saw Conley in the factory or anywhere else on that date, April 26th, 1913."

Frank concluded his poignant four-hour speech with these words: "Gentlemen, some newspaper men have called me 'the silent man in the tower,' and I kept my silence and my counsel advisedly, until the proper time and place. The time is now, the place is here, and I have told you the truth, the whole truth."

When he finished, the jury and the courtroom spectators were spellbound; some of the jurors were teary eyed. Many people felt the accused Jew had spoken the truth. His voice, his demeanor, everything about him gave the impression of a man being wholly open and honest.

After Frank, George Gordon took the stand. He was the attorney for Minola McKnight. He told the jury that during the course of the police investigation, Mrs. McKnight had been unlawfully detained in order to get information for the prosecution.

Nearly 200 citizens took the stand as character witnesses for Leo Frank. Most of them simply took the oath and gave their names, sometimes including their professions. Each stated that he or she had known Leo Frank for a certain time and that the defendant was of good character. The sheer number of people required considerable time to hear. In the grueling heat of Atlanta's July and August the jury no doubt became very tired of the seemingly endless procession of character witnesses. This was one of several mistakes made by Frank's defense counsel.

The prosecution closed its case with an impassioned speech by Hugh Dorsey. Holding Mary Phagan's clothes before the jury, the Solicitor snarled that the "fiendish degenerate" took the little girl's life. The dead girl's mother uttered a terrifying shriek.

Before the jury retired for deliberation, Judge Roan held a consultation at the bench. In the presence of the jury, the judge discussed with the chief of police and the colonel of the Fifth Georgia Regiment the best means of protecting Frank should he be acquitted. The militia was kept under arms that night. A "verdict of acquittal would cause a riot such as would shock the country and cause Atlanta's streets to run with innocent blood," wrote the *Atlanta Journal*. The judge also advised the defense counsel not to have Leo Frank present in the courtroom or to be there themselves when the verdict was rendered. There was genuine fear that if Frank were found "not guilty" the mob would lynch him and his lawyers.

Endnotes

1. From C. P. Connolly's *The Truth About the Frank Case*.

Chapter 4

THE VERDICT

Through the blistering days of summer the trial unfolded amidst the very real presence of an anti-Jewish mob spirit. The streets were thronged with people demanding the conviction of "the damned Jew." The crowd, some allegedly armed, applauded, jeered, and laughed throughout the trial. Judge Roan had made repeated, but timid, efforts to maintain a semblance of order.

Spectators in the courtroom sat directly behind the jurors. The jury could surely feel the palpable presence and sentiment of the crowd. Because of the heat, the windows in the city hall building were open and the heads of people standing in the street were practically level with the sills of these open windows. A group of men sat on the roof of a shed outside the window just ten feet behind the judge and the witness chair. "The mob was breathing vengeance in the very face of the judge and jury."

Near the end of the month-long trial, Frank's lawyers petitioned the court for a mistrial on the grounds of these various demonstrations—to no avail.

The emotions of the crowd had been stirred by persistent rumors and newspaper sensationalism. It was claimed, for example, that the tenets of the Jewish faith forbid the violation of a Jewess but condoned the rape of a Christian woman. Charges were made of Jewish money buying influence in Georgia.

Results of the southern baseball league and the standing of the Atlanta Cracker team were the only bits of news available to the jurors during the course of the Mary Phagan murder trial. The Crackers had a chance to overtake the Mobile Gulls and win their third pennant for the Gate City.

Once they were charged with deliberating a verdict, each jurist took a solemn oath never to reveal what transpired in the juryroom. Friendships that would last a lifetime, with anticipation of periodic reunions, were reported to have sprung up during the thirty days the twelve men were together. The jurors learned to call each other by nickname and, according to *The Atlanta Constitution*, these nicknames evoked laughter almost everywhere. A. H. Henslee was called "Big Newt," after Newt Lee and J. F. Higdon was dubbed "Luther Rosser," from the redoubtable defense attorney in the case. "Judge Roan" was the name chosen for W. M. Jeffries while J. T. Ozburn was "Christopher Columbus Barrett," after the discoverer of the blood spots in the "metal" room. Dr. David Marx's title went to Frederick Van L. Smith. Fred Winburn was called "John Black," after the city detective whom Luther Rosser cross-examined so fiercely, and M. S. Woodward was known as "Little Newt."

Descriptions of nicknames and close friendship, however, stand in sharp contrast to the reports of a terrorized jury. One juror, for example, reportedly said that unless the jury convicted Frank they would never get home alive. The spirit of the jury seemed very much in keeping with that of the mob, which seethed about the city hall building for the month-long trial.

At four minutes to five o'clock on Monday, August 25, 1913, this jury of Frank's peers filed back into the city hall courtroom. After four weeks of the greatest legal battle in Georgia history, a verdict had been reached in four hours. The courtroom had been cleared of morbidly curious onlookers. Only the newspaper men, Sheriff Mangum, his deputies, Solicitor Dorsey and Frank Hooper, and a few lawyers and close personal friends of the defendant were present. By not having Leo Frank present in his court at the time the verdict was rendered, Judge Roan had taken an "absolutely extraordinary" judicial step. Today, this move in itself would be grounds for a new trial. It would be a violation of constitutionally guaranteed due process of law.

A hush fell over that courtroom in Atlanta. With a trembling voice, Foreman Winburn read the verdict aloud: "Guilty!" The verdict was called out over the telephones to the three Atlanta newspapers. Word of the decision reached the street below almost immediately and a shout erupted from the waiting crowds. Hats went flying into the air and women wept and shrieked. The news of the verdict was chalked up on the scoreboard of a baseball game, and a wild demonstration of approval ignited in the bleachers. The end had come to the longest criminal trial in Georgia's history. Over the pandemonium outside the windows, the judge thanked the jury for their "faithful service and consideration of all details in this most arduous case."

When Solicitor Dorsey emerged from the city hall building, three muscular men swung him onto their shoulders and passed him over the heads of the crowd to his office across the street. With hat raised and tears streaming down his cheeks, the Solicitor of Fulton County looked on as the crowds wildly proclaimed its admiration.

It was more than fifty minutes before Frank, together with his wife at the Tower, learned of the verdict. Dr. Rosenberg, the Frank family physician, broke the sad news. Rabbi Marx was with the doctor. "My God!" Frank said, "even the jury was influenced by mob law. I am as innocent as I was one year ago." Lucille Frank wept, then fainted.

Three minutes after Foreman Fred Winburn announced the verdict in the trial, *The Atlanta Constitution* "Extra" hit the streets.

In the early morning hours of the following day, Joe McNeely, a black man, was taken from the Good Samaritan

Hospital in Charlotte, North Carolina, and shot to death by a mob of several hundred men. McNeely had been accused of shooting and mortally wounding a policeman named L. L. Wilson.

That same Tuesday, Newt Lee was given his freedom. His attorneys made an appeal in the newspapers on the old man's behalf for clothes, provisions, and a job. Lee's wife had left him, and his house was empty.

Leo Frank was brought before Judge Roan on Tuesday, August 26, and sentenced. The defendant was to "be by the Sheriff of Fulton County hanged by the neck until he shall be dead" between the hours of 10:00 A.M. and 2:00 P.M. on October 10, 1913. The accused pleaded his innocence once again. His defense counsel immediately filed a motion for a new trial, basing their petition on the grounds that several popular demonstrations heard by the jurymen during the trial prejudiced the case. A hearing for arguments on that motion was set by Roan for October 4. The original motion for a new trial was amended and that motion was heard on October 31, but the amended motion was overruled the very same day.

Jim Conley, an accessory after the fact to the murder by his own testimony, was still in jail. He would be convicted in February 1914 and serve a one-year sentence on a chain gang.

The Mennonite, a religious weekly journal of the Mennonite General Conference[1] of North America, carried a brief article about Frank's sentencing. Published by the Mennonite Book Concern of Berne, Indiana, this weekly journal was devoted to the interests of the Mennonite Church and the cause of Christ in general. *The Mennonite* is the only Christian magazine known to have mentioned anything about Frank's sentencing.

A fellow graduate of Frank's at Cornell University called upon alumni of that school to join in clearing his name. Letters of appeal were sent out to former Cornell grads recalling Frank's excellent undergraduate record.

The Jews of Atlanta and the surrounding countryside were naturally affected by the trial of Leo Frank. David Davis, a Jewish resident of the Gate City for the eight years preceding the Frank trial, which included the racial riots of 1906, says that a great upsurge of anti-Semitism followed in the wake of the preliminary police investigation into the murder of Mary Phagan.

"The Atlanta race riot, which began on September 22, 1906, was the most serious disturbance of the peace in Fulton County since the War Between the States."

A series of black assaults against white women triggered the riot. These attacks began in late 1905 and continued into the following year. Violence erupted on the night of September 22 after the press sensationalized four assaults that occurred that day. The bloodletting ceased only after four days. Two whites and ten blacks were dead and seventy people were wounded. James Woodward was mayor of Atlanta at the time. Another contributing factor was the intensely heated Georgia gubernatorial campaign that year (1906). The two leading candidates, Hoke Smith and Clark Howell, were both Atlantans. Clark Howell had become editor-in-chief of the *Atlanta Constitution* in 1897. The issue dividing the two men concerned the most effective way to keep blacks away from the ballot box.

In view of the smoldering racial unrest in Atlanta, which was still present during the investigative stages of their client's case, it would seem that Frank's lawyers were remiss in not seeking a change of venue for the trial. Moving the location several hundred miles from Fulton County, to Savannah perhaps, might have helped defuse some of the public fervor. But the defense counsel was perhaps overconfident. Their client was, after all, a businessman of unblemished character, whereas the State's witness had a history of drunkenness and incarceration. But most important, Jim Conley was a black man, and no court in the South had ever convicted a white man on the testimony of a black. Conley proved himself to be an able adversary during

Luther Rosser's cross-examination. Jim was street-smart; he had been in court before and knew how to handle himself. Rosser's failure to crack Conley's testimony after sixteen hours of cross-examination simply reinforced the credibility of the State's witness.

The points on which the State of Georgia built its case against Leo Frank went like this. Frank admitted to being the last person to see Mary Phagan alive. The girl never left the National Pencil Factory that Memorial Day but was killed on the second floor in the "metal" room near Frank's office. Frank dictated the murder notes to Jim Conley, who helped Frank take the body to the basement. Finally, the factory superintendent had been very nervous the Sunday after the killing. Though the charge of rape was never brought against him, testimony from the State's star witness portrayed Frank as a degenerate "womanizer."

The defense probably frustrated both judge and jury that hot summer by parading about 200 character witnesses into court on Frank's behalf. Frank's lawyers failed to vigorously pursue the forensic angle of the case. The Atlanta bacteriologist admitted later that he had discovered no resemblance between the strands of hair on the lathe in the factory's "metal" room and the hair of the dead girl. But the defense's most serious mistake was in not making a motion for mistrial at the time of crowd interference in the proceedings. This fact was brought out later in the Supreme Court record. Hence, Frank's lawyers bear at least partial responsibility for the outcome of the Phagan murder trial.

Leo Frank's trial in the United States has been compared with the Mendel Beilis blood libel trial in Russia and the Dreyfus Affair in France. There are some similarities in the anti-Semitism, the world-wide attention given these trials, and the Jewish responses. As early as March 1914, Rabbi Henry Berkowitz likened Frank to Beilis in a sermon delivered in Philadelphia. On the basis of circumstantial evidence, Menahem Mendel Beilis[2], a Jew, was accused of murdering a twelve-year-old Gentile boy named Andre

Yushchinsky near Kiev, Russia. The boy's mutilated body had been discovered in a cave on the outskirts of the city. The right-wing monarchist press immediately accused the Jews of killing the child to use his blood in religious rites.

Under the direction of M. Minschuk, Kiev police authorities discovered considerable evidence that the boy had been killed by a gang of thieves. Yet the chief district attorney, pressured by anti-Semitic elements, disregarded the police report and insisted on pursuing the blood libel against the Jews. Beilis was arrested on July 21, 1911 and sent to prison, remaining there two years before being brought to trial. Minschuk was condemned to prison for one year for manufacturing evidence to protect the Jews.

The government of Czar Nicholas II attempted to use Mendel Beilis to implicate the entire Jewish people in the charge of ritual murder. The case attracted worldwide attention and provoked international protest (see *The New York Times*, October 19, 1913). Beilis' trial finally took place from September 25 through October 25, 1913, and he was acquitted of the murder of Andre Yushchinsky.

In the celebrated Dreyfus Affair, there are similarities to the Frank case, too. In 1894, a French army officer named Alfred Dreyfus, a Jew, was arrested on charges of selling French military secrets to the Germans—treason! For this alleged crime he was court-martialed and sent to the penal colony on Devil's Island, off the coast of French Guiana. Anti-Semitic journalists launched a systematic campaign against the Jews, focusing on Captain Dreyfus. Common to Jews on all sides of the Dreyfus issue was a strong reaffirmation of their French patriotism. Captain Dreyfus was officially found innocent of all charges in 1906.

Before the 1880s, the anti-Semitic movement in France did not have popular support. When L'Union Generale bank crashed in 1882, the disaster was linked to Jewish financial manipulation. Edouard Drumont's two volume work, *La France Juive* (*French Jew*), was published in 1886. The Jews, Drumont argued, were members of an inferior race who had made themselves the masters of modern France. This author, a leader in the French anti-Semitic movement, blended traditional Christian anti-Semitism with racial discrimination.

The political machinations of the French military and Ministry of War in the Dreyfus case, as with the czarist involvement in the Beilis case, distinguish it from the Leo Frank affair. Other than the two appeals heard before the Supreme Court of the United States on Frank's behalf and the writ of habeas corpus petition filed in United States District Court, the United States government was not involved in the Frank case.

Forty-six years after Judge Roan sentenced Leo Frank to die for the murder of Mary Phagan, A. L. Henson published an obscure book called *Confessions of a Criminal Lawyer*. As a young man, Allen Henson had assisted the prosecuting attorney and his staff in the preparation of briefs for the Leo Frank appeal cases to be heard in U.S. District Court and the U.S. Supreme Court. He had read and analyzed every line of testimony from the original trial. And Henson recounted the way by which Judge Roan made up his mind not to grant a new trial for Leo Frank. William Smith, Jim Conley's attorney, had stopped by to see Judge Roan. Mr. Smith told the judge that the "verdict was only the echo of an angry mob!"

Smith went on to divulge his client's story. Jim Conley went to the pencil factory on Memorial Day expecting to be alone most of the time. He was to watch until Newt Lee came on duty as watchman about six o'clock. Conley had arranged for a man to bring him some corn whiskey at the factory. The whiskey was delivered at the door leading to the alley from the basement. Jim took some deep drinks and soon drained the bottle. Later, when his mind was clouded he saw a girl come into the factory. Conley followed her, and she screamed. They struggled and Jim remembered that he fought back. Then his mind went blank. Sometime later he remembered being in the basement. "He looked around and there was the girl, lying still, with a cord around her neck. He looked at her a long time and decided she was dead. He was scared. He didn't wait for Newt Lee, the nightwatchman, but hid the body the best he could, and left by the alley entrance."

Together, Judge Roan and William Smith concluded that this version of Conley's story was the truth. The judge was determined to grant the motion for a new trial. But he was also concerned about a widespread violent mob reaction to his decision. So, on the advice of a judicial associate (Judge Foster), Leonard Roan denied the motion for a new trial on October 31, 1913. By letting the case run its course through the appellate process, Judge Roan hoped the public excitement would subside. The governor of Georgia could, at a later date, decide on the case.

A letter signed by Judge Roan in December 1914 confirms his doubts of the original verdict in the Frank case. ". . . I allowed the jury's verdict to remain undisturbed," he wrote, "I had no way of knowing it was erroneous."

Shortly after Leo Frank's trial, Rabbi David Marx went to New York City to consult with Louis Marshall, president of the American Jewish Committee. The AJC was established in 1906 to aid Jews "in all countries where their civil or religious rights were endangered or denied." Rabbi Marx felt that Leo Frank's conviction was the result of an anti-Semitic outburst. The executive committee of the AJC considered the Frank issue for the first time on November 8, 1913, but resolved to take no official action. *The AJC did not want to be perceived as championing the cause of a Jew convicted of a crime!*

Although Louis Marshall counseled caution, he did not object to Jewish organizations giving "unpublicized assistance." Marshall's plan was to use the influence of important people to persuade southern newspapers to change public opinion in favor of Frank. In January 1914, Louis Marshall brought the Frank case to the attention of *New York Times'* publisher Adolph Ochs, who rose to Frank's defense.

Marshall also provided legal assistance and public relations advice to Frank's attorneys.

The AJC president later prepared and delivered the second appeal of Frank's case to the United States Supreme Court, arguing that Frank had been deprived of his constitutional rights under the due process clause of the Fourteenth Amendment to the Constitution. Frank, he argued, had not been in the courtroom when the verdict was rendered.

By 1914, many prominent American Jews, including Albert D. Lasker, Julius Rosenwald, and Jacob H. Schiff were providing money, time, and talent in support of Frank. As a result, the allegation circulated throughout Georgia that Frank's defense counsel used Jewish money to purchase influence. Georgia's establishment historian Lucian Lamar Knight wrote in 1917 that "the entire Hebrew population of America was believed to be an organized unit directing and financing a systematic campaign to mold public sentiment and to snatch Frank from the clutches of the law." But for American Jews to have ignored Frank would imply that Jews could be maligned and mistreated with impunity.

Unlike the American Jewish Committee, the Jewish community in California believed that Frank was a victim of blatant anti-Semitism. The California Jewish community (two percent of that state's population in 1915), felt that only a "massive popular campaign" would aid Frank's cause. Other Jewish individuals and communities openly attacked the Frank verdict in defiance of the wishes of Marshall and the AJC.

But Atlanta's Jewish community did not, in fact, assume an active role on Frank's behalf. In the South, Jews were not anxious to attract attention for fear of bringing on displays of anti-Semitism. It was rare for Jews to support publicly controversial issues; they were very conscious of their image in the eyes of Christians. On the other hand, in 1914, a Civic Education League was established in Atlanta by five Jewish lawyers. This organization was intended to raise the Jews' civic consciousness and encourage them to fulfill previously neglected obligations: to petition for citizenship, vote, serve on juries, and seek public office. Combatting civic apathy was seen as a means of bolstering the Jewish community's security.

Although there were random newspaper comments on the Frank case outside the South in 1913, it was not until the spring of 1914 that Frank's conviction became a national issue. But when it did, the majority of the nation's major metropolitan daily newspapers rose to Frank's defense. The controversy centered around whether the jury had convicted Frank because of legitimate evidence or because of intimidation by the mob atmosphere. The case became a cause célèbre, nearly matching public interest shown in the Sacco-Vanzetti case of the 1920s and the ordeal of the Scottsboro boys in the 1930s.[3]

The Frank case provided the first issue of national interest in which the concerns of blacks and Jews seemed in direct conflict. To the question: Did Frank, a Jew, kill a Christian girl or did Conley, a black, kill a white girl, the national newspapers focused on the latter.

Leo Frank, the Jew, was treated as a white man unjustly convicted of a crime "typically" committed by blacks. The theme of the "black monster," as the *New York Times* characterized Conley in March 1914, appeared in such major papers as the *Baltimore Sun*, *Chicago Tribune*, and *Washington Post*.

In reading the nation's press of 1914–1915, black Americans understandably felt that whites were again looking for a black scapegoat. By 1915, the system of segregation, known as Jim Crow, was firmly established and the efforts to substitute a black man for Leo Frank seemed but one more example of blacks being victimized by whites.

With the exception of the Frank case, there was little general hostility towards Jews by the black leaders of the early twentieth century. Black leadership included such men as Booker T. Washington, W. E. B. DuBois (founder of *Phylon*, the Atlanta University review of race and religion), and James Weldon Johnson, executive secretary of the National Association for the Advancement of Colored People (NAACP).

According to Eugene Levy, Jim Conley was not made a hero by the black press, but it was thought that he told the truth in his courtroom testimony. The black papers had no desire to see Frank hanged by the State of Georgia, nor did they wish to see a miscarriage of justice. But it was nonetheless felt that efforts by such reputable papers as the *New York Times* and *Chicago Tribune* to pin the murder of Mary Phagan on Jim Conley, because he was black, should be viewed with contempt. The only black editor who rejected Jim Conley's story and endorsed Frank's appeal for a new trial was Benjamin Davis of the *Atlanta Independent*, a black weekly that began publication in 1903.

The Seventh U.S. Census[4] estimated that there were 500 slaves in Atlanta in 1850. The first long-term contacts between Jews and blacks in Atlanta were between masters and slaves. At the end of the Civil War, all city ordinances that discriminated on the basis of race were repealed. Blacks were given the right to vote in Atlanta in 1868, the same year the State of Georgia expelled all blacks from its legislature. The Gate City's population in 1890 was over forty percent black; at the turn of the century that figure had decreased slightly, but ten years later the proportion of blacks in Atlanta's population had decreased to one-third.

Relations between the Jewish and black communities were normally cordial, although there were resentments and frustrations. Blacks tended to deflect local prejudices, which might otherwise have been directed against Jews.

Discussion of the Frank case in Jewish newspapers revolved around the extent and significance of anti-Semitism during the trial and its aftermath. The character and race of James Conley were of less concern to editors of Jewish papers than their counterparts on the metropolitan dailies or on black newspapers. However, the Jewish papers (including the *Boston Jewish Advocate*, the *Pittsburgh Jewish Criterion*, *The Jewish World*, the *St. Louis Jewish Voice*, and the *Cincinnati American Israelite*) frequently reprinted anti-Conley editorials from the daily papers.

While the case was attracting attention across the country, Leo Frank's attorneys were busy preparing appeals.

Endnotes

1. In 1910, there were only about 54,000 Mennonites in this country, and they were split into 11 groups.

2. See Paul Mendes-Flohr's and Jehuda Reinharz's edited work, *The Jew in the Modern World*.

3. Nicola Sacco and Bartolomeo Vanzetti had been tried and convicted for murder and robbery in Braintree, Massachusetts in 1921. There was widespread belief that the conviction had been influenced by the men's reputations as radicals. Public outcry forced a review of the case, even though a new trial was never granted. An advisory group to the state governor upheld the judicial procedure and the two were executed on August 27, 1927. Sacco and Vanzetti were widely regarded as martyrs.

On March 31, 1931, nine black youths were indicted for the rape of two white girls. After several trials and two U.S. Supreme Court reversals of conviction, five of the youths were convicted and sentenced, and four acquitted. Northern liberals and radicals charged anti-black bias in Alabama and made the case a cause célèbre. The Scottsboro Defense Committee, representing primarily liberal, non-Communist organizations, was largely responsible for ultimately freeing the young men.

4. The first census conducted in the country was in 1790.

Chapter 5

THE APPEALS

In their effort to win a new trial for their client, Leo Frank's defense attorneys stressed the procedural irregularities that regularly took place during the court proceedings. The defense submitted affidavits attesting to the alleged prejudice of two of the jurors towards the defendant. They also submitted affidavits from Atlanta residents who witnessed the trial and attested to the fact that the jurymen had heard the crowds outside the courtroom windows and had seen the public demonstrations.

Arguing for the State, Solicitor Dorsey and Attorney Hooper maintained that justice had been upheld. Judge Roan, as we have seen, denied the defense motion at the end of October 1913, although he stated that he was not thoroughly convinced of Leo Frank's guilt. His doubt arose from the character of the State's main witness, Jim Conley. But Judge Roan felt the jury had been certain Frank was guilty.

The judge's uncertainty provided a solid plank on which the defense built its next platform of appeal. A new trial was taken on writ of error to the Georgia Supreme Court by Luther Rosser and Reuben Arnold. Under a constitutional amendment adopted in 1906, the state supreme court was not permitted to reverse any capital case where no error of law had been committed in the trial. The weakness of evidence presented in a given case was viewed as irrelevant. The Georgia Supreme Court also could not investigate a case nor pass judgment upon a defendant's guilt or innocence. Its jurisdiction was confined strictly to matters of the law. Colonel Thomas Felder, the new attorney general, and Hugh Dorsey presented the State's case. On February 17, 1914, the court returned a judgment denying a new trial.

That same month, Frank's defense counsel asked the noted detective, William J. Burns, to assist them in their continuing investigation of the Phagan murder. The Burns Detective Agency in Atlanta had been involved in the Phagan murder investigation back in 1913, but William Burns himself had not gone to Atlanta to participate in the proceedings.[1]

While appeals were being prepared and investigations being carried out, Leo Frank was in the Fulton County jail in a barred cell measuring six-by-eight-feet. He kept a card-file index of everything printed about himself and the Phagan case. He had access to all the Atlanta and most of the southern newspapers. When interviewed by the *Atlanta Georgian* in late February 1914, he was wearing a neat, dark business suit, dark patent leather shoes, and a dark four-in-hand tie. His bed had a homemade quilt on it, and his cell had a table and chair.

In a telegram to the editor of the *New York Times*, Charles D. McKinney, acting secretary-manager of the Georgia Chamber of Commerce, declared that "Atlanta and the whole State of Georgia not only have no prejudice against a stranger, but we cordially invite manufacturers and investors, farmers, and the better clas [sic] of immigrants to make their homes and engage in business among us."

In March 1914, reports came to light suggesting that certain evidence presented in the Frank case was obtained under duress or ignored by the police authorities. Mr. W. J. Jenkins and his wife alleged that Detective John Black had tried to induce their daughter Lulu Belle to give false testimony against Leo Frank. The police reportedly bribed and threatened the girl. An affidavit issued by the newspaper delivery boy, George Epps, contained a denial of the boy's courtroom testimony. At the trial, Epps said that he caught the same street car as Mary Phagan and swore to the exact time of his actions. Epps claimed in the new affidavit that Detective Black coached him on exactly what to say.

Mrs. J. B. Simmons said she was not called to the stand because her testimony did not fit with the State's theory of the Phagan murder. While walking by the National Pencil Factory at about 2:30 P.M. the day of the murder, Mrs. Simmons claims she heard screams. Hugh Dorsey allegedly had tried to have the woman change the time in her story to 3:00 P.M. because Frank was not in the building at 2:30. He had gone home for some lunch.

Ruby Snipes, a seventeen-year-old white girl, swore that Jim Conley had attempted to attack her in April of 1911. In another sworn statement, Mrs. Hattie Miller, a young Atlanta woman, said that she had been offered $1,000 to testify falsely against Frank at his trial.

It was not until March 1914 that Christian clergymen went on record concerning the Frank case—although presumably Christian pastors and priests discussed the case prior to that time. In a letter to the editor of the *Atlanta Journal*, Reverend C. B. Wilmer, Rector of St. Luke's Episcopal Church in Atlanta, urged that some way be found for a new trial for the accused. Judicial murder had to be prevented. Dr. Wilmer was concerned not so much about the verdict as with the conditions surrounding the trial. He commented on the fact that not even the trial judge was fully convinced of Frank's guilt.

St. Luke's had been established during the Civil War by a chaplain in the Confederate army. Dr. Wilmer was called in 1900 and served as pastor until his resignation in 1924. "He never hesitated to champion the cause of the downtrodden and oppressed."

The pastor of Mary Phagan's Bible school, Dr. L. O.

Bricker, admitted that he, along with many others, were in such a state of mind during Frank's trial that proper exercise of judgment and decision was not possible. "This state of affairs reached a point that charged the very atmosphere of the courtroom with prejudice. An unbiased trial was impossible."

Dr. A. R. Holderly, pastor of the Moore Memorial Church in Atlanta, told his congregation that it would be "unfair to hang a sheep-killing dog upon the evidence upon which Frank has been convicted." Reverend Julian S. Rodgers, of the East Atlanta Baptist Church, spoke in favor of a new trial for Leo Frank during his sermon on March 15, 1914.

The Rome Tribune and *The Albany Herald*, both newspapers of Georgia, ran editorials in March 1914 urging that a new trial be held so that justice could prevail. The sentiment in favor of granting Frank a new trial seemed to be growing, as evidenced by the flood of letters from Georgia to the *New York Times* in the spring of 1914.

And one of the twelve men who had been on the jury during Frank's trial finally replied to the calls from Atlanta pulpits for a new trial for the defendant. J. T. Ozburn argued that the jury had heard all the testimony and had sufficient intelligence and honesty to weigh the evidence without prejudice. The ministers attacking the Frank verdict are "holier-than-thou gentlemen," said Ozburn.

On March 22, two more Atlanta pastors issued strong demands for a new trial. Reverend F. A. Lines, of the First Universalist Church, devoted his entire sermon to the Frank case. Mob conditions had surrounded the trial, he charged, and in convicting the defendant the jury had responded to the pressure of the crowds. "The Church, the Christian people of this city and State are on trial."

That same Sunday a leading Atlanta clergyman, Reverend G. L. Hickman, talked about a new trial for Leo Frank in the prelude to his morning sermon: "If Leo M. Frank is

MARY PHAGAN. The little girl found murdered at the National Pencil Factory. *(Atlanta Journal & Atlanta Constitution)*

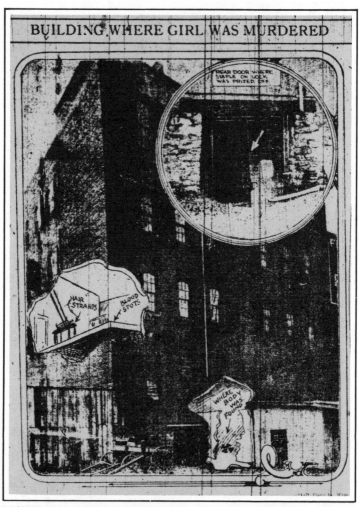

NATIONAL PENCIL FACTORY. The building at 37-41 South Forsyth Street in Atlanta which was home to the National Pencil Factory. *(Atlanta Journal & Atlanta Constitution)*

BOOKKEEPER ACCUSED OF MURDER

JOHN M. GANTT. An early suspect in the Phagan murder was John Gantt, former bookkeeper of the National Pencil Company. *(Atlanta Journal & Atlanta Constitution)*

ARTHUR MULLINAX. A streetcar conductor arrested in connection with the murder of Mary Phagan, Arthur Mullinax was soon released by police. *(Atlanta Journal & Atlanta Constitution)*

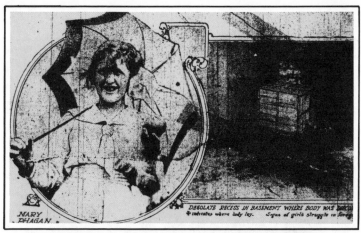

PRETTY YOUNG VICTIM AND THE SITE OF HER MURDER. *(Atlanta Journal & Atlanta Constitution)*

MARY PHAGAN'S FAMILY AND BLOOMFIELD'S UNDER-TAKER ESTABLISHMENT.
(Atlanta Journal & Atlanta Constitution)

LEO M. FRANK.
(Atlanta Journal & Atlanta Constitution)

MARIETTA MOURNS AS BODY IS LOWERED INTO GRAVE

MARIETTA MOURNS ITS LOSS.
(Atlanta Journal & Atlanta Constitution)

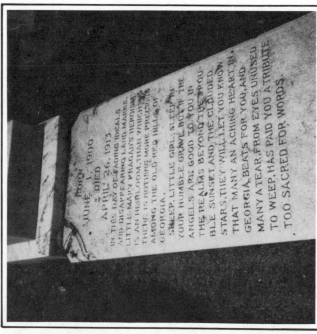

MARY PHAGAN's GRAVESITE IN CITIZENS' CEMETERY, MARIETTA, GEORGIA. The local United Confederate Veterans (Marietta Camp No. 763) erected a memorial at the head of the little girl's grave. A marble stone with a two-paragraph inscription covers the grave itself. *(Robert Seitz Frey)*

ATLANTA CITY DETECTIVES.
(Atlanta Journal & Atlanta Constitution)

HE IS DETAINED BY THE POLICE

HELD ON SUSPICION OF MURDER. Factory superintendent
Leo Frank was held by police on suspicion of murder.
(*Atlanta Journal* & *Atlanta Constitution*)

TWO WITNESSES IN THE CORONER'S INQUEST. Miss Daisy Jones and George W. Epps were called before Coroner Paul Donehoo. (*Atlanta Journal* & *Atlanta Constitution*)

JUDGE LEONARD STRICKLAND ROAN. Judge Roan served as the trial judge in the Phagan murder case.
(*Atlanta Journal* & *Atlanta Constitution*)

Top row, left to right: Solicitor General Hugh Dorsey and Reuben Arnold, attorney for Frank. Bottom row: Frank A. Hooper, aiding prosecution, and Assistant Solicitor General E. A. Stephens.

THE ATTORNEYS. Far left: Sketch of defense attorney Luther Z. Rosser. Top row, left to right: Solicitor General Hugh M. Dorsey and Reuben Arnold, lawyer for Leo Frank. Bottom row, left to right: Frank A. Hooper, aiding the prosecution, along with Assistant Solicitor General E. A. Stephens. (*Atlanta Journal* & *Atlanta Constitution*)

**FRED WINBURN,
JURY FOREMAN.**
*(Atlanta Journal &
Atlanta Constitution)*

REPRESENTING STATE IN FRANK TRIAL

Left to right: Solicitor General Hugh M. Dorsey, Assistant Solicitor E. A. Stephens, and Attor-

FOR THE PROSECUTION. Hugh Dorsey, E. A. Stephens, and
Frank Hooper represented the State of Georgia against Leo Frank.
(Atlanta Journal & Atlanta Constitution)

Members of Mary Phagan's Family Who Are Attending Frank Trial

MARY PHAGAN'S AUNT, MOTHER, AND SISTER. Miss Mattie Phagan, Mrs. J. W. Coleman, and Ollie Phagan.
(Atlanta Journal & Atlanta Constitution)

THE PHAGAN WOMEN.
(Atlanta Journal & Atlanta Constitution)

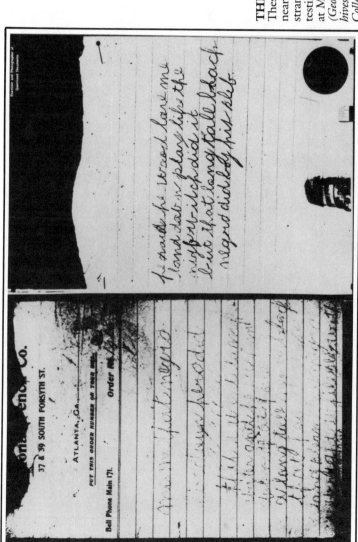

THE MURDER NOTES.
These two notes were found near Little Mary Phagan's strangled body. Jim Conley testified that he wrote them at Mr. Frank's instruction. *(Georgia Department of Archives and History; Slaton Collection; AC# 00-070)*

LEO AND LUCILLE FRANK AT THE TRIAL.
(Atlanta Journal & Atlanta Constitution)

innocent, give him a fair chance to prove that he is innocent. If he is guilty, let him pay the penalty."

The Frank case was also on the agenda at the Fortieth District Convention of the Independent Order of B'nai B'rith held in Atlanta on March 30.

The efforts of Leo Frank's defense counsel to secure a new trial through appeal to the Georgia Supreme Court had been damaged by the retracted affidavits from Reverend C. B. Ragsdale and his parishioner, Mr. R. L. Barber. Ragsdale, a Baptist minister, and Barber had sworn that they overheard a black man identified as Jim Conley confess that he had murdered Mary Phagan. Later, they changed their statements. Attorney Reuben Arnold obtained an order from Judge Ben H. Hill striking from the motion for a new trial the amendment establishing the Ragsdale affidavit as a part of the grounds for a new hearing. Judge Hill sat in the Criminal Division of Fulton County Superior Court.

His initial affidavit was a deliberate "frame-up," Ragsdale claimed, and went on the charge that he had been bribed with several hundred dollars. But Luther Rosser and Reuben Arnold insisted the pastor's testimony had been volunteered freely. Reverend Ragsdale resigned his pastorate and refused to be interviewed on the subject.

During the last week of April 1914, the *New York Times* published a letter written by Leo Frank to the "People of Atlanta." Frank was incensed that Chief Newport Lanford, head of the detective department, could serenely announce that the charge of perversion had never entered into the case. That charge had been the very thing which was the driving force in his road to the gallows, Frank maintained. He asked if his case should not be reconsidered now that the perversion "charges" had been dropped. Was he to be hanged on the word of a "creature" such as Conley? "Is it possible that my life of decency is to weigh as nothing?"

A motion was filed in the Superior Court of Fulton County on April 16, 1914, to set aside the verdict against

Leo Frank. Judgment was rendered against Frank on June 6. The Supreme Court of Georgia affirmed that judgment five months later, after the lower court's decision had been taken up the appellate ladder on a writ of error.

During the summer of 1914, national attention was focused on the gathering war clouds in Europe. By summer's end, the Allies were at war with the Central Powers.

Leo Frank's defense counsel now directed their appeal to the nation's capital. Application for a writ of error to review the Georgia Supreme Court's judgment was made to Justices Joseph Rucker Lamar and Oliver Wendell Holmes of the United States Supreme Court. Counsel premised their petition on the fact that Frank had been absent from the courtroom at the rendering of the verdict. Both justices denied the application, although Holmes was not convinced that Frank had received due process of law in light of the threatening crowds.

The defense then petitioned to be heard by the entire Court. Their request was granted, but the appeal was refused on December 7, 1914, and was not accompanied by any written opinion.

Leo Frank then petitioned to the U.S. District Court of Northern Georgia to discharge him from custody. U.S. District Judge William T. Newman denied the writ of habeas corpus four days before Christmas, in 1914.

In October of the same year an extremely promising development occurred. William M. Smith, the lawyer who had represented Jim Conley during the Frank trial, announced that he was ready to join forces with the defense. In a public statement, Smith unequivocally called Jim Conley the murderer. Conley, then working in the Bellwood convict camp, seemed indifferent to this new development. In February 1915, a second and final appeal was made to the U.S. Supreme Court. And it was Louis Marshall, lawyer and president of the American Jewish Committee, who prepared the defense brief. Born in Syracuse, New York, to German Jewish immigrants, Marshall graduated from Columbia University Law School in 1876 and was admitted to the New York bar in 1878. Although he had maintained a low profile in the Frank affair, he played a very significant role in assisting and supervising Leo Frank's defense counsel and in arguing the second appeal of the Frank case before the Supreme Court of the United States[2] (237 U.S. 309): *Leo M. Frank, Appellant* v. *C. Wheeler Mangum, Sheriff of Fulton County, Ga.* Marshall was assisted by Henry C. Peeples and Henry A. Alexander; Attorney General Warren Grice and Solicitor General Hugh M. Dorsey represented the State of Georgia.

Mr. Marshall built the defense around the hostile atmosphere surrounding the trial, Frank's absence from the courtroom at the time the verdict was rendered, and the mob action after the verdict had been delivered. Solicitor Dorsey announced that if Leo Frank obtained his freedom from the Supreme Court, he would attempt to have Frank indicted by the grand jury on one or two other charges, namely, criminal assault and perversion. The aura of perversion hung over the entire Frank case. The Jew from Brooklyn was viewed and portrayed as different from other men. Tom Watson's "Jew pervert" was a powerful image. According to one New York magazine, during the entire appeal process a mob in the Atlanta area kept up its threats and heightened the level of tension.

On April 19, 1915, the Court rejected[3] the defense motion, 7–to–2. In stating the dissenting viewpoint, Justices Oliver Wendell Holmes Jr.[4] and Charles Evans Hughes clearly recognized and deplored the influence of the mob during Frank's trial. Justice Holmes wrote that "we think the presumption overwhelming that the jury responded to the passions of the mob."[5]

Later (in *Moore* v. *Dempsey*; 261 U.S. 86), the Court found for defendants, who had grounds for defense similar to those of the Frank case. The accused included Frank Moore, Ed Hicks, and J. E. Knox, all black men. E. J.

Dempsey was Keeper of the Arkansas State Penitentiary. The legal brief for this case is dated October 1922.

Georgia law permitted one final recourse for Leo Frank's defense attorneys, namely, to petition Governor John Slaton for clemency through the Georgia State Prison Commission. From the initial date of October 10, 1913, Frank's execution had been moved first to April 17, 1914, then to January 22, 1915, and finally to June 22, 1915. And the pressure on Slaton to commute Frank's sentence was becoming more intense every day.

Jews and Christians alike were urged to write to Governor Slaton asking for executive clemency for Leo Frank. Dr. Joel Blau, during a talk at the Madison Avenue synagogue in New York in December 1914, contended that "we Jews are not seeking to shield a criminal." Every *Christian* pulpit, he said, ought to speak out on the case.

American Socialist leader Eugene Victor Debs, a five-time Presidential hopeful, declared that race prejudice made Leo Frank's trial a farce. "The South is blinded by race prejudice, one of the inheritances of chattel slavery. . . . It is in this atmosphere and environment that Frank, 'the damned Jew,' has been railroaded." The U.S. Constitution had been violated, Debs argued, and its protection denied a citizen charged with a crime in a prejudiced community.

In a Sunday morning service in Rochester, New York, held the last week of 1914, Dr. William Rosenau, of Baltimore, said that in the great American democracy there is still the occasional outbreak of feeling against the Hebrew. "The Leo M. Frank trial in Atlanta is an example of this." Rosenau was Vice Chancellor of the Chautauqua.

The widow of Congressman William H. Felton, Representative from Georgia's 7th District, wrote a letter to the *New York Times* printed in mid-January 1915. Mrs. Felton, then nearly eighty, claimed that "there is no 'Jew-baiting' in Georgia. . . . Those of Hebrew lineage are most highly respected in every instance where they are known to be good citizens. I do not forget that the Southern Confederacy placed one of its highest positions in the care of Judah P. Benjamin."[6]

By the fall of 1914, although America had not entered the war in Europe, it was the focus of national attention—especially after the battle of Ypres, where thousands of men on both sides were slaughtered. This prompted one New York magazine to raise this question: At a time when men are being killed by the thousands in war, why should the quandary of whether *one* man lives or dies seem important? In answer to its question, the magazine said that there are times when the death of one man may be of more consequence to the future welfare of the human race than the loss of an entire regiment or army corps. That man was Leo Frank.

By January of 1915, it was estimated that Governor John Slaton had received more than fifteen thousand pieces of correspondence about the case from all over the country, including a letter from the presiding judge at Frank's trial. Most of the letters requested that the governor commute the defendant's sentence. The legislatures of Arizona, Texas, Louisiana, Michigan, Pennsylvania, West Virginia, and Tennessee passed formal resolutions to that effect. Letters were sent to the governor's office from the president of the University of Chicago, the dean of Yale College, and future Nobel laureate, Jane Addams, famous for Hull House in Chicago. Several state governors and United States senators also petitioned on Frank's behalf. North Dakota's governor asked John Slaton to consider commutation in order to buy time for both Leo Frank and the State of Georgia to throw new light on the case. The governor of Nevada was convinced that Frank should not suffer the death penalty on any evidence brought out so far. Nevada's governor wrote to Governor Slaton on Frank's behalf, although he was aware that he was violating established ethics of gubernatorial conduct. Governors did not, as a rule, interfere in the internal affairs of another state. But the governor of Arkansas wrote: "The Jewish people in our state are very solicitous about this case, and, if you could see your way clear and feel that the interests of justice would be served by a commutation of this sentence to life imprisonment, it would meet with general approval."

On January 20, 1915, Mrs. J. W. Coleman, mother of Mary Phagan, filed a damage suit against the National Pencil Company. She asked for ten thousand dollars for the death of her daughter. The suit, which named both Leo Frank and Jim Conley, sought to demonstrate that the company was responsible for the safety of its employees while they were on its premises.

That same January day, a mob took a young black man away from a deputy sheriff and lynched him inside the city limits of Vicksburg, Mississippi. The victim had been arrested for stealing some cattle.

In March, Judge Leonard Strickland Roan[7] died of a blood clot at Polyclinic Hospital in New York. According to his relatives the judge made no written or verbal statement on the Frank case before he died. His brother did not feel that Roan's illness had been brought on or even aggravated by the widespread public discussion of the trial and sentence. But Roan's sister claimed he worried about the case a great deal. And Judge Roan had written from The Berkshire Hills Sanitorium in late 1914: "After many months of continued deliberation I am still uncertain of Frank's guilt." The letter was addressed to Rosser and Brandon and Reuben R. Arnold, attorneys for Leo Frank.

On Sunday, April 25, 1915, Reverend S. Edward Young delivered a sermon at the Bedford Presbyterian Church at Nostrand Avenue and Dean Street, in Brooklyn. The pastor called for a nationwide appeal on behalf of Leo M. Frank, using Deuteronomy 19:10 as the basis for his sermon. That passage from the Bible reads: "Lest innocent blood be shed in your land which the Lord your God gives you for inheritance, and so the guilt of bloodshed be upon you."

The issues involved in the Frank case, said Dr. Young, "affect the whole country and the vital teachings of religion.

. . . The element of incalculable seriousness is the convicting of any American citizen on account of his race or religion." The fact that prejudice against the Jew was the real accuser in the Frank trial must not be tolerated. "Against it cry out the Old and New Testaments. . . ." Dr. Young said that race prejudice is the worst possible indictment of the Christian religion, which would seem to imply that Christianity bears some responsibility for anti-Jewish prejudice.

Evangelist William Ashley "Billy" Sunday[8] also commented on the Frank case during his sermon at the Tabernacle, in Paterson, New Jersey, on the night of May 11, 1915. He said that if he were governor of Georgia, Leo Frank would go free tomorrow. These words brought loud applause from the crowds.

Mrs. Frank was informed in early May that "petitions are coming in daily" to *The Muskogee Times-Democrat*, a leading daily newspaper of Oklahoma. That same month, *The Illinois State Journal* sent her 1,104 "signed cards petitioning the governor of Georgia to grant a commutation of sentence to your husband." San Francisco's *Daily News* had received six thousand petitions from its subscribers. Lucille Frank worked untiringly to keep her husband from the gallows. "I beg the American people to save my husband's life, because he is innocent."—was her continuing plea. "Every bit of evidence produced at the trial," said the plump, dark-haired Mrs. Frank, "shows completely that my husband is not guilty. In the end I know his name will be cleared."

Fifteen thousand petitions for clemency—making up a package weighing 75 pounds—were collected from all over the State of Ohio and delivered to Governor Slaton in mid-May.

But Governor Slaton hoped and believed he would never be called on to decide the fate of Leo Frank. In a letter dated April 28, 1915 to Senator Lawrence Sherman, the governor wrote: "I retire . . . in June, and I doubt if the case will reach me before that time." He was wrong.

Four judges of the Appellate Court of Chicago signed petitions urging clemency. In addition, a mass meeting dubbed "Leo M. Frank Day" was held in the Windy City. The speakers included three Christian clergymen: the Right Reverend Samuel Fallows, the Reverend P. J. O'Callaghan, the Reverend S. J. Siedenberg. Also scheduled to speak was Clarence Darrow, who would later defend John T. Scopes at Dayton, Tennessee, in the famous "Monkey Trial" in 1925.

The president of the American Federation of Labor took time to write to the governor of Georgia: "Frank did not have a free, fair, impartial trial," wrote Samuel Gompers. "May I not appeal that your great prerogative be exercised in commuting the sentence of Leo M. Frank from death to a life term of imprisonment?"

By now Leo Frank had the support of almost all of America's major newspapers, including many in the South. For a time, the coverage of the case challenged the war in Europe for national attention. And a little eight-year-old boy named Floyd, from Ohio, wanted to be Leo's friend: "I want Jesus to let you free," the first-grader wrote, so that you can "come home an (sic) see your Mama." Little Floyd sent along one of his arithmetic papers for Mr. Frank to see because he had been given a "100" on his "numbers." This was only the second letter the boy had ever written.

But, counteracting the flood of petitions on Frank's behalf that poured into Governor Slaton's office during 1914 and the first half of 1915 was the "palpable menace of mob violence," anonymous threats to let Frank die, and political rewards promised by Thomas E. Watson if Frank's execution were carried out. The promised rewards were probably quite tempting to Slaton, who had solicited and received the former Populist leader's support during the Georgia gubernatorial race in 1912. According to historian Charlton Moseley, perhaps no other man in Georgia in the early twentieth century was more in accord with Ku Klux Klan principles, particularly that of anti-Catholicism, than

Thomas Watson. Watson used his *Jeffersonian* magazine as a forum to attack Leo Frank, selling 87,000 copies per week during the peak of the commutation controversy in June of 1915.

Thomas Edward Watson was born in McDuffie County, Georgia. After attending public schools he entered Mercer University in Macon in 1872. But lack of finances forced him to leave Mercer in his sophomore year to teach school. He studied law until admitted to the Georgia bar in 1875 at the age of nineteen. He began his practice in Thomson, Georgia, where he also published his *Jeffersonian* magazine. Watson married Georgia Durham in 1878, and the couple had two children. By the age of 36, Watson had "forged to the very front [of the state] as a lawyer and public man." In 1890, he was elected as a national representative to the Fifty-Second U.S. Congress. He died in September 1922 from an attack of bronchitis and asthma. The Ku Klux Klan sent a cross of roses eight feet high to his funeral at "Hickory Hill."[9]

Watson's campaign against Frank, staged through the pages of his *Jeffersonian*, was very effective in arousing the opposition. Typical of the mail it inspired is this letter in the "John Marshall Slaton Collection" at the Georgia Department of Archives and History from Moultrie M. Sessions to a Mr. Hanford, dated May 17, 1915. Sessions, a lawyer who lived outside of Atlanta, argued that Leo Frank indeed deserved to be hung. "All the stuff about race prejudice was lugged into this case by Frank's own attorneys for the purpose of muddying the waters," wrote Sessions. Frank "has gotten up a great deal of false sympathy over the United States. . . . If Leo M. Frank had not been a 'Jew' he would have been hung months ago." Leo and Lucille Frank received a postcard from Charleston, South Carolina, care of the "Mansion of Aching Hearts," an obvious reference to Governor Slaton's former home. The face of the postcard read: "ALL the lies they tell about the Jews are true." The word "Dutch" had originally appeared but was crossed out and "Jews" had been written.

The Georgia Prison Commission met on May 31, 1915, in special session to hear Frank's appeal for commutation. The commission and the governor had received a six-page letter from Jim Conley's lawyer. "There exists a large number of the strongest lines of evidence," wrote Attorney William Smith, that "reveals the error of charging Leo M. Frank with having any part in the murder of Mary Phagan. . . . I BELIEVED IT WAS MY DUTY TO SPEAK. I HAD HELPED TO DESTROY AN INNOCENT MAN. . . . BEFORE GOD, MY SOLE PURPOSE IS TO UNDO THE WRONG I HAVE HELPED TO DO. . . . With all the earnestness and seriousness of my life, I appeal to you not to let him die."

"Poor boy.
He is innocent.
Will you let him die?"

Slaton and the commission also were petitioned by Attorney Arthur Powell on Frank's behalf. Arthur Powell's partner, Mr. Hooper, had taken part in the prosecution of the Phagan murder case. During the trial proceedings, Powell had advised Judge Leonard Roan, at the judge's request. "Toward the close of the trial he [Judge Roan] sent for me and told me that his (the judge's) life was being threatened, that the temper of the crowds about the trial was such that he believed if the defendant was present at the verdict he would be lynched and that there was danger to his counsel if they were present. . . . To any critical mind there must be grave doubt of his guilt."

The vote against clemency was 2–to–1! Although Frank's guilt was questioned in the mind of at least one of the commissioners—T. E. Patterson—the board refused to recommend for clemency. Wrote Patterson: "If we take the evidence of the case outside that of Conley and Leo M. Frank, we find that both Frank and Conley had equal opportunity and motive for committing the crime." In his decision, Patterson weighed the letter written by Judge Roan in which he was still uncertain of Frank's guilt. The commissioner also pointed to the dissenting opinion of Chief Justice Fish and Justice Beck of the Georgia Supreme Court. "In the language of the Supreme Court this case depends largely upon circumstantial evidence, if not altogether."

Now there was only one last hope for Leo Frank—commutation of his sentence by the governor.

John Slaton was born in Merriwether County, Georgia, the son of William Franklin and Nancy Jane (Martin) Slaton. His father was an educator and the Slatons had a large family—2 boys and 4 girls. John graduated with an M.A. degree in 1886 from the University of Georgia, and was admitted to the Georgia bar in 1887.

Slaton began the practice of law in Atlanta in 1887 as a member of the firm of Glenn, Slaton & Phillips. Benjamin Z. Phillips, a Jewish attorney, was the junior partner. The firm later became known as Rosser, Slaton & Hopkins. Luther Rosser later served on Leo Frank's defense counsel.

In 1896, Slaton was elected on the Democratic ticket from Fulton County to the Georgia House of Representatives. He married Sarah Frances Grant Jackson in 1898; the couple had no children. Slaton became president of the Georgia Senate about 1909 and from that position became governor in 1911, when Governor Hoke Smith resigned to take a seat in the U.S. Senate. He was elected governor in 1912 and, through re-election, served until June 1915. Both Hoke Smith[10] and John Slaton advocated Progressive reforms[11].

John Slaton was also chairman of the board of Trinity Methodist Episcopal Church, South, and a member of the Masons and the Elks.

During the week of June 14, 1915, Governor Slaton held hearings on the commutation appeal for Leo Frank. That same week he had to deliver the commencement address at the University of Georgia in Athens. And he was also preparing to leave office.

On Monday of that week, Solicitor General Hugh Dorsey spoke for three hours opposing commutation. Contending that the trial evidence was overwhelmingly against the defendant, Dorsey also pointed to his conviction being upheld by both the Georgia Supreme Court and the United States Supreme Court. The case against Frank, according to Dorsey, was complete even without the testimony of Jim Conley. To commute Frank's sentence would be to invite the reign of the mob in Georgia.

Following Dorsey's arguments, the Reverend C. B. Wilmer launched a strong appeal for commutation, speaking as a representative of a committee of ministers. "The appeal," he said, "was not based on mercy." A plea for mercy would be based on a confession of guilt. "The appeal which I make is based on moral grounds and on a sense of justice. . . . We appeal against the provincial prejudice which has been evident against outside interference and against the prejudice of Gentiles against Jews."

The petition which Reverend Wilmer read[12]

appealed for clemency on the grounds that commutation would not change the jury's verdict or reflect on the Solicitor or the courts; that a life sentence would vindicate the severity of the law; that time might disclose new facts about the crime, and that commutation would be an act both of justice and humanity.

Because of differing viewpoints among the ministers who signed this petition, "they had not deemed it advisable to include appeals additional to those stated."

Pastor Wilmer continued to address the governor:

Several matters have been injected into this case which tend to befog it, and it is with reluctance that I discuss them in public. A prejudice has been engendered between Jews and Gentiles. Even if it were true, as charged by some, that the friends of Frank have done anything of a wrongful character in his behalf, it would not be something for you to consider in an appeal for commutation. . . . class prejudice has been brought into this case—a prejudice between employee and employer. This was obvious before, during, and since the trial. Then, politics has been injected into this case; it also should be eliminated.

I wish briefly to refer to the atmosphere of this community before and during Frank's trial. . . . Even should we admit that there was no suggestion of violence whatever on the part of the spectators at the trial, it should be remembered that psychological influence is far more subtle and far more calculated to affect the mind of a brave man than mob violence.

Wilmer also questioned the methods of the Atlanta detectives in gathering evidence in the Frank case. This caused Solicitor Dorsey to reply that the detectives were "as 'good men as Dr. Wilmer or any other wearer of the cloth in Atlanta.' " *The New York Times* noted that "Dr. Wilmer has shown unusual interest in the case. The wife of Governor Slaton is a communicant of his church."

Meanwhile, mail was continuing to pour into the governor's office asking the governor to grant clemency. "In the name of Christ Jesus and for the respect of your high office, don't have the stain of this man's blood on your hands," a pastor wrote from New Orleans. Reverend Mackay from Greensboro, Georgia, pointed out that, "even those who are firmly convinced of his guilt think that it would be a terrible risk for the State to inflict the death penalty in view of the many doubts in the case."

On June 20, 1915, Governor John Slaton made a courageous decision and committed political suicide by commuting Frank's sentence to life imprisonment. The next day he left office.

Endnotes

1. In an interview with the *New York Times* in December, 1914, Burns was of the opinion that the "false charge of perversion undoubtedly had caused the mob clamor" for Leo Frank's conviction. The

detective had offered a $5,000 reward for anyone who could produce facts supporting the perversion charge, but no one came forward. Burns said that every man connected with his Atlanta office had been arrested at one time or another and all fined on the assumption that they were associated with an unlicensed detective agency. But his agency was licensed, Burns maintained. He went on to say: "Prejudice against Frank? It is so strong, so all-embracing, so fostered by the police and those to whom a reversal of his conviction would be a blow that any person favoring Frank is a marked man in the city [Atlanta]."

2. Members of the Supreme Court at the time Frank's appeal was considered were Mahlon Pitney, Joseph McKenna, Oliver Wendell Holmes Jr., William Rufus Day, Charles Evans Hughes, Willis Van Dovanter, Joseph Rucker Lamar, and James Clark McReynolds.

3. The majority opinion was written by Justice Mahlon Pitney. Born in 1858 and educated at the College of New Jersey (Princeton), Mahlon Pitney was elected to the U.S. House of Representatives (1895–1899) and was a member of the New Jersey Senate. He was nominated for the Supreme Court by President William Taft in 1912. He served on the Court for ten years, retiring in December 1922. Justice Pitney died in Washington, D.C., two years later. (See *Guide to the U.S. Supreme Court*.)

4. Born in Boston on March 8, 1841, Oliver Wendell Holmes was the son of Oliver Wendell Holmes Sr. and Amelia Lee (Jackson) Holmes. His father was a professor of anatomy at Harvard Medical School and was also a poet, novelist, and essayist of renown. The younger Holmes graduated from Harvard in 1861 as class poet. He served in the Massachusetts Twentieth Volunteers during the Civil War, being wounded three times in battle and leaving the army as a captain. Admitted to the Massachusetts bar in 1867 after completing his legal studies at Harvard the previous year, Holmes practiced law in Boston for fifteen years. During that time he also taught constitutional law at his alma mater. In 1882 the governor of Massachusetts appointed Holmes, then a full professor at Harvard Law School, to a seat as associate justice of the Massachusetts supreme court. Dr. Holmes served there for twenty years. Theodore Roosevelt nominated Oliver Wendell Holmes Jr. for the United States Supreme Court in 1902. His twenty-nine years on the Court spanned the terms of Presidents Roosevelt, Taft, Wilson, Harding, Coolidge, and Hoover. Holmes died two days before his 94th birthday in Washington, D.C., in 1935. He and his wife, Fanny Bowdich Dixwell, never had any children. She had died in 1929. (See *Guide to the U.S. Supreme Court*.)

5. See Appendix 2, Justice Holmes' Dissent.

6. Judah Benjamin, a Jewish lawyer and statesman, was successively attorney general, secretary of war, and secretary of state of the Southern Confederate government.

7. Leonard Roan, born in 1849, was the husband of Miss Willie Strickland from Fairburn, Georgia. They had three sons and two daughters. The judge was a member of the First Methodist Church in Fairburn.

8. A former major league baseball player, "Billy" Sunday was ordained by the Chicago Presbytery in 1903. He proclaimed an ultra-conservative evangelical theology, preaching divine wrath rather than divine love.

9. See Comer Vann Woodward's *Tom Watson: Agrarian Rebel* and the *National Cyclopedia of American Biography*.

10. The governorship of the State of Georgia passed among many hands in the sixteen years from 1906 to 1921. Hoke Smith, a lawyer and former Secretary of Interior, was elected governor in 1906. Smith advocated many Progressive reforms, including increased appropriations for public schools, the establishment of juvenile courts (so children would not be tried as adults), and the abolition of the convict lease system. This system allowed for the placement of convicts with individuals or companies who leased the labor of the convict from the State. Smith resigned his office in November, 1911, to assume a senatorial seat in the United States Congress.

As president of the Georgia Senate, John Marshall Slaton became acting governor on November 16, 1911. He served until a special election was held in January of the following year. Joseph Mackey Brown won the special election, and held the governorship until June, 1913. Brown's term saw no major reform efforts. Defeated in his bid for a seat in the U.S. Senate by Hoke Smith in 1914, Brown later became an author.

11. After the Phagan murder, members of the California Progressive movement charged that Georgia lagged behind in enacting changes on the Progressive agenda. If there had been regulations mandating inspections of factories and factory conditions, the Progressives argued, the murder might have been less possible. As a group, the California Progressives did not couch their arguments about the Frank case in terms of capital punishment and anti-Semitism, but generally conceived of equality only in political and economic terms. There was no "vigorous ideological offensive against the barriers of race and nationality." Progressivism was alive in California in 1913–1915, even though it had eclipsed as a movement in most other parts of America. See Gerald S. Henig's article, "California Progressives React to the Leo Frank Case."

12. Wilmer's petition had also been presented to the Georgia Prison Commission several weeks before by Reverend John E. White, pastor of the Second Baptist Church in Atlanta. Organized in 1854, the church claimed three United States senators, four governors of Georgia, two members of the Supreme Court, six judges of the Superior Court, and

ten mayors of Atlanta among its distinguished parishioners. Dr. John White served there as pastor from January 1901 until August 1915. He also was president of the Georgia Baptist Convention and "a dynamic force in the civic life of the community."

Chapter 6

THE COMMUTATION

Throughout his twenty-seven months in prison, Leo Frank received mail from friends and from people all over the country. A man from Hayti, Missouri, sent a cartoon from the *St. Louis Post-Dispatch* "with the idea of showing to you that all of the world is not cruel or cold." In the drawing a mighty hand and forearm labeled "MOB SPIRIT" is crushing the limp body of "LEO FRANK." "It is an awful thought that the human family lust for the blood of a human being, but thank God we are becoming more civilized," this unknown friend wrote in his letter. The man also wished Frank a Merry Christmas that year—1914.

A few months before, Frank received notice from the National Pencil Company that his monthly salary of $150 would be cut to $100. He wrote to Sig Montag, letting him know how grateful he was for the money. "I also wish you to know that I consider the monthly check, which you so kindly send me, but a loan, which, when brighter days come, I shall endeavor to repay."

Frank had petitioned the prison commission for clemency in April 1915. About six weeks later, Maurice Kovnat of the AntiCapital Punishment Society of America, headquartered in Chicago, wrote him a two-page letter. "Our Society has most probably been the first to nationally work on your behalf," wrote Kovnat. Many of the society's prominent officers, he said, have written letters to the governor and the prison commission.

But Frank's most steadfast correspondent was his wife, Lucille. Many of her letters begin with "My own," "Dearest," or "My dear Honey" and they swell with love and caring. She also sent news of family and friends amidst an unending refrain of longing to be together. The letters must have made his burden just a little easier to bear.

Guns from the Austrian and German armies pounded Lemberg in Galicia on June 21, 1915, the day that Governor John Slaton commuted Leo Frank's sentence to life imprisonment. Frank had been taken from the Tower to the train terminal at about midnight the night before. Accompanied by two deputies, the prisoner met Sheriff Mangum at the station and the four men boarded the Central of Georgia train for Macon. The conductor in charge of their Pullman car, Captain L. B. Irwin, said Frank had a cloak pulled up around his head and pretended to be ill. Several other men left the Tower at about the same time Frank did in order to decoy anyone who might have been watching. Two hours and forty-five minutes later, Leo Frank was put into an automobile in Macon and driven the thirty miles through the countryside to the Milledgeville prison farm, where he was registered as Convict No. 965. The next day he issued a statement thanking Governor Slaton and once again affirming his innocence.

The *Atlanta Journal* carried a statement from the governor in the June 21 edition. He said he had received more than a hundred thousand letters from people all over the country requesting clemency, and then proceeded to review the salient details of the prosecution's case against Frank as well as the defense strategy. "The mystery in the case is the question as to how Mary Phagan's body got into the basement," said Slaton. Jim Conley testified that he had helped Frank take the girl's body down to the basement in the elevator on the afternoon of April 26, 1913. Yet Conley also testified that on the *morning* of April 26 he had defecated in the elevator shaft in the basement. The next morning at 3:00 A.M., when the detectives went down to the basement by way of the ladder, they found human excrement in the elevator shaft in "natural condition." Because the elevator only stopped by hitting the ground in the basement, excrement left there on the morning of April 26 could not have been found intact on the morning of April 27, if Frank and Conley had used the elevator to carry the girl's body to the basement. Conley had contradicted himself under oath. In addition, with his slight physique, Frank could not have carried the girl's full body down the ladder to the basement.

Governor Slaton also pointed out that the wound on the top of Mary Phagan's head was one that bled freely. Yet the spot on the second floor "metal" room, where Conley testified he found the murdered girl's body, did not have blood on it. In addition, microscopic examination of the strands of hair found on the lathe there did not match the victim's hair.

The virtue of Mary Phagan was not violated on the day she was murdered, Slaton concluded, after sifting through more than a thousand pages of evidence from the case. The governor also pointed out that the solicitor general admitted in his written argument that Frank was convicted on the basis of circumstantial evidence.

Pastors Who Petitioned the Governor and the Prison Commission to Commute Leo Frank's Sentence

REV. G. R. BUFORD, Moore Memorial Presbyterian Church, Atlanta

REV. CHARLES W. DANIEL, Pastor, First Baptist Church, Atlanta

REV. H. M. DuBOSE, Pastor, First Methodist Church, Atlanta

REV. R. O. FLINN, Pastor, North Avenue Presbyterian Church, Atlanta

REV. C. LEWIS FOWLER, Pastor, College Park Baptist Church, Atlanta

REV. A. H. GORDON, Pastor, Ponce DeLeon Baptist Church, Atlanta

REV. W. R. HENDRIX, Pastor, Saint Mark's Methodist Church, Atlanta

REV. W. E. HILL, Pastor, West End Presbyterian Church, Atlanta

REV. A. R. HOLDERB(L)Y, Pastor, East Point Presbyterian Church, Atlanta

REV. R. J. HUFF, Pastor, Eagan Park Baptist Church, Atlanta

REV. A. M. HUGHLETT, Presiding Elder, Methodist Church, Atlanta

REV. JERRE A. MOORE, Pastor, Harris Street Presbyterian Church, Atlanta

REV. FRITZ RAUSCHENBERG, Pastor, College Park Presbyterian Church, Atlanta

REV. RUSSELL K. SMITH, Rector, Epiphany Church, Atlanta

REV. JACOB L. WHITE, Pastor, Tabernacle Baptist Church, Atlanta

REV. JOHN E. WHITE, Pastor, Second Baptist Church, Atlanta

REV. C. B. WILMER, Rector, Saint Luke's Episcopal Church, Atlanta

Source: John Marshall Slaton Collection (AC # 00–070)
        Box 42
        Georgia Department of Archives and History

In commuting Frank's sentence to life imprisonment, Governor Slaton said he believed he was carrying out the will of Judge Roan. "I can endure misconstruction, abuse, and condemnation, but I cannot stand the constant companionship of an accusing conscience," the governor wrote. "Two judges of the supreme court of Georgia doubted; two judges of the supreme court of the United States doubted; one of three prison commissioners doubted," wrote Slaton. Obviously he doubted, too.

The same issue of the *Atlanta Journal* editorialized that "the governor has shown wisdom and courage in his performance of an act of simple justice, and time will vindicate his moderation." That the jury had reached a verdict of guilty was not surprising, the editorial said, due to the circumstances and conditions that surrounded the trial. No human court or jury could have done differently.

In the aftermath of Slaton's decision to commute Frank's sentence, martial law had to be declared in Georgia and was in effect the day Nathaniel E. Harris assumed the office of Governor. The National Guard was stationed at the governor's mansion, and the demonstrators marching outside cried: "We want John M. Slaton, King of the Jews and traitor Governor of Georgia."[1] The woods around ex-Governor Slaton's home were filled with several hundred angry people, and Slaton and his wife were induced to leave Atlanta until tensions subsided. John Slaton had always been popular in Atlanta, and the public reaction against him reveals the depth of the emotional response his pardon of Frank had aroused.

The Mennonite was the only Christian journal to mention the commutation. But oddly enough, after this, it was silent on the Frank case; whereas after mid-August 1915, other Christian magazines that had never mentioned it began discussing the Frank case.

The Jewish community was traumatized by the events that followed Governor Slaton's decision. Jewish businesses were boycotted in several sections of Georgia (including Marietta), and in Atlanta, Jews had to organize groups to keep watch on the mob that marched on the governor's mansion. Jewish parents kept their children out of the downtown area for fear they might be hurt. How could this be happening in America, they wondered.

Several weeks after Leo Frank's transfer to the prison farm at Milledgeville, he was attacked while he slept by J. William Creen, a fellow inmate. His throat was badly slashed with a butcher knife and he nearly died. Only the quick action of a surgeon, who was also a prisoner, saved his life.

Thomas Watson, in his *Jeffersonian*, urged that a petition be circulated asking for clemency for William Creen, who was serving a life sentence. Governor Harris later was presented with the petition and he personally interviewed the assailant after the attack.

Shortly after the attempt on Frank's life, Governor Harris learned that a mob from Cobb County, Georgia, planned to go to Milledgeville and execute Frank. But Harris alerted the National Guard and the attack was forestalled.

Throughout the summer of 1915, Thomas Watson continued his incessant editorial assault on Frank. Now he also attacked ex-Governor Slaton—and his wife, as well—and openly advocated lynching Leo Frank. No record, however, shows that Tom Watson was there at Frank's lynching or at the ceremony that gave birth to the modern Ku Klux Klan. Indeed, back in 1913, Watson evidently had been offered five thousand dollars to defend Leo Frank, but turned it down. (Alexander Brin, of *The Boston Traveler*, informed Mrs. Frank "that a movement has been started here [in Boston] to make it possible to suppress Tom Watson's paper 'The Jeffersonian'. Prominent citizens of Massachusetts are united in the effort. . . .")

Except among the hard line anti-Semitic community, which was kept in continual agitation by Watson and his *Jeffersonian*, the public reaction to Slaton's commutation of Frank met with widespread approval. U.S. Senator Irving Joseph, of New York, wrote to John Slaton at the end of June, when the former governor and his wife were in New York City. "Under the circumstances you showed great moral and physical courage," the Senator said, "for which your fellow citizens throughout this great nation admire you."

The Jewish press from Atlanta to San Francisco lauded the former governor's courage and action. "There is no honor comparable to that which causes a man to sacrifice life *or* ambition in the cause of justice," wrote *The American Jewish Review* of Atlanta. In San Francisco, *The Jewish Times* declared that "a justice-loving community must feel grateful towards ex-Governor Slaton for the stand he has taken. He has proven himself to be one of the most fearless and broadest minded men in the United States." Present-day Atlanta has a street named Slaton Drive.

Meanwhile, Leo Frank lay in the Milledgeville hospital ward reading his mail, which included a letter from the Cornell Class of '06 secretary offering "heartfelt congratulations on the splendid stand taken by the Governor." As he lay recovering from the slashing of his throat, the frightened young man could only wonder what would happen next.

Endnotes

1. See Nathaniel E. Harris, *Autobiography: The Story of an Old Man's Life with Reminiscences of Seventy-Five Years.*

Chapter 7

THE LYNCHING

Shortly before 10:00 P.M. the night of August 16, 1915, seven automobiles carrying twenty-five men drove into the little town of Milledgeville. *The Macon Telegraph* would later describe this group as "avenging angels." When the men arrived at the outer walls of the state penitentiary, they quickly overpowered and gagged the two guards stationed there. While four men stood watch over the subdued prison guards, others using electrician's pliers, snapped the barbed wire entanglements surrounding the penitentiary.

Inside the grounds, one group of men subdued Captain J. M. Burk, superintendent of the prison. He was getting ready for bed when he was summoned to the door of his home by a guttural voice and loud knocking, then hand-cuffed and forced to lead this group three hundred yards from his house to the main gate of the prison. Another group of men had gone to the home of Warden James E. Smith and held him at gunpoint. The warden's wife fainted into her husband's arms.

At the gate to the prison, Chief Night Guard Hester was ordered to put up his hands. Meanwhile, five men grabbed Frank from the hospital ward. He was handcuffed, and one of the captors grabbed him by the hair. The prison super-intendent said that Frank never uttered a word as he was dragged toward the waiting cars, although he was groaning in pain.

With Frank captured, all the men sped away in automobiles in the direction of Eatonton, evidently heading for Atlanta. The entire operation inside the prison building lasted less than seven minutes.

The taillights of the automobiles had barely merged with the Georgian darkness when the prison authorities sounded the alarm. The telephone was useless, because the wires had been cut on the telegraph and telephone lines connecting Milledgeville with Macon and Atlanta. All the wires to the prison farm had also been severed, but a single telegraph strand, connecting Milledgeville with Augusta, had been overlooked, and it was over this line that news of the kidnapping was sent. The men had also cut the gas line on Warden Smith's car.

A courier was sent to the home of Captain Ennis, commandant of the Baldwin Blues, Milledgeville's detachment of state militia. Messengers were also sent to the homes of other Baldwin County officials, including Sheriff Terry. Soon guards from the prison and other police officers were after the mob. This urgency could have been prompted by a desire to apprehend an escaped prisoner, because early reports suggested the mob which took Frank away might have been a group of his friends.

The entire Board of the state prison commission happened to be at the Milledgeville penitentiary the Monday night Frank was kidnapped. Commissioners Davison, Rainey, and Patterson had arrived late on August 16 to begin preliminary work on the improvements planned for the penitentiary, which had been approved by the state legislature. They were spending the night at the home of the prison superintendent and apparently slept through the abduction, waking only to see the cars speed away.

The kidnapping would have been much harder to execute a few weeks before. Because of the daily rumors about plans to take Frank out of the prison, the roads around Milledgeville had been guarded and additional men had bolstered the guard at the penitentiary. On the night of August 16, however, prison guards were few and the roads were open.

At the prison, a coil of rope had been thrust into Leo Frank's face and another prisoner had overheard the mob leader say that they were planning to take Frank to Marietta, 175 miles away. Frank was handcuffed, and the wound in his neck was obviously hurting. It was a torturous ride, lasting seven or eight hours.

Why did the mob choose Marietta? Why did they risk detection to drive so far? It would have been quicker and simpler just to have shot Frank at the prison. But Marietta was the hometown of Mary Phagan. Frey's woods was where the little girl had played as a child. It was an appropriate place to hang the man the vigilantes were sure had killed her. The mob members called themselves the Knights of Mary Phagan; and this lawless act brought into being a new chapter of the Ku Klux Klan.

A brown grass rope, half an inch thick, was thrown over the limb of an oak tree about twelve feet off the ground. He was told to climb onto a table, and the rope was put around his neck. The table was then kicked out from under him. The lynch mob felt they had "performed a duty to Southern womanhood and to Southern society." Only the onset of daybreak prevented their placing Frank's body on Mary Phagan's grave. The last statement Leo Frank uttered was: "I love my wife and my mother more than I love my life."

Readers of *The Washington Post* awakened on Tuesday, August 17, 1915, to learn that "Mexicans Attack U.S. Cavalry Post," "U-Boat Bombards Coast of England," and "Russian Front Cut by Bavarian Wedge." That same morning, the headlines in the upper left corner of the paper read: "Leo Frank Taken from Prison by Armed Men; Vow to Put His Body on Mary Phagan's Grave." Unknown to the Washington paper editors, by the time this edition was on the street, Leo Frank was dead.

Around 7:00 A.M. on August 17, 1915, outside the little town of Marietta, Georgia, William J. Frey saw four automobiles speeding along the road in front of his house. He thought he saw someone matching Leo Frank's description wedged between two men in the back seat of the second or third car. Frey was a former Cobb County sheriff. He owned a grove of woods and a cotton gin house along Roswell Road two-and-a-half miles east of town. Today Marietta still has streets named Roswell Road and Frey's Gin Road.

At around 7:30 A.M., Frey drove into Marietta, where he learned that Frank's body had been found hanging from a tree in his own woods. He had driven right by it on the way into town; the leaves of summertime had hidden the gruesome sight.

A curious crowd was gathered in the grove of oaks close to his gin house by the time Frey returned. News of the discovery had spread over the countryside like fire through a barn of dried tobacco. The road next to the wood was clogged with people coming from both directions. Across the road was the cottage where Mary Phagan once lived with her parents.

The sight of Leo Frank's body hanging from an oak tree came into view as William Frey and his companions, Gus Benson and W. W. Yaun, entered the thicket. One end of the rope was around Frank's neck, and had been tied in a hangman's knot. The other end was tied to a sapling some twenty feet away. Frank's bare feet, tied together at the ankles with grass rope, were roughly four feet off the ground. His body swayed in the morning breeze.

A white handkerchief covered the dead man's face. Frank's body was clothed in a thin, white pajama jacket with the letters L.M.F. stitched in red thread on the left side of the chest. The letters were sewn there by his wife, Lucille. The sleeves of his jacket had been cut, bit by bit, by the pocketknives of souvenir hunters. From the waist down,

Frank was wrapped in a dirty piece of brown cloth that looked like khaki. His hands were cuffed in front of him.

A trickle of blood had run down from Frank's neck onto the pajamas. The wound that had almost ended his life thirty days earlier was now gaping open.

After the lynch mob had fled the scene at about eight o'clock that morning, the first curious onlookers had found Frank still alive. His body was warm, and there was the faint throb of a pulse. But no one cut him down then. He hung there and died!

As the sun came through the stand of trees that morning, the body Frey and his companions saw looked almost tranquil. Frank's hands were limp and held together by the handcuffs, giving the image of a man praying. He seemed part of the forest.

The crowd came in droves to see Frank's lifeless body. They took pictures, even craning their necks to be part of the camera's record. One man stood by the suspended body with his hand on Frank's leg as if he were a sports fisherman with his prize catch. Wisps of the hemp rope used to hang Leo Frank were also collected, once his body had been cut down. This behavior was not uncommon; at lynchings souvenirs were often collected, and wanting to be part of the picture was typical of the crowd reaction.

As the crowd pressed to see Frank's corpse, a frenzied man, eyes blazing like a maniac, ran up to the body and shook his fist: "Now we've got you!" he screamed. "You won't murder any more little innocent girls! We've got you now! We've got you now!"

At this point Newton Morris, a former judge of the Blue Ridge circuit, shouted for attention: Turn Frank's body over to an undertaker, he urged. But the frenzied man demanded it be burned so that there would not be "a piece of it as big as a cigar." Finally the judge persuaded the crowd not to burn the body. Someone cut Frank down and Judge Morris called for an undertaker.

When the undertaker's men arrived in a horse-drawn

wagon, the frenzied man reached out and struck the body as it was being carried. The undertaker's men dropped Frank's corpse, and the maniac started to grind Frank's face with his heel. The judge begged the man to stop, while the undertaker's assistants grabbed the body and loaded it onto the wagon. They jumped into the wagon and the big horse started toward Marietta at a gallop.

Judge Morris and a companion, John Wood, ran from the grove and followed in Wood's automobile. They overtook the wagon on the outskirts of Marietta, transferred the body to Attorney Wood's car, and raced for Atlanta—with a large crowd in pursuit.

From the moment it was known that Frank's body had been taken into the undertaking establishment of Greenberg & Bond, thousands of curious onlookers crowded the building at Houston and Ivy streets hoping to see the body. The corpse had been hidden in a garage at the rear of the undertaker's address, but its location was soon known and a crowd gathered, which included hundreds of women and children. An estimated fifteen thousand people viewed Frank's body, coming into Greenberg & Bond at the rate of fifty to sixty a minute. It took fifty policemen, under the command of Captain Dobbs, to keep order. Among those viewing Frank's body was city detective John Black, who had arrested Frank on the Tuesday morning following the Phagan murder.

Hundreds of pictures of Frank's hanging body were sold for twenty-five-cents apiece. Licenses were issued to three Atlantans to sell picture postcards of the body. However, within a few days, the Atlanta city council passed an ordinance making it unlawful to sell photographs of the body of a person who had been hanged illegally. But the ordinance did not prevent people from obtaining pictures of Frank's lifeless body for several years after the lynching.

About ten years before Frank was hanged in Frey's grove, the Atlanta City Council and Chamber of Commerce had issued a pamphlet, which said: "Atlanta is an orderly city and scenes of mob violence have never occurred here. There has never been a lynching or a forcible rescue of prisoners, and the bloody scenes which have saddened the history of other communities are wholly absent from the records of Atlanta's life."

William Frey was offered two hundred dollars for the big oak tree on which Leo Frank was hanged. Frey declined the money, but was forced to hire a watchman to guard the tree from souvenir hunters. Plans were made to build a concrete wall around the tree to mark the spot where the "alleged slayer of Mary Phagan" died.

Chapter 8

THE BURIAL

At 12:01 P.M., August 18, the body of Leo Max Frank began the trip back to Brooklyn on Southern Railway passenger train No. 36. Mrs. Frank, her brother-in-law Alexander Marcus, and Rabbi David Marx were among those who accompanied the casket to New York. Mrs. Frank was dressed in the clothes of mourning. She had been preparing to visit her uncle in Athens, Georgia when she learned of the lynching.

The Pullman car, "Valdosta," stood on the track parallel to the baggage car in which the coffin was placed. Leo Frank had ridden in the drawing room of the "Valdosta" two months earlier when he was secretly taken from Atlanta to the Milledgeville prison farm.

Security was tight the night before the train left for Brooklyn. Police Chief Mayo asked his men not to take sides with the crowd, even though some of his officers collected souvenirs the morning before in Frey's grove. But surprisingly, few people gathered at the terminal as Frank's body was loaded onto the waiting train. His casket was a plain pine box, painted black.

Leo Frank's parents, Rudolph and Rae Frank, heard of their son's death on August 17. They drew the blinds in their home at 152 Underhill Avenue, in Brooklyn, and did not answer the phone or the doorbell. Callers at the Frank home were met by Otto Stern, Leo's brother-in-law.

Governor John Slaton, who commuted Frank's death sentence to life imprisonment, was in San Francisco with his wife attending an exposition. When he learned of the lynching, he expressed unqualified condemnation of the deed. Slaton claimed that the lynching would never be condoned by the citizens of Georgia, but Mayor James G. Woodward of Atlanta warned the ex-governor and his wife not to return to their state. The mayor, who was also in California at the time, suggested that Slaton would be in dire danger if he did so. Speaking before the California State Assessor's Association, Mayor Woodward defended the lynching as fulfilling the will of the people and declared that Frank suffered just penalty for an unspeakable crime. Woodward, a former printer, served four terms as mayor of Atlanta between 1899 and 1916. (On one occasion, in November 1908, he had been discovered drunk in that city's "red light" district.)[1] There was rebuttal in Georgia to Mayor Woodward's California speech. Reverend W. F. Smith, pastor of the First Methodist Church in Valdosta, spoke of the mayor's "unwise and damaging speech" during his sermon on Sunday, August 22, 1915.

Speaking before the San Francisco Center of the California Civic League on August 17, 1915, John Slaton said he would return to Georgia by mid-September. He and his wife planned to live out their lives in that state.

Leo and Lucille Frank had spent less than five years together. And now, on the afternoon of August 18, 1915, she was taking her husband to New York to be buried. She had endured the long court appeals and suffered the endless barbed editorials about her husband. She had thrilled to his commutation, despaired at his near fatal wounding, and, now, suffered his hanging to a tree. As the long train thundered towards New York, Mrs. Frank seemed on the verge of collapse. She had taken a sleeping potion, but awakened from time to time. "Oh, God, my Leo," she moaned. "They took my Leo away from me, but I have him back now—but only for a short time. I won't feel at ease until I see him lowered into the grave. Vengeance? I want no vengeance. All I ask is to be left alone. My Leo is gone forever. What can I do?"

Riding in the train with Mrs. Frank was Rabbi Marx.[2] He had been called to the pulpit of the Atlanta Hebrew Benevolent Congregation (later called Temple) twenty years earlier and he held the post for more than fifty years. Rabbi Marx, a friend and staunch supporter of Leo Frank, led the established German Jewish community of Atlanta, and Leo Frank's wife and uncle were members of his group. The rabbi had been born in the South, graduated from Hebrew Union College in Cincinnati, and was a perfect ambassador[3] between the German Jews of Atlanta and the Christian public. The best way to prevent anti-Jewish feeling, he believed, was to assume the identifying marks of the surrounding Christian community. German Jewish worship services were performed in a Christianized format and traditional Jewish dress and grooming were changed to match the general styles of the day.

In a selection preserved in the *Official History of Fulton County* (1934), Rabbi Marx maintained that Jews "constitute no special group. They are integrated into the life of Atlanta, share in that life, in its weal and woe—in its efforts to build a better and a greater city."

While making that somber trip northward, Rabbi Marx must certainly have gone over in his mind the many changes that had taken place in the small German Jewish community of Atlanta since the early 1880s. Social and economic conditions in Russia and the promise of a better life in the West had caused a massive number of Russian and Eastern European Jews to pull up stakes and cross the Atlantic to America. Rabbi Marx tried to act friendly towards his twelve hundred Russian brethren who had settled in Atlanta by 1910. But he was concerned that their large number threatened to undo the social and professional bonds with the

Christian community the long-established German Jews had worked so hard to develop. Rabbi Marx also felt Leo Frank's conviction for Mary Phagan's murder was caused by an anti-Semitic outburst brought about in large part by the presence of so many Russian Jews in the center of town and he had gone to New York City after the trial to talk with Louis Marshall of the American Jewish Committee to express his concern.

Leo Frank was laid to rest in the Cypress Hills District of Queens Borough in New York on August 20. To maintain family privacy, less than twenty mourners were on hand for his burial. The casket was taken hastily to the cemetery, to avoid the curious onlookers. Rabbi Marx conducted the service. Three days later Leo Frank's earthly belongings were sent back to his wife from Milledgeville onboard the Georgia Railroad. The bill of lading read: a bale of bedding, an ice water cooler, a box spring, and one box of books.

Although he referred to Frank's lynching as a consummate outrage, former Governor John Slaton declared he would prefer to have Frank lynched by a mob than to have him hanged by judicial mistake. And the former governor went on to say that every man who was engaged in the lynching should be hanged as an assassin.

Governor Nathaniel Harris[4], who took office in June 1915, riding on Tom Watson's political support, also pledged a thorough investigation into the lynching of Leo Frank. Harris was notified by Marietta's Mayor Dobbs shortly after 10:00 A.M. on Tuesday, August 17 of Frank's death. The governor took the train that night from Fitzgerald, Georgia, to Atlanta to help the prison commission in its inquiry. The governor later offered a reward of fifteen hundred dollars for the "first three convictions of participants" in the Frank lynching.

The Knights of Mary Phagan were from Marietta, the hometown of the murdered girl. This self-appointed "vigilance committee" included a clergyman, an ex-sheriff, and two former Superior Court judges. However, no member

of this lynch mob was ever brought to justice. The grand
jury that investigated the lynching reported to the court
that they were unable to find evidence against anyone,
despite offers of interviews by the lynchers to reporters. Officials
at the Milledgeville penitentiary were also exonerated.

Historian Leonard Dinnerstein notes that at least one of
the Knights of Mary Phagan came to know what Frank
must have felt in the early morning hours of August 17,
1915. Fred Lockhart, also known as D. B. (Bunce) Napier,
was nearly lynched by a mob in Shreveport, Louisiana, in
April 1934. He reportedly drove the car that took Frank on
his final journey from Milledgeville to Marietta. There has
been some speculation that a member of the Phagan family
was among the lynch mob, but this is unsupported by any
evidence.

Denunciation of Frank's lynching came from varied quarters. Secretary of the Navy Daniels issued a formal statement calling the lynching of Leo M. Frank "the worst blot
upon the name of the state [of Georgia]." Louis Marshall,
who acted as attorney for Frank in the U.S. Supreme Court,
looked at the crime as "an ineffaceable blot upon the name
of Georgia." Dr. C. B. Wilmer, an Episcopal minister from
Atlanta, deplored the mob spirit. Reverend Wilmer called
Atlanta's Mayor James Woodward and the *Jeffersonian's* editor, Tom Watson, "a menace to public safety." The Leo
Frank Protest League, an organization of about two hundred men and women which included suffragist Bella New-
man-Zilberman, planned to send a statement to all of the
state governors protesting the great injustice done to Frank.

On Wednesday, August 18, the same day Leo Frank's
body was put on the train for New York, a newspaper
reporter named O. B. Keeler sat in the living room of his
Marietta home listening to the Victrola. Just as the band
broke into "The Robert E. Lee Medley," there was a step
on the veranda outside the open door. A knock soon
followed. Mr. Keeler went to the door and stepped outside.
After asking his name, a man handed Keeler an envelope.

Then he turned and walked out into the summer night. Keeler did not know who the messenger was. When he opened the envelope Keeler found a wedding ring and a typewritten note which said: "Frank's dying request was that his wedding ring be given to his wife. Will you not see that this request was carried out?" The note also warned Keeler not to try to discover the identity of the man who delivered the envelope.

Leo Frank never expected to have to make such a last request. In a letter to Deputy U.S. Marshall Maurice Klein, written July 4, 1915, Frank spoke of again taking up the fight which would lead to vindication and liberty.

Just ten days before he was hanged, Leo Frank wrote a letter to Dan Lehon, the southern manager of the Burns Detective Agency. His neck wound was healing rapidly, Frank said, and the scar would probably not be very noticeable. He was still very weak from losing so much blood and was confined to bed continuously. His wife, Lucille, was a "ministering angel," who had supported him wonderfully in his struggle to live. "Surely God has let me live and aided me in this dark hour for a brighter day, which must be near at hand."

Endnotes

1. See George J. Lankevich, *Atlanta: A Chronological and Documentary History 1813–1976.*

2. David Marx served as Rabbi of the Temple from 1895 until 1946, and Rabbi Emeritus from 1946 until his death in 1962. Dr. Marx had been preceded by Dr. Leo Reich (1888–1895), and was followed by Jacob M. Rothschild.

3. The rabbi delivered an opening prayer in the Georgia State Senate in 1898.

4. Born in Jonesboro, Tennessee, Nathaniel Edwin Harris was the son of a physician and Methodist minister. His parents, Alexander and Edna (Haynes) Harris, had eleven children. Nathaniel was the eldest. He married Fannie Burke in 1873 and the couple had seven children. After his first wife died, Harris married Hattie Gibson Jobe, in 1899.

Harris served in the Confederate Army during the Civil War, then graduated from the University of Georgia in 1870. Nathaniel Harris was the last Confederate veteran to serve as governor of the State of Georgia. Leo Frank's uncle, Moses Frank, also served in Lee's army. After practicing law in Macon, Georgia, Harris was elected to the Georgia House of Representatives where he served four years. He was instrumental in the establishment of the Georgia Institute of Technology.

Although adequately fulfilling the duties of the State Executive Office, Harris was very unpopular. He had to face the economic problems of the First World War, the reemergence of the Ku Klux Klan, and Prohibition. Harris did secure passage of a compulsory education law. In 1916, Hugh Dorsey defeated Harris in the Democratic gubernatorial primary by a margin of more than thirty-six thousand votes.

Chapter 9

THE PREJUDICE

Leo Frank was convicted on the strength of a black man's testimony—truly a rare event in the South in the early years of the twentieth century. Certainly the words of a black man were almost never taken over those of a white man. And Frank was convicted by an all-white jury.

The same day in August 1915 on which Leo Frank was lynched in Frey's woods, a black man named John Riggins was shot about a hundred times near Bainbridge, Georgia. Riggins had been accused of attacking a white woman, the wife of a prominent tobacco man in the lower section of Decatur County. There was no trial, no appeals. Yet the people of this county were described in one Atlanta newspaper as some of the most conservative and level-headed folks in that part of Georgia. John Riggins was twenty-three years old. Before he was killed, he was carried before his alleged victim for identification. She said he was, indeed, her assailant.

In the early years of this century, blacks living in the South were by far the most frequent targets for lynching. Although the South had about half as many people as the North and West at this time, it had more than seven times the number of lynchings as the other two sections combined. Only five states in the entire country could say they had no lynchings between 1889 and 1918[1]. Of the 96 people lynched in America in 1915, 53 were black and 43 were white. Georgia headed the list with 17 mob killings. Some of the lynching victims were innocent of any crime and the majority had committed only minor offenses. More often than not, members of the lynch mobs were never brought to justice.

Leo Frank was lynched at a time when lynchings in the United States were on the decline. Most significantly, Frank, a white man, was lynched at a time when that lawless act was directed primarily against blacks. There were two other whites lynched in Georgia in 1915, but one would have to go back six years, to 1909, to find record of another white man lynched there.

In 1906, an article appeared in *The Independent* that viewed anti-Semitism as being responsible for the Dreyfus Affair in France. It asked: "Is the Dreyfus case possible in America?" The conclusion was no, because anti-Semitism had not yet reached the pitch of intensity here that it had in Russia, Austria, Germany, and France. To be sure, a subconscious anti-Jewish feeling existed and showed itself in many small ways in the larger American cities where Jews formed a distinct class. But we in this country, it was noted, are no better than other nations insofar as racial antipathies. Witness our treatment of blacks and the Chinese.

By 1913, however, the attitude toward Jews, at least in the South, appeared to be changing—for the worse. An article appearing in *Colliers* in 1915, written by C.P. Connolly, who was also a lawyer, said that the heart of the Frank case was "politics, prejudice and perjury."

Connolly had carried on correspondence with Leo Frank during the fall of 1914. "What I want to do is to vindicate your good name before the people of the United States," he wrote Frank. "My heart is in the work." In another letter he said: "How such a mass of falsehood and suspicion could be built up around you is amazing. . . . Do not worry. Keep up your spirits." And after studying the case exhaustively, this prosecuting attorney from Montana concluded that "Frank is the victim of the police fastening the crime on him as the result of a public opinion which demanded conviction."

Justice William Lawlor of the Supreme Court of California came to a similar conclusion, after discussions with Connolly, Daniel Lehon of the Burns Detective Agency, Burns himself, and Governor John Slaton. "The case was without parallel in the history of the United States," the associate justice wrote Lucille Frank, "Your lamented husband was innocent of murder."

Leo Frank was not a black and he was convicted on the contradictory testimony of a black man of questionable character who was known to be drinking on the day of the murder. And he was lynched by a white mob at a time when even the lynching of blacks in the South was declining significantly. Obviously, some other emotional prejudice was afoot; and in the seven decades since this pre-World War I tragedy, we have had a prolonged opportunity to study the climate that produced the verdict and the ghastly aftermath that would inflict such an ugly stain on the legal system of Georgia.

How have the major historians[2] viewed the role of anti-Semitism in the South in general and the Frank case in particular? The established nativist philosophy on minority groups made the Jew suspect in the South. "The Jew usually personified all the fears of the rural masses concerning dissent from orthodox religious Protestantism. The Jew was a stranger. . . . In addition, he was usually successful in business, a fact no doubt quickly noted in depressed agrarian areas," wrote one historian. Many historians have drawn a distinction between popular and upper-class anti-Semitism. Popular anti-Semitism is linked with political and economic issues, whereas upper-class anti-Semitism is a variety of snobbery. The barbarous treatment of Leo Frank was "apparently the venting of pent-up hatreds against his race and position. . . . It is very likely that the absence of similar cases in the South was due entirely to the fact that the aloofness and disjoined social position of the Jew provided an absence of opportunities." There were, of course, many concerns and emotions churning in and around the courtroom in Fulton County during July and August of 1913: "A rising crime rate and anxiety over law and order, an increasing rigidity and punitiveness in racial discipline, an embattled defense of sexual purity, [and] a baffled rage at industrial oppression." Leo Frank was hated intensely for being a Yankee outsider and was seen as a deviant "who incarnated all the alien forces that threatened the traditional culture."

Writing on anti-Jewish prejudice in the United States in 1914, Rabbi Bernard Drachman maintained that knowledge "will drive from the heart of the Gentile all hatred of the Jew and relegate anti-Jewish prejudice, in America and all countries, to the limbo of forgotten things."

In 1914, Edward A. Ross, a University of Wisconsin professor, recorded some of his personal and professional observations about the Eastern European Hebrews in America. The Hebrews in this country endeavor to control the immigration policy, Professor Ross argued. "The literature that proves the blessings of immigration to all classes in America emanates from subtle Hebrew brains." A former Populist-turned-Progressive and a radical, Ross lent academic support to the anti-immigration sentiment in the United States. Why would the Jews favor open immigration in the United States? The answer, according to Ross, was that they wanted to get their brethren out of the "Pale of Settlement" in Russia. The Pale had been established in April 1835 as the area in which Jews could live and carry on business. By 1897, nearly five million Jews lived in the Pale and conditions in Russia had grown steadily worse since 1880. After the 1917 Revolution, the Pale was dissolved.

Ross pointed out that the Jewish immigrants would live in the dirtiest poverty to avoid hard muscular labor. And, of course, "none can beat the Hebrew at a bargain, for through all the intricacies of commerce he can scent his profit. . . . Pent within the Talmud and the Pale of Settlement, their interests have become few, and many of them have developed a monstrous and repulsive love of gain." Most of the crimes committed among the Hebrew immigrants were supposedly for gain. The Gentile, Ross said, resented having to engage in an undignified scramble in order to maintain his trade or his clientele "against the Jewish invader."

One of the professor's comments is very relevant to the Frank case. "The fact that pleasure-loving Jewish businessmen spare Jewesses, but pursue Gentile girls, excites bitter comment." The stigma of perversion hung over Leo Frank's head from the time of his arrest. D. M. Parker of Baxley, Georgia, in a 1915 letter to the editor of the *New Republic* said that his state "has sought in the conviction of Frank to redress a monumental wrong, a crime against an innocent working girl, committed by a fiend. . . ."

Dr. Ross also said that in certain parts of the country, "the readiness of the Jews to commit perjury has passed into proverb." He noted that Hebrews drove down the ethics of the professions, such as medicine and law. And sounding not unlike the Nazis, Ross spoke of the "prosperous parasitism" of the Jew.

Positive Jewish traits, such as an emphasis on education and learning, the professor interpreted as a means to a Jewish end, namely, making money. Acquisition of knowledge was simply another example of Jewish acquisitiveness. As for religious ideas, Jewish immigrants were described as "so stubborn that the Protestant churches despair in making proselytes among them."

These thoughts by an established university professor suggest how at least some members of the intellectual establishment viewed the Jews at a time when Leo Frank's defense counsel was pursuing the appeal process through the courts of Georgia.

An influential Protestant weekly magazine in Chicago, *Christian Century*, published only one brief reference to the Frank case from 1913 to 1915. On the other hand, it printed two articles which questioned the legitimacy and necessity of Jewish religious expression and collective Jewish identity in the twentieth century.

In his *Christian Century* article, "Inadequate Religions: How the Religion of Jesus Christ Fares Amid the Wreckage of Ancient Faiths," Robert Elliott Speer wrote that: "Nineteen hundred years ago, to the best of all the non-Christian religions—the religion between which and all the other non-Christian religions a great gulf is fixed, Judaism—Jesus Christ came, and that, the best of all religions, He declared to be outworn and inadequate. The time had at last come, He taught, to supplant it with the full and perfect truth that was in Him." For Robert Speer, Jesus was the only source of human salvation. The author maintained further that "if the missionary enterprise is a mistake, it is not our mistake; it is the mistake of God."

In the other *Christian Century* article, W. J. Lhamon explored the question: "Why does the Jew remain?" After discussing a book written by a Jewish scholar of Talmudic literature at Cambridge University, Lhamon asked:

> How shall we understand the age-long abiding of this strange people? Have they still a message to the world, and is that why they stay? Or have they delivered their message? Have they given their best to the world? And are they ready to melt into the greater group, the brotherhood of the world in process of redemption? Is it not pride of race that holds them now, and the habit of separateness? And will not these inferior forces give way under the disintegrating rationalism indicated above? Their message of monotheism—Christianity has received it, and improved it, and is bearing it on to the world with a speed and power never dreamed of by the Jews. Their message of monogamy—that too has been accepted by Christianity, and rendered more secure in her hands than ever it was in the hands of Moses and David. Their message of atonement—that has

become priceless with Christians, and by them has been win-
nowed of sacramentalism, and sweetened by the love and blood
and prayers of Israel's greatest Son, and is being proclaimed to
the world by fifty times as many millions as the Jews can boast.

Why do they linger?

Historians and social scientists have offered two basic
theories of the rise of anti-Jewish discrimination in the
United States. One is that a visible pattern of anti-Jewish
discrimination began to develop in America in the last
twenty-five to thirty years of the nineteenth century. Associated with this line of thinking is the idea that the general
American conception of the Jew always contained both
positive and negative elements. In effect, the "average
American" held ambivalent feelings about Jews.

The other theory holds that an essentially positive public
attitude towards Jews in America underwent a fundamental
shift in the second decade of the twentieth century. Ambivalent attitudes towards Jews on the part of non-Jewish
Americans are not part of this model. The period from
1890 to 1900 is viewed not as anti-Semitic, but "actually
marked by distinct philo-Semitism."

It should be noted, however, that there is a distinct lack
of historical research on American anti-Semitism. There are
very few works that attempt to analyze the causes of American anti-Semitism based on historical investigations. For
example, most of the studies from the 1930s (when serious
scholarly attention to American anti-Semitism first developed) to the late 1950s, were only descriptive. Anti-Jewish
discrimination was discussed in an evolutionary manner,
with little interpretation of the historical information. In
addition, less historical attention has been given to the Jews
in the South than in any other section of America. Knowledge of southern Jewish life is therefore less than thorough.
The works of historians Jacob Marcus and Bertram Korn
stand as significant exceptions to the general neglect of the
Jewish experience in the South.

According to the second theory, the American obsession

with fear of the Jew which began in the period 1913 to 1920 was essentially something new. This fear was manifested in economic and social discrimination, even in political action. For the most part, this anti-Semitism was produced by the First World War, a time when many Americans rejected every tie with Europe. Large numbers of East European and Russian Jews had, of course, emigrated to the United States beginning in the 1880s and this continued through to the war years.

In addition to the fear of foreigners during this period, the disappointment of many radicals and reformers who somehow came to blame the Jews for their failure after 1900, contributed to the rise of anti-Semitism. One group of radicals and reformers were the bimetalist supporters, who advocated currency reforms in the American monetary system. Bimetalism called for the use of both gold and silver as the monetary standard of value and currency; and the bimetalists sought to explain their defeats throughout the 1890s by looking to an external power, often focusing on the international Jewish banker.

The suspicion of the currency radicals regarding Jewish financial control of the world's purse strings was supplemented by the cloak of mystery in which the American popular mind had wrapped the Jew. However, the conviction that there was a strange and mysterious Jew in the United States did not assume the same demonic character transmitted from the Middle Ages to nineteenth-century Europe. Rather, the emphasis in this country was on interpretations of the mission of Israel, which went back at least two hundred years to Cotton Mather. Mather was a Puritan clergyman and writer, best remembered for his part in the Salem witch trials of 1692. He compiled a history of the Jews in 1714 as part of his *Biblia Americanuum*, a work which contains misinformation about the Jews, at the same time expressing the urgent need to convert them.

Even though the Jew was perceived in the American popular mind to be mysterious, this mystery did not include elements of the demonic passed from generation to generation among the Christian population of Europe since the eleventh century. During the Middle Ages, the Jews were accused of blood libel or ritual murder (as in Norwich, England, in 1144 and Blois, France, in 1171), desecration of the Eucharist host, the communion wafer, which is the symbolic body of Christ (as in 1243), and well-poisoning (as during the Bubonic Plague of 1348–49). Blood libel, which referred to the Jews' allegedly using the blood of a Christian (usually a child) in their religious rites, resulted in massacres and expulsions of Jews.

The authoritative book of Jewish commentary, the Talmud, was believed to conceal secrets of Jewish magic. Official ecclesiastical concern was so great that there were four major Church-sponsored Talmud burnings, including one in Paris, France. Many people believed that Jewish religious ritual required the blood of Christians. The charge of ritual murder often surfaced around Passover time, when it was thought that Jews used the blood of a Christian child to prepare the matzo for the Passover meal. Russia's Beilis affair, in 1911, was a modern example of this ancient charge. During the Middle Ages, Jews were also portrayed as the enemy and potential destroyer of Christianity and Christendom, and as such were seen to be evil, sinister, and, indeed, the devil himself. The Jews were perceived to be essentially different from Christians. How else, it was argued, could Jews sustain their stubbornness in the face of the Christian truth.

These medieval European conceptions of the Jew did not take deep root here in America. With few exceptions, Jews and Judaism have been allowed to live and grow here without the severe impediments of European and Russian governmental, religious, and popular anti-Semitism. And there is nothing in the American Jewish experience in any way similar to the major expulsions of Jews from European nations and states: from England, in 1290; France, in 1306, 1322, and again in 1395; Spain, in 1492 (the same year in which Columbus is credited with discovering the New World); and Portugal, in 1497. Expulsion, enforced ghettoization, and economic restriction were a way of life for Jews during the Middle Ages in nearly all parts of Europe.

The theory of anti-Semitism, which holds that the anti-Jewish sentiment and actions of the years 1913–20 were not previously seen in the United States, includes the notion that there were stereotypic images of Jews that took shape over the course of the second half of the nineteenth century. Twentieth-century prejudices were, therefore, not built completely on an empty foundation. By 1900, there was a clearly defined Jewish stereotype in the collective American mind.

Jewish interest in money was the most important part of this distortion. The great fortunes of the world were seen to be controlled and manipulated by greedy Jewish fingers. The Jewish link to finance, so this theory holds, was strengthened by the growing preoccupation of the American public with money, particularly following the economic depression of 1893. And during the 1890s, the American stereotype of the Jew "involved no hostility, no negative judgment." The impact of this stereotype was blunted by the fact that it was merely one of many ethnic prejudices prevalent during that period of intensive immigration.

To account for the sense of fear from which the idea of a Jewish conspiracy supposedly grew, this theory points to the city as an object of dread and fascination. To the city, and particularly New York, entire parts of the South and West felt themselves in bondage. In the United States, Jews, more than any other group, were associated with the city through their dealings in commerce. "If all trade was treachery and Babylon the city, then the Jew—stereotyped, involved in finance, and mysterious—stood ready to be assigned the role of arch-conspirator."

In the context of this theory, Leo Frank was perceived to be from the dreaded Yankee city of Brooklyn and could be counted among the well-to-do of Atlanta. Because of the blurred conception of German and East European Jew in the popular Atlanta mind, Frank would also have been seen as one of the group of foreigners invading the Gate City.

The other major theory of the rise of anti-Semitism in the United States is more complex because it contains the ideas of several historians. The period when anti-Jewish discrimination emerged in America is seen as early as the 1870s and as late as the 1890s. (The period from 1870 to 1890 in this country has been called the Gilded Age.) The longstanding ambivalence toward the Jew in American public attitudes is also emphasized.

In the imagination of nineteenth-century America, Jews were both the instruments as well as unwilling witnesses of Divine purpose, and they represented the virtues and vices of modern business. The religious aspects of the popular conception of the Jew reach back to the writings and teachings of Saint Paul, who believed the Torah or Jewish scriptures had been superceded by the Cross as the means of man's salvation. In the centuries that followed, Jews came to be seen as living reminders of God's victory in Christ and also as necessary players in the pageant of final redemption.

The official Church dogma toward the Jews in the medieval period held that Jews were to serve as witnesses to the truth of Christianity. As witnesses, they were to be protected, yet subject to limitations. Jews could not hold public office; in certain countries they had to wear special Jewish clothing, including a yellow "Jew badge" and headgear; and they were prohibited from building new synagogues or houses of worship. The enforced wearing of the yellow star by the National Socialists (Nazis) during the 1930s and early 1940s had its origin in the official policies of the Roman Catholic Church during the Middle Ages.[3]

According to one line of thinking, the Southern image of the Jew had always been ambivalent: half biblical patriarch (Abraham, Isaac, and Jacob are considered the biblical patriarchs) and half Christ-killer; half legitimate entrepreneur and half Shylock[4], the ruthless usurer in Shakespeare's *Merchant of Venice* (1595). Usury is money-lending at extremely high rates of interest, and it is considered to be a sin in Roman Catholic teachings.

Although anti-Jewish prejudice did exist in nineteenth-century America, it was largely offset by other ideas that emphasized the essential equality of all white men and the many opportunities available for those who worked hard—the Protestant work ethic. A distinction needs to be made, however, between actual social relations and stereotypes or ideas. The prevalence of good relations in the nineteenth century does not mean that American attitudes toward Jews were ever completely favorable.

Unfavorable attitudes about an ethnic group do not necessarily determine social interaction with members of that group on an individual level. Because Jews as a group were viewed to be foreign, preoccupied with money, and mysterious did not necessarily mean that each individual Jew directly was branded with that stereotype. In the South, as well as other sections of the country, non-Jews who resented Jews and desired to restrict their political influence nevertheless accepted the usefulness of Jewish merchants and artisans to the local economies.

Prejudice and discrimination are not the same thing, nor does discrimination necessarily follow directly from prejudice: Prejudicial attitudes may lead to actual discrimination for many reasons; and conflicting attitudes and feelings frequently exist side by side. But for practical reasons these deep prejudices are not always allowed to come to the surface.

Insofar as nineteenth-century Atlanta is concerned, several factors blunted the expression of the negative elements in the popular conception of the Jew. The relatively small numbers of West European Jews in Atlanta before 1880, the assimilationist tendencies of the Jewish community there, and the involvement of Jews in general public life contributed to their acceptance by the Atlanta populace.

Furthermore, Jews benefited from the doctrine of white supremacy; and in Atlanta more than any other Southern community, entrepreneurial ability was thought to be a special virtue. What changed the character and public conception of the Atlanta Jewish community was the arrival of the Russian Jewish immigrants. This new horde produced a wave of anti-Jewish discrimination, and it was the catalyst that inspired the anti-Semitic outbursts that dominated the Frank trial and led to the tragedy.

It has been suggested that regional attitudes have had more negative impact on Jews in the South than in other sections of the United States. In the last third of the nineteenth century, many Jews in the South "served as scapegoats for a society unable to cope with—or recognize—the major sources of its grievances." The rural population, for example, held Jews responsible for economic turmoil, as a result of people feeling in bondage to the merchant or peddler. Many Jews were small merchants and peddlers, traditional occupations brought with them from Europe, for a host of complex social, ecclesiastical, and political reasons. Leading personalities in Southern communities also sanctioned negative images of Jews.

Whether the rise of anti-Semitism is marked at 1870–90 or 1913–20, the causes of this phenomenon are significant. Again, two theories are advanced, one economic, the other ideological.

According to the economic theory, "discrimination issued not from primarily irrational, subjective impulses but rather from a very real competition for social status and prestige." Stereotypes made discrimination possible, but did not create it. "In times of economic crisis or when the poor felt particularly victimized, the predatory Jew reappeared in public discussions." Conditions that heightened white antagonisms against blacks in Atlanta, such as the racial riot of 1906, also worsened relations between Jews and non-Jews. According to Leonard Dinnerstein, these conditions revolved around a discontented urban working

class forced to endure low wages, crowded and uncomfort-
able tenement housing, and little hope for any improvement
in the future. The fear of racial pollution inflated the
negative conditions created by the economic upheaval. By
the 1890s, the Jews were considered to be racially and
religiously different and inferior within a pattern of southern social thinking dominated by conformity.

Supporters of the economic theory suggest that the anti-
Semitism, which most closely affected American Jewry from
1830 to 1930, owed very little to stereotypic thinking or
ideological sources. During the Gilded Age, the established
pattern of urban life in America was disrupted by the
general struggle for rank, status, and privilege. Anti-Semitic
demonstrations provided a tool to stabilize the social ladder.

Although several historians maintain that discrimination
began at the top of American society and spread downward,
others argue that "discrimination can arise more or less
simultaneously at every social level where a crush of appli-
cants poses an acute problem of admission. Discrimination
is probably much less a game of follow-the-leader than one
of limiting the followers." According to this theory, Jews in
America met with little economic discrimination before
about 1910, because they had not entered the popular labor
markets. Anti-Jewish social discrimination came much earlier, however.

Three periods of intense anti-Semitism in America have
been identified—and they correspond with similar periods
in Europe: the 1880s and 1890s, the years after the First
World War, and the 1930s.

The last two decades of the nineteenth century saw the
Dreyfus affair in France along with the anti-Semitic writings of Edouard-Adolphe Drumont and Karl Eugen Duehring in France and Germany, respectively. The years immediately following the First World War were marked by
the rise of the Ku Klux Klan, immigration restrictions in
the United States, Henry Ford I's *Dearborn Independent*,

widespread distribution of the *Protocols of the Elders of Zion* in Europe, and the formation of the National Socialist (Nazi) political party in Germany. The rise of Nazism in Germany and anti-Semitic regimes in Poland and Hungary darkened the 1930s.

The German economist and philosopher Karl Eugen Duehring was one of the early advocates of *racial* anti-Semitism and was to have a profound influence on the development of German anti-Semitism in the 1880s. Duehring argued in *Die Judenfrage als Racen-Sitten- und Culturfrage* that "a Jewish question will still exist, even if every Jew were to turn his back on his religion and join one of our major churches. . . . Jews are to be defined solely on the basis of race, and not on the basis of religion." Nazism promoted racial anti-Semitism, although it drew heavily on the images of the Jew nurtured by religious anti-Semitism and the support of populations exposed to anti-Jewish religious teaching and preaching.

Beginning in May 1920, the Ford-owned *Dearborn Independent* of Dearborn, Michigan, carried anti-Semitic propaganda for nearly seven years. A May 22, 1920, article was entitled "The International Jew: The World's Problem." *The Protocols of the Elders of Zion*, with its theme of a Jewish conspiracy to rule the world, was serialized in the Ford journal. Even the combined efforts of President William Taft, President Woodrow Wilson and a group of 119 distinguished Americans, and the Federal Council of Churches could not convince the automobile manufacturer to abandon his project. Finally, in 1927, when a Jewish attorney from Detroit brought a libel suit against the *Dearborn Independent,* Ford repudiated his anti-Semitism and issued a public apology that appeared in the nation's leading daily newspapers. But anti-Semitic literature supported by Ford's money continued to enjoy wide circulation.

Concocted in Paris in the last decades of the nineteenth century by an unknown author working purportedly for the Russian secret police, the *Protocols of the Elders of Zion* were probably intended to influence the policy of Czar Nicholas II toward the interests of the secret police. They were first published in Russia at the beginning of this century and then translated into several languages after the First World War. They were distributed in the United States by Ford under the title, *The Jewish Peril*, an anti-Semitic literary hoax intended to show the existence of an international Jewish conspiracy intent on world domination. Adolf Hitler's obsession with a worldwide Jewish conspiracy was apparently derived, in part, from the *Protocols of the Elders of Zion*, which was translated into German in 1920. This work continues to enjoy circulation in the Soviet Union, certain Arab nations, and, more recently, in Japan.

In the 1880s and 1890s, there were primarily three groups in American society that harbored and manifested significant anti-Jewish feelings: Agrarian rebels in the Populist movement; certain eastern patrician intellectuals (such as Henry Adams, Brooks Adams, and Henry Cabot Lodge); and the immigrant, urban poor. What these disparate groups had in common was a pervasive social discontent and nationalistic aggression. Each group discovered itself to be at a particular disadvantage in the dislocations of the industrialization process in America. The poor were discontented because industrialization often exploited them; the patrician class because it displaced them from positions of influence.

The Industrial Revolution spread to the United States from England and Germany following the Civil War. In England, industrialization had developed in the period 1750–1850; German industrialization began after 1850. The brothers Henry and Brooks Adams were historians. Henry Cabot Lodge, a United States Senator from Massachusetts, was a conservative Republican who led the fight against the Treaty of Versailles and the League of Nations after the First World War. "It is not too much to say that the Greenback-Populist tradition activated most of what we have of modern popular anti-Semitism in the United States," one historian concludes. There, in fact, has been a persistent link between anti-Semitism and money and credit obsessions. Individuals advocating this obsession included Congressman Thaddeus Stevens, Henry and Brooks Adams, poet Ezra Pound, and Right Reverend Charles Coughlin. The latter, a Roman Catholic priest and radio orator in the period after the Great Depression, envisioned currency reform schemes such as the abolition of the Federal Reserve System.

Historian Richard Hofstadter argues that populism cannot be viewed simply in the narrow sense of the People's or Populist Party of the 1890s. Rather, it should be viewed as the larger trend of thought originating at the time of Andrew Jackson's presidency (1829–37) and coming together after the Civil War in the Greenback, Granger, and anti-monopoly movements.

The Greenback party was a political organization formed between 1874 and 1876 to promote currency expansion in the wake of the 1873 depression. Its membership was primarily western and southern farmers and it mostly dissolved after the 1884 national election. Taking its name from the National Grange of the Patrons of Husbandry, the Granger movement was an agrarian organization which expanded rapidly after the economic panic of 1873.

Populism expressed the discontent of many farmers and businessmen with the far-reaching economic changes of the late 1800s. It was the first modern political movement of practical importance in the United States to insist that the federal government accept some responsibility for the common welfare. It was also the first popular movement to attack industrialism.

Populist thinking has survived to the present day as an undercurrent of popular and "democratic rebelliousness and suspiciousness along with nativism." Populists were not alone in conceiving the events of their own day to be a conspiracy. The entire flow of American history after the Civil War was viewed by the Populists as a conspiracy of international money power. The farmer, for example, was not seen as a "speculating businessman, victimized by the risk economy of which he is a part, but rather a wounded yeoman, preyed upon by those who are alien to the life of folkish virtue." This conspiracy view of history was developed in the novel entitled *Caesar's Column*, by Populist leader Ignatius Donnelly. It was the Populist writers who identified the Jew with the usurer and the "international gold ring," the central theme of American anti-Semitism at the time. Populist anti-Semitism was almost entirely verbal, however. It was a rhetorical style, not a tactic or program and it did not result in exclusion laws, riots, or pogroms. The Populists did exhibit—in particularly virulent form—a fear and suspicion of the stranger.

The conduct of Georgia Populist leader and politician Thomas E. Watson had direct bearing on the Leo Frank case and its ultimate tragedy. During 1914–15, *Watson's Magazine* and *The Jeffersonian* "fanned the flames of anti-Semitism with an unrelenting storm of slanderous commentary." Leo Frank was a "Jew Pervert," a degenerate, and a Sodomite according to *Watson's Magazine*. Governor John Slaton was "the infamous governor" for having commuted Frank's sentence.

As late as 1899, however, Watson was vigorously condemning medieval practices against Jews. This well-mannered and charming southern gentleman also defended a Jew against the charge of murder. Fifteen years before Leo Frank was lynched, Watson assisted in the defense of a merchant named Sigmund Lichtenstein. This young Jew had been charged in Adrian, Georgia, with killing a Gentile, the first cousin of the town's mayor. Historian Louis Schmeir notes that Thomas Watson finished his thirty-minute closing oration to the jury by saying that "No Jew can do murder."

The people most adamant in their demands for the conviction of Leo Frank were the committed followers of Tom Watson. Many historians, however, find little evidence that the Populists as a group were more anti-Semitic than other groups in American society. The Populists provide an excellent example of diverse and conflicting attitudes towards Jews existing side by side in the collective American mind. Populists and other currency reformers who envisioned the "Shylocks of Europe" arrayed against the working farmers and businessmen of America were precisely those groups most deeply imbued with and influenced by the best traditions of American democracy and Christianity.

Two contrasting interpretations of American anti-Semitism have emerged. The first, given its fullest expression in the writing of Carey McWilliams, appeared in the 1930s. This view included "a worried and aroused sensitivity to ethnic conflict, an interest in its conservative or reactionary manifestations, and an economic interpretation of its origins. . . . American anti-Semitism was traced to the industrial revolution of the 1870s and was attributed to the assault of big business upon our democratic heritage."

The second interpretive theory, labeled neo-liberal or revisionist, was given its fullest expression around 1950. This approach minimizes the impact and pervasiveness of anti-Semitism in America and finds the origins of anti-Semitism in the realm of ideas rather than economic forces. The harmony and unity of American society are emphasized.

There is the tendency to concentrate on the need of the anti-Semite for a scapegoat in both theories. Neither viewpoint is prepared to accept the "role that the minority group itself plays in the conflict situation." The target of discrimination may, in fact, participate in and contribute to the discriminatory process. The tendency among certain groups of Jews to voluntarily separate from society has led to a general perception of "clanishness." Separation limits the contact necessary for the possibility of general public understanding.

*
**

Leo Frank was a family man, Cornell graduate, and superintendent of a business, who was lynched for a murder many thought he did not commit. And his murder occurred in the twentieth century just outside the largest and fastest growing city in the South.

Almost four years after Leo Frank was hanged in a tree outside of Marietta, United States District Attorney H. Alexander recalled the Frank case at a mass meeting held in Atlanta. The meeting was to protest the persecution and murder of Jews in Poland and other countries of Eastern Europe; but not until the real murderer in the Phagan case was found and convicted, said the district attorney, could the people of Georgia protest Poland's crimes.

But it should also be noted that the American Jews themselves were not without anti-Semitic prejudices such as existed at the time of the Frank trial and lynching. By 1915, Moses Alexander of Idaho was the only Jew to reach the position of state governor in America. Although Governor Alexander felt Jews should be active in politics, he also thought they should stop thinking of themselves as a distinct religious nation and "become true citizens of the United States on a broad basis of Christian brotherhood."

In an interview in Boston with *The Christian Science Monitor*, the governor said he would not appoint any Jews to office during his administration. He went on to say that "if the Jew would take a more liberal view of life and its Christian relations and not pay so much attention to making money, he would go a long way toward establishing a more liberal condition for himself."

Moses Alexander did not wish to be seen as a Jew, but as a citizen of the United States. If the State of Idaho were filled with and governed by Jews, the governor said he would move out.

*
**

At this date, more than seventy years removed from that day when little Mary Phagan was murdered, it is still difficult to assess the prejudices and emotions that dominated the period. But perhaps the instinctive assessment of the Atlanta pastor, Dr. Luther O. Bricker, provides us with the best clue as to what happened in Georgia in 1913. Dr. Bricker, of course, knew little Mary Phagan, having taught her in his Bible School, and he revealed his thoughts back at the time of her murder, shortly before he died in 1942. He wrote: "My own feelings, upon the arrest of the old negro night-watchman, were to the effect that this one old negro would be poor atonement for the life of this little girl. But, when on the next day, the police arrested a Jew, and a Yankee Jew at that, all of the inborn prejudice against the Jews rose up in a feeling of satisfaction, that here would be a victim worthy to pay for the crime."[5]

Endnotes

1. In the thirty years, from 1889 to 1918, 3,224 people were lynched by mobs in this country—702 whites and 2,522 blacks. Nearly 80 percent of the victims were black. Georgia led the nation "in this unholy ascendancy," with 386 lynchings, followed by Mississippi (373), Texas (335), Louisiana (313), and Alabama (276). The number of whites lynched decreased steadily from 1903. Women accounted for 1.5 percent of the total number of people lynched during this period. The summer of 1915 saw seven lynchings in Georgia, all for alleged murder and/or rape. See *Thirty Years of Lynching in the United States 1889–1918*.

2. See works by Leonard Dinnerstein, John Higham, Oscar Handlin, Richard Hofstadter, and Steven Hertzberg.

3. See also Joshua Trachtenberg's *The Devil and the Jews: The Medieval Conception of the Jew and Its Relation to Modern Anti-semitism*.

4. Steven Hertzberg, "The Jewish Community of Atlanta from the End of the Civil War to the Eve of the Frank Case" in the *American Jewish Historical Quarterly* (1973).

5. See L. O. Bricker, "A Great American Tragedy" in the *Shane Quarterly* (1943).

Chapter 10

THE EPILOGUE

After more than seventy years and the deaths of all the principals in the case, the questions of guilt and innocence seem to lose much of their meaning. The legacy left by the Frank case was one of pain and bitterness and for the Phagan family there is still the anguish caused by the murder of a beautiful little girl.

The Phagan family went separate ways in the 1920s, with many members of the family moving out of Georgia, and Mary Phagan (the great-niece of the murdered girl) says that the tragedy they all had suffered in 1913 contributed to the exodus. Ollie Phagan, she believes, moved to Virginia. Ollie's daughter is still living. Little Mary Phagan's brother, Charlie, has a daughter who now makes her home in Texas. Mary Phagan is the oldest of her father's children.

There was also the sadness and loneliness of the Franks and Seligs, who lost their loved one to the hangman's noose. After Leo Frank was buried in New York, Lucille found employment in a woman's dress shop outside of Georgia for several years. When she returned to Atlanta, she worked in a department store for a time. She was also active in the work of the Hebrew Temple, and she spent the majority of her remaining years protesting her husband's

131

innocence. Although a young woman at the time of Leo's death, Lucille never remarried. And according to friends, she always proudly signed her name, "Mrs. Leo Frank." Lucille Frank died on April 23, 1957, at the age of sixty-nine. The Franks never had children.

The trial testimony, the affidavits, the letters, and the interviews strongly suggest that Jim Conley murdered little Mary Phagan. Alonzo Mann believed Conley was guilty, as did William Smith, Judge Powell, and Attorney A. L. Henson. When asked her reaction to the lynching, Mary Phagan said that her family had strong feelings on that subject—but she would not state what those feelings were.

Jim Conley served a year in a chain gang for being an accessory after the fact in the killing of Mary Phagan. He was convicted on February 24, 1914, and sentenced to a year in jail, ensuring that the former factory sweeper could not be tried again for Mary Phagan's murder. In 1919, Conley was shot and slightly wounded while trying to break into a drug store in Atlanta owned by Arthur Conn, also a black man. For this crime he was sentenced to serve twenty years in the state penitentiary. The Atlanta police picked him up in 1941 for gambling and arrested him once again, in 1947, on a charge of public drunkenness. Conley died in 1962.

The Knights of Mary Phagan who rode in automobiles that night in 1915, formed the core of the new Ku Klux Klan, which had been disbanded in 1869. In the late fall of 1915, "Colonel" William Joseph Simmons[1] (the title was honorary in the Woodmen of the World), a preacher, salesman, and fraternal organizer from Alabama, became the new Imperial Wizard of the Invisible Empire.

The inauguration ceremony for the new Ku Klux Klan took place at midnight on Thanksgiving Eve, 1915. Colonel Simmons had hired a sightseeing tour bus to drive his followers eighteen miles from Atlanta to Stone Mountain, which towers sixteen hundred feet above the surrounding plain, the largest mass of exposed granite in the world.

Using flashlights, the men picked their way to the top and erected a "crude altar and a base for the cross of pine boards which Simmons had brought there that afternoon." The cross was padded with wood shavings and soaked with kerosene. Colonel Simmons touched a match to the cross, and beneath its fiery blaze the Ku Klux Klan was reborn. A Bible open to Romans 12 was part of the ceremony. "The passions and prejudices of the modern Ku Klux Klan had been widely accepted dogmas in the South for generations before the secret, terroristic society was revitalized."[2]

The following year an area of Stone Mountain was dedicated as the site for a carved memorial to the Confederacy. This striking carving of Jefferson Davis, Robert E. Lee, and Thomas "Stonewall" Jackson on the sheer face of the mountain is the focal point of present-day Stone Mountain park.

The State of Georgia gave the new K.K.K. corporate rights by issuing it a charter. Membership in this fraternal order was open to native-born, white, Protestant males 16 and older. Blacks, Roman Catholics, and Jews were not permitted to become members. In 1921, the Klan acquired the former Atlanta home of Edward M. Durant, at the corner of Peachtree Road and East Wesley Road, which would serve as an Imperial Palace. It was not until 1947 that Georgia revoked the Klan's charter. Despite its heritage, "the Georgia Klan seldom directed its violence toward Jew, Roman Catholic, and Negro."

And Mary Phagan's memory lived on within the Ku Klux Klan in northern Georgia. The Klan wanted to observe a "Mary Phagan Remembrance Day" in the 1970s, and in 1983 it laid a wreath on the girl's grave in Marietta after a march through town. With the War Veteran's monument at the head of Mary's grave, there seems to be a strong link from Confederacy to Klan to the memory of the murdered girl.

Perhaps Governor Slaton had not really done Leo Frank a favor by commuting his sentence. If he had been executed by the State, he would not have suffered the throat slashing and would at least have had the dignity of a few last words with family and friends. If he had been awaiting pardon, he might have spent sixty years languishing behind bars with no real hope of release.[3]

The families of John Slaton and William Smith have had to endure years of threats and criticism, and in the wake of the lynching, the Jewish community in Atlanta lived with trauma and fear for decades. The wound left by the Frank case on Atlanta's Jews was very slow to close. One former resident of the Gate City contends that it was only with the bombing of the Temple there on October 12, 1958, that a scar began to form.

Janice Rothschild Blumberg calls it "The Bomb That Healed."[4] Her late husband, Jacob Rothschild, was rabbi of the Hebrew Benevolent Congregation (the Temple) at the time of the bombing. Nineteen fifty-eight was a time in an era when reprisals for speaking out on civil rights drew very violent reactions. The outpouring of general community support in the wake of the bomb blast helped to restore the confidence of Jews living in Atlanta. Though money was not requested, thousands of dollars were sent to the Temple by concerned Christian individuals and church groups.

And Alonzo Mann lived nearly seventy years with a burdensome secret. The violence in 1913 led to more violence in 1915, which, in turn, produced years of fear, guilt, and pain.

The Frank case affected the political lives of several prominent Georgians and altered the course of Georgia politics for decades. Governor John M. Slaton was an immediate political casualty. Only three years earlier in 1912, Slaton had won the governorship by one of the largest margins ever. The ex-governor and his wife, having been warned by Atlanta's Mayor Woodward not to return to Georgia, went on an extended tour of America and the world. When he returned to Georgia, Slaton resumed his practice of law in Atlanta. The University of Georgia conferred upon him an honorary LL.D. degree in 1922, and

Oglethorpe University in Atlanta did the same a few years later. In 1928, the former governor was unanimously elected president of the Georgia Bar Association. He was defeated in a bid for the U.S. Senate in 1930. Slaton died on January 11, 1955 at the age of eighty-eight. William Smith died a year later. Mrs. Slaton had died in 1945.

The fact that John Slaton was not only able to return to Georgia but was also able to assume positions of some authority may be related to Tom Watson's death. Had Watson lived for another fifteen to twenty years, Slaton's personal and professional life would probably have been quite different. Tom Watson himself rode the tide of state public support to a seat in the United States Senate in 1920. His victory, by a margin of nearly 40,000 popular votes, was over his former ally Hugh Dorsey. But then, Watson died in September 1922 from an attack of bronchitis and asthma.

In 1916, Solicitor Hugh M. Dorsey faced disqualification during other litigation. By his own admission, he had accepted a $1,000 fee from the family of two sisters who had disappeared and were presumed murdered. But this did not hurt Dorsey's[5] political ambitions. He was elected governor of Georgia in 1916, running unopposed. He was supported by Thomas E. Watson, whose incendiary writings in *Jeffersonian* magazine had much to do with inflaming public feeling against Leo Frank in Atlanta and throughout Georgia.

Dorsey charged that an "enormous slush fund" had been created to ensure his defeat in the gubernatorial election. He named former Governor John Slaton as a major contributor to the fund and argued that Slaton had written letters to various people claiming Dorsey to be unfit for the governorship. In a statement issued before the Georgia primary election in 1915, Dorsey said that "the attitude of that race [Jewish] in the Frank case and in every criminal case in which a Hebrew is a defendant has demonstrated the fact that the successful prosecution of a Hebrew is regarded by members of that race as persecution." Louis Marshall of the American Jewish Committee called Dorsey's statement an "attempt to seek votes by stirring up religious animosity." Dorsey was reelected unopposed to the governorship in 1918. During his second term in office, he was known for his "fearless denunciation of lynching."

In 1921, Dorsey wrote and distributed a pamphlet called "The Negro in Georgia" expounding on the need to end outrages against blacks. He believed that compulsory education for blacks and whites alike, conferences with both races to discuss interrelations, and proper religious instruction would improve relations between blacks and whites.

In addition to the political repercussions, the lynching of Leo Frank affected Georgia's sentiment toward American intervention in the war in Europe. At a time when the honor of the State of Georgia was blemished by the Frank case, patriotism emerged as a significant statement of pride and closeness to the Union. In an effort to rid themselves of recently embarrassing associations with Tom Watson and his anti-Wilson stand, most Georgians tended to embrace the most nationalistic cause of all—preparedness for war.[6]

Perhaps the most enduring legacy of the Frank case is the role it played in the formation of the Anti-Defamation League of B'nai B'rith in 1913. B'nai B'rith (Sons of the Covenant) was founded in New York City in 1843 and it is the world's oldest and largest Jewish service organization. Initiated with the help of Adolf Kraus, the Anti-Defamation League (ADL) works under the auspices of B'nai B'rith. Through education, vigilance, and legislation, the ADL has sought to provide "concerted action against the constant and ever increasing efforts" to diminish the good name of the Jew. The Leo Frank tragedy was the ADL's first case. For over sixty-five years, the league collected information and conducted interviews on the Phagan murder and Frank trial and lynching. In 1982, it appeared that finally the ADL's first case would be resolved.

**
*

Memory of the trial and lynching of Leo Frank has been kept alive over the years in films, novels, plays, and nonfiction accounts. Prior to the lynching at Marietta, Sam Adelstein and George Delands produced a film called *The Frank Case*. But their Rolands Feature Film Company was forbidden to exhibit the film by the Commissioner of Licenses in New York. It was alleged that Commissioner Doll's decision was based on disapproval of the Frank film by the national board of censors. Adelstein and Delands challenged the Commissioner's ruling in the New York Supreme Court.

The novel, *Death in the Deep South*, by Ward Greene[7] appeared in 1936 and served as the basis for a 1937 film about the Frank case, "They Don't Forget." *Death in the Deep South* is set in the 1930s, after the Frank and Scottsboro cases were no longer in the public eye. *Leo. M. Frank: The Martyr Jew* was the title of a little booklet by Azalia E. De Steffani, probably printed before 1920. And Arthur Powell published a book in 1942 called *I Can Go Home Again*. Judge Powell sat on the judicial bench with Leonard Roan while Roan was charging the jury in the Phagan murder trial. "I know who killed Mary Phagan," Powell wrote, "but I know it in such a way that I can never make the information public so long as certain people are living." Arthur Powell died August 5, 1951. He had said he would write down what he knew about the real murderer, but no letter or statement has ever been found. However, Powell did believe that Hugh Dorsey had "conscientiously followed his duty as he saw it" in the Frank case. Hugh Dorsey, 77, died three years before Powell. The former solicitor general and governor was then serving as Judge of the Superior Court of Fulton County.

In 1952, Francis Busch included the Frank case in his series of books on "Notable American Trials." Four years later, Charles and Louise Samuels' treatment of the Frank tragedy, *Night Fell on Georgia*, was published.

One of the most important books about the Frank case was Harry Golden's *A Little Girl Is Dead*, published in 1965. Charles Wittenstein, the ADL lawyer instrumental in the pardon of Leo Frank, says that Golden's book was his first real acquaintance with the Frank issue. In academic circles, Dr. Leonard Dinnerstein's *The Leo Frank Case*, published in 1968 by Columbia University, has served as the standard work.

The television series "Profiles in Courage," inspired by John F. Kennedy's Pulitzer-Prize winning book, covered the aftermath of the Leo Frank trial in 1965. The Frank episode was shown only once, "then withdrawn following threat of a lawsuit by Tom Watson's great-grandson, Atlanta attorney Tom Watson Brown." Brown "opposed seeing his great-grandfather portrayed as an illiterate, dishonest, back-country demagogue," and rightly so. Actor Walter Matthau played Governor Slaton in the show.

The play "Night Witch" was written by Barbara Lebeau and performed in Atlanta at the Academy Theater. "Night Witch" was the expression used in the murder notes found near the body of Mary Phagan. These words probably referred to "a Negro legend about a ghost—the night witch—which killed little children by strangling them with a cord as they slept." Radio station WRFG (Radio Free Georgia; 89.3 FM) planned a two-hour program on the Leo Frank case several years ago. The first hour was to be a "documentary composed of the reminiscences of Atlantans who remember the episode." The second hour was to feature a panel of humanists who were to "discuss broader questions posed by the episode in an attempt to set the case and Atlanta in a context that will help us understand the pre-World War I period."

NBC television officials recently announced that the network will make a four-and-a-half-hour mini-series based on the Leo Frank case, with Academy Award-winning actor Jack Lemmon in the starring role of John Slaton, the governor of Georgia who commuted Frank's sentence.

Produced by George Stevens Jr., much of *The Ballad of Mary Phagan* was filmed during May and June of 1987 in and around Richmond, Virginia. The script "is based on work by Pulitzer Prize-winning author Larry McMurtry." The producer said that a script had been available in 1982, but network management felt at that time that there was not enough public interest to warrant a television drama.

And down through the years, little Mary Phagan has also endured in our folk music and poetry:

This ballad[8] is from Ubapah (Deep Creek), Utah, circa 1925–27:

> *Little Mary Phagan*
> *She went to town one day;*
> *She went to the pencil fact'ry*
> *To get her little pay.*
> *She left her home at seven,*
> *She kissed her mother goodbye;*
> *Not one time did that poor child*
> *Think that she was going to die.*
>
> *The wicked villain met her,*
> *With a brutal heart we know;*
> *He laughed and said, 'Little Mary,*
> *You go home no more.'*
> *He crept along behind her*
> *Till they reached the metal room;*
> *He laughed and said, 'Little Mary,*
> *You've met your fatal doom.'*
> *Newt Lee was the watchman,*
> *And when he turned his key,*
> *Away down in the basement*
> *Little Mary he could see.*
> *He called for the policemen*
> *Their names I do not know;*
> *They came to the pencil factory*
> *And told Newt he must go.*

Judge Roan passed the sentence,
You bet he did not fail;
Solicitor Hugh Dorsey,
He sent the brute to jail.
Astonished at the question
The villain failed to say
Why he killed little Mary
Upon that holiday.

Her mother sits a-weeping,
She weeps and moans all day;
And hopes to meet her darling
In a better world some day.
Now come all you good people,
Wherever you may be;
Suppose that little Mary
Belonged to you or me.

Mrs. Pearl Flake from Atlanta gave this version between 1939 and 1941:

Leo Frank he met her,
With a brutish heart and grin;
He says to little Mary,
'You'll never see home again.'

She fell down on her knees
To Leo Frank and pled.
He picked up a stick from the trash pile
And beat her o'er the head.

The tears rolled down her cheeks,
The blood rolled down her back;
For she remembered telling her mother
What time she would be back. . . .

Nemphon was the watchman;
He went to wind his key;

And 'way down in the basement
Little Mary he could see.'

They took him to the jailhouse
And locked him in a cell;
That poor old innocent Negro
Had nothing he could tell. . . .
Judge Roan passed the sentence;
He passed it very well;
The Christian doers of heaven
Sent Leo Frank to hell.

Another version of the ballad blames the janitor, Jim Conley:

When she got to the factory
The janitor let her in.
Instead of giving her her pay,
He did a dreadful sin.

Many long hours her mother wept
Over that evil day,
For Mary was her sole support
With her little pay.

The sheriff he was a wise good man,
He never flicked a hair;
He let them string that janitor up
And left him hanging there.

All versions have the same meter and can be sung to the same tune despite their differences in content.

There is also a poem that deals with Mary Phagan's murder. It has ten numbered stanzas, and obviously was written before the commutation of Leo Frank's sentence in June 1915.

Mary Phagan[9]

Bright as the morning light
And modest as the dew,
Came little Mary on the trolley car,
As often she did do.

Came to draw her money
And to see the parade that day;
She knew not that a murder
Was hiding on her way.

She entered the building gaily,
Straight to the office she went;
She reached her hand to get her pay,
And so her life was spent.

While within the building,
And near the metal room,
She fought for that which is dearer than life,
And so she met her doom.

Now, while in that building,
Though virtuous and modest, too,
She was brutally murdered
By the Negro or the Jew.

The sad, broken hearted mother,
As she cries and mourns all day,
Looking for her darling child
Who can never come back that way.

The voice of the people
Is the voice of God they say,
So let us pray while we wait,
To hear what the court may say.

A message came from heaven.
Tis in the bible today.
That whatsoever a man soweth
That shall he also reap that way.

Sweet as the fragrance of a dewey rose,
Pure as the drifted snow,
She died, defending her virtue,
By the cruel cord & blow.

Made a little below the angels
Her blood cries to heaven today;
Vengeance is mine, Saith the Lord,
And I will surely repay.

O God of [love] and mercy,
Thou knowest the guilty one
[Save?] the Governor of a sovereign state,
By ruling that Justice be done.

Endnotes

1. Born near Harpersfield, Alabama, in 1880, Simmons was the son of a country preacher. He served in the Spanish-American War and later began a career in the ministry of the Methodist Episcopal Church, South. He left the ranks of the clergy to become a salesman of fraternal insurance for the Woodmen of the World. "His varied career also included a brief term as Instructor of Southern History at Atlanta's faltering Lanier University," Kenneth T. Jackson noted. See also Ernest Volkman's *A Legacy of Hate.*

2. On December 6, 1915, *The Birth of a Nation*—the first full-length motion picture in American history—opened to a wildly enthusiastic audience in Atlanta. The film, based on a novel of the Civil War and Reconstruction by Thomas Dixon and directed by David Ward Griffith, told the story of a "vanquished South" rescued just in time by the "hard-riding horsemen of the Ku Klux Klan." William Simmons was able to persuade the theater manager "to grant him free admission to see *The Birth of a Nation* time and again." The film electrified audiences in the Old South for decades, and more than fifty million people nationwide

eventually saw the white-hooded riders save the day. See Kenneth T. Jackson's *The Ku Klux Klan in the City 1915–1930,* Charlton Moseley's "Latent Klanism in Georgia, 1890–1915," and David Chalmers' *Hooded Americanism.*

3. A man named Tom Mooney (1885–1942) was convicted by the California courts in 1915 of murder and sentenced to life imprisonment. Not until twenty-four years later was he pardoned from jail. Mooney had been convicted on testimony known by the prosecuting officers to be perjured. (See Mark DeWolfe Howe's *Holmes-Laski Letters.*)

4. "The blast was more than a shock. It was a shock treatment. For Jew and non-Jew alike the bomb released long buried thoughts about themselves and each other. It blasted through the southern moderates' wall of silence. All of 'the right people', from Georgia Governor Marvin Griffin to President of the United States Dwight D. Eisenhower, had 'the right thing to say' about the bombing and said it for publication." *(As But A Day)*

5. Hugh Manson Dorsey succeeded Nathaniel Harris as governor in 1917. Like Slaton and Harris, Dorsey was a Methodist. Born in Fayetteville, Georgia, he was the son of Rufus Thomas, an eminent jurist, and Sarah (Bennett) Dorsey. Dorsey graduated with an A.B. degree from the University of Georgia in 1893, then studied law at the University of Virginia for one year. He was admitted to the Georgia bar in 1894 and started practice in 1895 in Atlanta with Dorsey, Brewster & Howell, his father's firm. He was a member of that firm until 1916, resuming connection with it after his second term as governor in June 1921. In 1910, Governor Joseph Brown appointed him Solicitor General of the Atlanta Judicial Circuit to complete the unexpired term of Charles D. Hill. He subsequently was elected to that position and served until his resignation in 1916 to assume the office of governor of Georgia. One of the high points of his career as Solicitor was his brilliant 9-hour summation speech at the end of Leo Frank's trial.

Dorsey married Mary Adair Wilkinson in June 1911. He was the father of two children, and belonged to the Masons. His father-in-law, James Marion Wilkinson, was the vice-president of the Georgia & Florida Railroad.

Thomas William Hardwick, a Protestant lawyer, became governor in 1921 following the two terms of Hugh Dorsey. Hardwick failed in his reelection attempt in 1922 because he had waged a campaign against the Ku Klux Klan, demanding an end to the mob violence in Georgia. Clifford Mitchell Walker assumed the office of governor in 1923. He ran unopposed and was reelected unopposed once again in 1924.

During Walker's administration, Georgia received national criticism for its officially sanctioned cruelty to the prisoners. Walker angered the

Ku Klux Klan when the use of the lash in prison camps was abolished through his efforts.

Both Governor Slaton and Hugh Dorsey were members of many of the same clubs and fraternal organizations in Atlanta, including the Masons, Capital City Driving Club, Piedmont Driving Club, and the Odd Fellows.

6. See Milton L. Ready's "Georgia's Entry into World War I."

7. Events in Ward Greene's book were similar to the Frank case, but had certain distinct differences. The accused, Robert Edwin Perry Hale, was not Jewish, although he was a northerner. The setting was a business school in the South of the 1930s. The victim, thirteen-year-old Mary Clay, had been murdered and raped on Confederate Memorial Day. Suspects included Mary's boyfriend and a black elevator operator at the school. At one point Hale was compared to Leo Frank, with the idea conveyed that Frank had been innocent while Hale was not.

A local barber was directed by a police detective (under instructions from the prosecutor) to leave town during Hale's pre-trial investigation. This barber could verify Hale's whereabouts at the most likely time of the murder, thereby damaging the prosecution's case. The prosecutor was, like Hugh Dorsey, trying to make his way in politics and needed a conviction to advance his career. Hale's course mirrored Frank's insofar as he was found guilty, sentenced to hang, his sentence commuted by the governor, and then he was lynched. Greene never resolved the drama as far as telling the reader who did the killing, whether Hale or another.

8. From Olive Woolley Burt, *American Murder Ballads and Their Stories* Oxford University Press, 1958.

9. This poem was found in the Special Collections Department of the Robert W. Woodruff Library of Emory University in the "Atlanta Miscellany Box" 572 #2. Its origin is unknown.

Chapter 11

THE PARDON

Although he testified only briefly at the trial, fourteen-year-old Alonzo Mann[1] was also at the pencil factory on that overcast Saturday morning in August of 1913. Mann, an office boy at the factory, was "standing in a stairwell moments after the crime." In a sworn statement, Mann said he saw Jim Conley carrying the limp body of the girl on the first floor of the factory near the trap door that led to the basement. But *his affidavit came nearly seven decades after the fact*.

Jim Conley saw young Alonzo that Memorial Day and threatened to kill him if he ever mentioned what he had witnessed. Alonzo took a trolley home and told his mother what had happened. His mother cautioned him not to become involved, although Mann did testify at the trial. After Leo Frank was convicted of the murder, Alonzo's mother and father told their son there was nothing anyone could do to change the jury's verdict. So young Alonzo learned to live with his vision of Jim Conley carrying the dead or unconscious Mary Phagan in his arms.

Occasionally, Mann would tell his story to friends and relatives, but no one really listened to him or took him seriously. Once, when he was in the service during World War I, he fought with somebody from Marietta, Georgia, about it. Another time, he hired a lawyer who chose not to pursue the story. In the 1950s, Mann gave information about what he saw in 1913 to a reporter from the *Atlanta Constitution and Journal*; the editor supposedly said the story would not be run because the Atlanta Jewish community would not want to have the case brought up again. The editor was probably correct; and, of course, Mrs. Frank was still alive then. During the 1960s and 1970s, the Seligs, Lucille Frank's family, had asked ADL's attorney Charles Wittenstein to quiet publicity about the case. The trial and lynching of Leo Frank had left such scars on the collective memory of the Jews in Atlanta that they were afraid to raise the issue for fear of bringing back the rabid anti-Semitism they remembered.

Wittenstein is a pleasant, white-haired man in his late fifties. Except for a span of about fifteen months, he has lived in Atlanta continuously since 1952. For fourteen years, he served as the Director of the American Jewish Committee and worked an equal time as Southern counsel for the Anti-Defamation League of B'nai B'rith. And he maintains that if Mann had convinced someone of his story fifteen years earlier than he did, the ADL could have done very little with it. Support within the Jewish community simply would not have been there. Jews in the generation that had lived through the Frank tragedy would not have favored any effort to seek a pardon.

A reporter from *The Nashville Tennessean* was the first person to give a receptive audience to Alonzo Mann. And it came about through a rather circuitous series of events. Jerry Thompson, a reporter for the *Tennessean*, had infiltrated the Ku Klux Klan in Alabama as part of an assignment to investigate Klan involvement in a mayoral race. Thompson joined two competing Klan groups—one led by David Duke and the other by Bill Wilkinson. After about fifteen months he surfaced and began publishing articles about the Klan. Death threats soon followed. The publisher of the paper, John Seigenthaler, hired two bodyguards for

Thompson, one to live full-time at his farm and the other to go with Thompson on speaking engagements; he had become very popular as a speaker. He also went on temporary leave from the *Tennessean* in order to write a book about his experiences, eventually titled *My Life in the Klan*. One day when Thompson and his live-in guard (Robert Mann) were relaxing, the guard asked Thompson if he would be interested in doing a story on a famous murder case. Alonzo Mann—known to friends as Lonnie—was the bodyguard's close relative.

When Thompson first told Seigenthaler that he had new information on a case that took place seventy years ago in Atlanta, the publisher said the readers of the *Tennessean* would not be interested. Thompson and his friend, fellow reporter Robert Sherborne, later went to a trailer home in Bristol, Virginia, to visit Lonnie Mann and hear his story. They called Seigenthaler from Bristol. When Thompson told him that it was the Leo Frank case, Seigenthaler[2] said to move on it. The publisher knew about the tragedy.

A team from the *Tennessean*—including Jerry Thompson, Bob Sherborne, Sandra Roberts, and Nancy Warnecke Rhoda—spent several months pouring over court records and published accounts[3] of the Frank case to confirm Mann's story. The newspaper's credibility was at stake. Several minor discrepancies in Mann's recollection of events that Memorial Day were eventually resolved through sheer relentless research. Thompson and Sherborne seemed to believe Mann's story immediately, but Sandra Roberts remained skeptical. When the facts had been assembled, Alonzo Mann was subjected to three tests to determine the truthfulness of his account. Seigenthaler first met Mann at the cross-examination conducted by the newspaper's research team, the deputy managing editor, and Bill Willis, the *Tennessean*'s lawyer. When Mann referred to Conley, he called him "Jim" or the "black man." He seemed to have been genuinely afraid of Conley, but according to Seigenthaler, Mann did not brand Conley the murderer out of any

special animus for blacks. *Alonzo Mann was white*.[4] It was
difficult not to believe him, Seigenthaler said, although the
publisher tried to stay distant and objective. Bill Willis
concluded that Mann was a credible witness after the cross-
examination. In addition to this, Mann underwent a psychological stress evaluation and a polygraph test.[5] "He
passed both analyses impressively."

From what Charles Wittenstein saw of him, Alonzo
Mann was a sincere, conscientious, decent Christian man
who took his Christian responsibility seriously. Mann felt
that he had to unburden himself before he met his Maker.
He suffered from a heart condition and had undergone
surgery to implant a pacemaker. His story was a confession
in contemplation of death. Seigenthaler confirms that Mann
was deeply religious. He remembers Mann saying that he
wanted to get his story out so Jesus would understand him
better. On the fourth day of March 1982, Mann swore an
affidavit which said in part that "Leo Frank was convicted
by lies, heaped on lies." "Jim Conley, the chief witness
against Leo Frank, lied under oath. I know that. I am
certain that he lied. I am convinced that he, not Leo Frank,
killed Mary Phagan. I know as a matter of certainty that
Jim Conley—and he alone—disposed of her body." When
the *Tennessean*'s story ran on March 7, 1982[6], in a special
section of the Sunday edition, the public response was
nothing short of phenomenal. The wire services picked up
the story and great interest in the case was generated in
Georgia. Overall, according to Seigenthaler, the response
was positive. The Jewish community was worried, but very
interested. A few letters with Klan overtone were sent to
the paper. In looking back on the case, Seigenthaler feels
that Frank was not well represented legally. His lawyers
were counting on the jury *not* to convict on the word of a
black man. There is absolutely no doubt in Seigenthaler's
mind that two of the jurors had made "lynch statements"
prior to the trial. They wanted Frank dead before any
witnesses were called.

In addition to supervising the research efforts at the *Tennessean*, Seigenthaler also encouraged the governor of Georgia to assist in the pardon process as much as possible. The publisher contacted Bert Lance[7], seeking his assistance too.

Charles Wittenstein spent four years on the Frank case serving as an advocate on behalf of Frank's innocence[8]. Wittenstein's grandfather-in-law, Arthur Heyman, had been a law partner of Solicitor General Hugh Dorsey. Heyman (of Dorsey, Brewster, Howell and Heyman) was called by the defense as a character witness for Leo Frank during the trial, but the move backfired, because Prosecutor Dorsey knew that Heyman did not know Frank that well. Dorsey was able to exploit the fact that Heyman was testifying to the character of a person he saw only a few times a year, such as during High Holy Days.

The ADL, the American Jewish Committee, and the Atlanta Jewish Federation submitted an application to the Georgia State Board of Pardons and Paroles on January 4, 1983 requesting a full pardon for Leo Frank. Alonzo Mann's affidavit was the primary document in the application, which also included affidavits from Jim Conley with numerous internal inconsistencies; statements from Annie Maud Carter[9], Conley's girlfriend (who said he had confessed the murder to her several times); and John Slaton's written commutation of Frank's sentence. Mann had made statements asserting Conley's guilt on March 4, 1982, and again on November 10, 1982 in Atlanta. He was videotaped when making his statement in Atlanta and his words were "recorded by a court reporter in the presence of representatives of the Parole Board." Dale M. Schwartz acted as lead counsel in the pardon effort.

The ADL argued not that Leo Frank was denied a fair trial, but that he was innocent based on the new evidence provided by Alonzo Mann—the position also taken by the Jewish community in Atlanta.

The National Conference of Christians and Jews formally

supported the pardon, as did the Christian Council of Metropolitan Atlanta, and the Black-Jewish Coalition wich was chaired by the Reverend John Lewis. Support from these groups took the form of communication to the Pardon and Parole board and to local newspapers.

But there was opposition to the posthumous pardon. About 200 robed Ku Klux Klan members marched in Marietta on Saturday, September 3, 1983, where they heard a speech by Dr. Edward R. Fields, a former chiropractor who headed the New Order Knights of the Ku Klux Klan. Fields is also editor of the *Thunderbolt*, a publication of the National States Rights Party based in Marietta. From time to time the *Thunderbolt* (which has a national circulation of about 15,000, mostly among right-wing extremists) runs a story on the Frank case, quoting liberally from Tom Watson's *Jeffersonian*.

The Klan's march that day ended at the grave of Mary Phagan in Citizens' Cemetery, where they laid a large wreath. Across town, Marietta's mayor and members of the City Council joined a counter-demonstration that attracted about 300 people at the First Baptist Church. The town council had granted the Klan a parade permit, but said it did not agree with the views of the white supremacist organization. In retrospect, Charles Wittenstein feels that the Klan march probably helped the ADL's case.

Opposition to the pardon also came from James Phagan and his daughter Mary. James Phagan's father was Joshua Phagan, the brother of Little Mary Phagan who was murdered in 1913. Mary Phagan, the great-niece of the murder victim, still lives in Marietta. She was born in Washington state when her father was a master sergeant in the United States Air Force. James has since retired from the United States Postal Service.

Mary Phagan was about thirteen-years-old before she realized who the great-aunt was that she had been named for. Today at thirty-three, Ms Phagan teaches blind and visually handicapped children near Atlanta. She bears a striking physical resemblance to her great-aunt. I've had to live as two people, Ms Phagan says, people see me as the Little Mary Phagan of long ago and as Mary Phagan of today. Although she has no children, she said that she probably would not name any daughter for her great-aunt. She simply wants the case to be forgotten and live a "normal" life.

James Phagan and Mary Phagan objected to a resolution sent by the Georgia Senate in March 1982 to the Board of Pardons and Paroles. It had requested an investigation "and, if the evidence indicates that Leo Frank was not guilty, the board should give serious consideration to granting a pardon to Leo Frank posthumously." James Phagan "sent a letter to the board answering each point of the resolution, arguing that no new evidence has been submitted to warrant a pardon." Mann's affidavit, said Phagan, was not evidence.

In an interview with *The Atlanta Constitution* James Phagan emphasized that he did not support or believe in the K.K.K. "Nearly ten years ago," he said, he "denied the organization's request to use the Phagan name in a 'Remember Mary Phagan Day.'"

Throughout 1983, considerable public support for Frank's pardon emerged. Atlanta newspapers editorialized in favor of it and Governor Joe Frank Harris let it be known he supported the efforts. The ADL went into the 1983 hearing that December fully expecting victory. But on December 22, 1983, the five-member Georgia State Board of Pardons and Paroles denied Leo M. Frank a posthumous pardon. Alonzo Mann, then eighty-five, was in Atlanta's state capital pressroom when the announcement by Silas Moore, deputy director of central operations for the board, came. The board's chairman Mobley Howell[10] wrote that "for the Board to grant such a pardon, the innocence of the subject must be shown conclusively. In the Board's opinion, this has not been shown." Alonzo Mann cried when he heard the decision.

In 1982 there were only two types of pardons granted by

the board: a pardon of forgiveness and a pardon of inno-cence. Both types were designed for cases where judge, prosecution, defense counsel, and witnesses were all alive. A pardon of forgiveness essentially meant that a person was, indeed, guilty, but because of an upright life following prison, the State grants forgiveness. A pardon of innocence meant that innocence must be shown beyond any doubt whatsoever.

The ADL did not want and would not accept a pardon of forgiveness. That left only the pardon of innocence, but this was impossible to obtain seventy years after the fact, when all principals in the case were dead. In 1983, the ADL had been doomed from the start, but did not know it. Later, it argued that innocence beyond any doubt was unknown as a standard in American law.

The parole board was flooded with mail denouncing its finding. The Christian Council of Atlanta "joined Jewish groups in condemning the board's action." But James Pha-gan supported the board's decision: "I feel satisfied that Justice prevailed," he said.

According to Dale Schwartz, the son of William M. Smith was very helpful in the 1983 effort to secure pardon for Frank. Walter Smith, still an attorney in Atlanta, said in an interview with the *Atlanta Journal and Constitution* that his father (who had been Conley's attorney) "felt a great degree of guilt, because he had been deceived by Conley, [and] that he had lent his efforts to convict an innocent man." The elder Smith's efforts on Leo Frank's behalf had put him in constant danger. According to his son, people felt William Smith had "become a traitor to his client."[11]

After the board's December 1983 decision, the ADL dropped the case for awhile. Later Louis Kunian, a Jewish businessman, contacted the board and "asked renewed board consideration of the Frank case." By this time Dale Schwartz was preoccupied with other matters, so Charles Wittenstein presented the arguments before the board.[12]

In this second round of pardon proceedings, the ADL

JIM CONLEY. A floorsweeper at the National Pencil Factory, James Conley was the State's main witness against Leo Frank. *(Atlanta Journal* & *Atlanta Constitution)*

WITNESSES FOR THE STATE. From left to right: Miss Grace Hicks, Police Detective John Black, and Harry Scott of the Pinkerton Detective Agency. *(Atlanta Journal & Atlanta Constitution)*

ALONZO MANN AS A BOY. Alonzo Mann testified at Leo Frank's trial. *(Nancy Rhoda, Nashville Tennessean)*

N. V. DARLEY. Mr. Darley was Assistant Superintendent of the National Pencil Factory.
(*Atlanta Journal* & *Atlanta Constitution*)

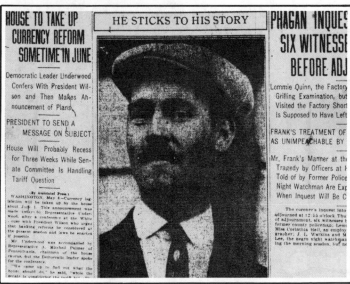

HOUSE TO TAKE UP
CURRENCY REFORM
SOMETIME IN JUNE

Democratic Leader Underwood
Confers With President Wilson and Then Makes Announcement of Plans

PRESIDENT TO SEND A
MESSAGE ON SUBJECT

House Will Probably Recess
for Three Weeks While Senate Committee Is Handling
Tariff Question

HE STICKS TO HIS STORY

PHAGAN INQUES
SIX WITNESSE
BEFORE ADJ

Lemmie Quinn, the Factory
Grilling Examination, but
Visited the Factory Short
is Supposed to Have Left

FRANK'S TREATMENT OF
AS UNIMPEACHABLE BY

Mr. Frank's Manner at the
Tragedy by Officers at F
Told of by Former Police
Night Watchman Are Exp
When Inquest Will Be C

LEMMIE QUINN. Lemmie Quinn, a foreman at the National Pencil Factory, testified at the coroner's inquest and at the trial.
(*Atlanta Journal* & *Atlanta Constitution*)

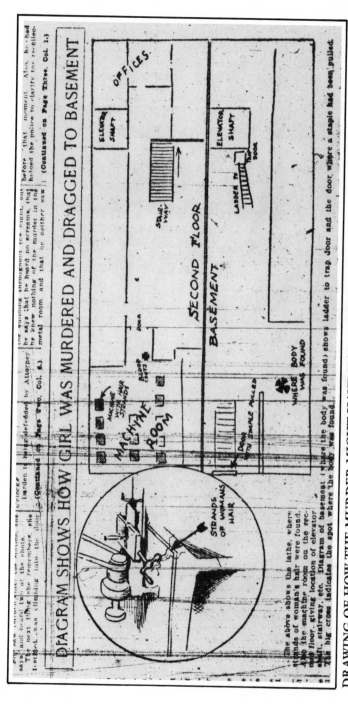

DRAWING OF HOW THE MURDER MIGHT HAVE HAPPENED.
(Atlanta Journal & Atlanta Constitution)

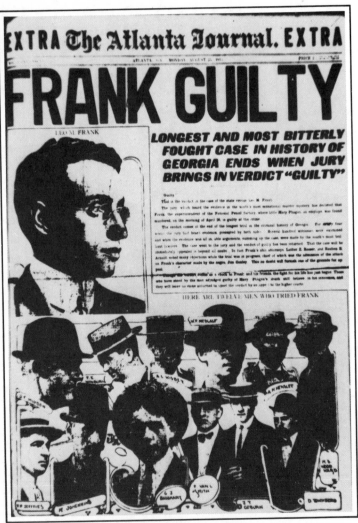

THE "EXTRA" OF THE *ATLANTA JOURNAL* — August 25, 1913.
(Atlanta Journal & Atlanta Constitution)

Vol. XLVI—No. 71. ATLANTA, GA. TUESDAY MORNING, AUGUST 26, 1913.—SIXTEEN PAGES.

FRANK CONVICTED, ASSERTS INNOCENCE

LIND QUITS MEXICO; WILSON'S MESSAGE GOES TO CONGRESS

The President Will Personally Present Views on Situation to Joint Session of House and Senate.

CONFERENCE IS HELD AT THE WHITE HOUSE

Wilson Reads Message to Two Congressional Foreign Relations Committees and It Is Given Approval

MESSAGE ON MEXICO

FARM CURRENCY WINS IN CAUCUS

Paper Based on Agricultural Products on the Same Basis an Commercial Paper for Banking Purposes.

ATTENDANCE MARK SOUGHT BY LOCALS

Want 200,000 for the Season. "Birmingham Must Be Beaten," Is Slogan—Field Day Wednesday.

GUILTY, DECLARES JURY

LEO M. FRANK.

LEO FRANK'S HISTORY.

WAITS WITH WIFE IN TOWER FOR NEWS FROM COURTROOM; FRIENDS TELL HIM VERDICT

"I Am as Innocent Today as I Was One Year Ago," He Cries—"The Jury Has Been Influenced by Mob Law"—"I Am Stunned by News," Declares . . . Rabbi Marx, One of Prisoner's Closest Friends—Defense Plans to Carry Case to Supreme Court in Order to Secure New Trial—Judge Roan Will Defer Sentence For a Few Days.

OVATION FOR JURY AND SOLICITOR GIVEN BY CROWD WAITING ON STREET.

Judge Roan Thanks Jurymen for Services During Four Long, Hard Weeks, and Tells Members He Hopes They Will Find Their Families Well—Courtroom Was Cleared by Order of Judge Before Jury Was Brought in to Give Its Verdict—"I'm Sorry for Frank's Wife and His Mother," Says Solicitor Dorsey.

LEO FRANK CONVICTED.
(*Atlanta Journal & Atlanta Constitution*)

A COURAGEOUS GOVERNOR. Governor John Marshall Slaton
received pleas from all over the country to spare Frank's life. Slaton also
received political enticement and threats, both in an effort to have Frank
executed.
(Atlanta Journal & Atlanta Constitution)

THOMAS EDWARD WATSON. A powerful politician and lawyer of
Georgia, Tom Watson fanned the flames of hatred in his *Jeffersonian* and
Watson's Magazine.
(Atlanta Journal & *Atlanta Constitution)*

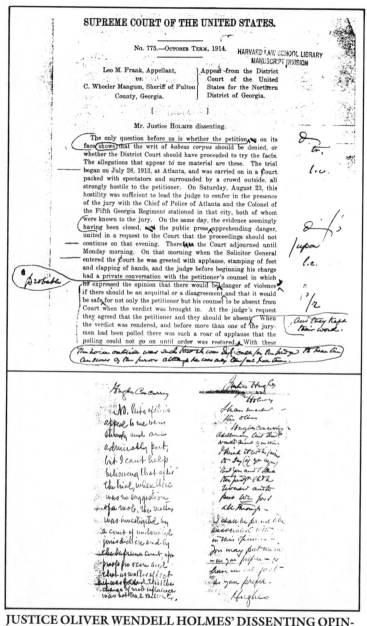

SUPREME COURT OF THE UNITED STATES.

No. 775.—October Term, 1914.

Leo M. Frank, Appellant,
vs.
C. Wheeler Mangum, Sheriff of Fulton County, Georgia.

Appeal from the District Court of the United States for the Northern District of Georgia.

[ ]

Mr. Justice Holmes dissenting.

The only question before us is whether the petition on its face shows that the writ of *habeas corpus* should be denied, or whether the District Court should have proceeded to try the facts. The allegations that appear to me material are these. The trial began on July 28, 1913, at Atlanta, and was carried on in a Court packed with spectators and surrounded by a crowd outside, all strongly hostile to the petitioner. On Saturday, August 23, this hostility was sufficient to lead the judge to confer in the presence of the jury with the Chief of Police of Atlanta and the Colonel of the Fifth Georgia Regiment stationed in that city, both of whom were known to the jury. On the same day, the evidence seemingly having been closed, and the public press apprehending danger, united in a request to the Court that the proceedings should not continue on that evening. Thereupon the Court adjourned until Monday morning. On that morning when the Solicitor General entered the Court he was greeted with applause, stamping of feet and clapping of hands, and the judge before beginning his charge had a private conversation with the petitioner's counsel in which he expressed the opinion that there would be danger of violence if there should be an acquittal or a disagreement, and that it would be safe for not only the petitioner but his counsel to be absent from Court when the verdict was brought in. At the judge's request they agreed that the petitioner and they should be absent. When the verdict was rendered, and before more than one of the jurymen had been polled there was such a roar of applause that the polling could not go on until order was restored. With these

JUSTICE OLIVER WENDELL HOLMES' DISSENTING OPINION. Justice Holmes' handwritten comments as well as Justice Charles Evans Hughes' notes have never before been published. Hughes wrote that he was proud to be associated with Holmes in this opinion. *(Oliver Wendell Holmes, Jr. Papers, Harvard Law School Library)*

THE LYNCHING IN FREY'S GROVE.
(Georgia Department of Archives and History)

(Atlanta Journal & Atlanta Constitution)

The Atlanta Journal.

VOL. XXXIII. NO. 175.　　ATLANTA, GA., TUESDAY EVENING, AUGUST 17, 1915.　　LAST EDITION　　PRICE 2 CENTS

LEO FRANK FORCIBLY TAKEN FROM PRISON; HE IS HANGED TO A TREE NEAR MARIETTA; HIS BODY HAS BEEN BROUGHT TO ATLANTA

JUDGE NEWTON A. MORRIS, of Marietta, addressing the crowd assembled in Frey's Grove, where Frank was lynched, asked any members of the mob which was about to cut down, when having spring suspended from an oak tree. The crowd voted to sustain the appeal of Judge Morris and the body was removed from its grave and transferred to an undertaker's wagon.

1,002 PERISH WHEN GERMAN SUBMARINE SINKS A TRANSPORT

British Transport Royal Edward, Loaded With Troops, Is Torpedoed and Sunk in the Aegean Sea

GERMANS SCORE NEW VICTORY OVER RUSSIANS

Captured —Three —sk Fall

PEOPLE THRONG TO SCENE WHERE BODY DANGLES FROM ROPE

U. S. ACCEPTS OFFER OF GERMANY TO PAY DAMAGES FOR FRYE

Government Also Agrees That Disputed Treaty Provisions Be Submitted to Arbitration at The Hague

ASKS KAISER AS TO FUTURE OPERATIONS

Note Is Regarded in Washington as Putting Noted Case Well on Way to Final Settlement

After Urging the Crowd Not to Indulge in Further Demonstrations, Judge Morris Hurries Frank's Body to Atlanta

Leo M. Frank's dead body, which is now in the hands of an

HORSES STOLEN IN Frank's Last ... ...

FIRES MENACE CITY

LEO FRANK HANGED NEAR MARIETTA.
(*Atlanta Journal* & *Atlanta Constitution*)

CHARLES F. WITTENSTEIN. The Southern counsel for the Anti-Defamation League of B'nai B'rith, Mr. Wittenstein was instrumental in the pardon of Leo Frank.
(Robert Seitz Frey)

ALONZO MANN HOLDING PHOTO OF HIMSELF (Right)
AND HIS TWO BROTHERS (c. 1910).
Nashville Tennessean, Nancy Rhoda)

ALONZO MANN BY THE GRAVE OF MARY PHAGAN.
(Nancy Rhoda, Nashville Tennessean)

**ALONZO MANN AFTER SUCCESSFULLY COMPLETING
A POLYGRAPH EXAMINATION.**
(Nancy Rhoda, Nashville Tennessean)

DRAWING BASED ON ALONZO MANN'S AFFIDAVIT. An artist's interpretation of the confrontation between Alonzo Mann, then 14, and Jim Conley, holding the limp form of Mary Phagan on the first floor of the National Pencil Factory. (Pat Mitchell, *Nashville Tennessean*)

based its petition on the State's culpability in the Leo Frank case. The State had violated its obligation, ADL claimed, to protect its prisoner from the lynch mob and the State had not prosecuted any member of the lynch mob. Therefore the State foreclosed efforts to prove Leo Frank's innocence. The lynch mob and the State's failures had aborted the judicial process, the ADL argued. Implicit in this position was the message, "repent your sins." The board should do something to atone for the wrongs committed by the State. The ADL pointed out that the board was not limited by the Georgia Constitution to only two forms of pardon and asked the board to come up with a remedy that met the unique circumstances of a unique case.

The crucial evidence, said the Anti-Defamation League, was what Charles Wittenstein called the "shit in the shaft" argument. Jim Conley's final testimony was that he had helped Leo Frank take the Phagan girl's body down from the second floor to the basement in the elevator. Yet a pile of human feces that Conley admitted depositing in the elevator shaft early Saturday was found to be intact the following Sunday morning—after the murder. If Conley and Frank had indeed used the elevator, the excrement would have been flattened. The ADL used Allen L. Henson's chapter on the Frank case from his book published in 1959, and also drew upon Pastor Luther Bricker's comments about a poor black man not being fit to atone for such an atrocious murder.

A senior from Harvard University, who was doing his thesis on executive pardon as seen through the Frank case, also became involved in the formal pardon process. Clark J. Freshman ('86) acted as a liaison between the ADL and the parole board, "a lubricant in the process," said Wittenstein. "He confirmed for the us [the ADL] that, based on his conversations with the board, there was a possibility positions could be bridged and he suggested some areas of possible agreement." The board apparently wanted to heal old wounds.

Wittenstein never filed a second written motion before the board; he delivered instead an oral argument, which the board considered to be a motion.

On March 11, 1986, nearly seventy-three years after being convicted for murder by the Superior Court of Fulton County, Leo Max Frank was officially pardoned by the State of Georgia. The ADL's first case was closed. But Alonzo Mann, whose testimony cleared Frank, had died in 1985[13] at the age of eighty-seven, never learning of the pardon of the man he knew was innocent.

The official pardon said: "The lynching aborted the legal process, thus foreclosing further efforts to prove Frank's innocence. It resulted from the State of Georgia's failure to protect Frank. Compounding the injustice, the State then failed to prosecute any of the lynchers." The pardon also alluded to the atmosphere surrounding the trial.

The ADL did not receive a significant amount of hate mail in response to its role in the pardon process and Wittenstein said he was grateful the New York office of the ADL had allowed the Atlanta office to "quarterback" the pardon effort.[14]

Mary Phagan said in June 1987 she was angry when the pardon was first made official. She felt she and her father had not been notified far enough in advance of the final announcement. Her own anger has subsided since then, she says, but some members of her family are still very bitter. Mary is also very much against the NBC mini-series; she simply does not want the affair to receive any more publicity. When asked who she believed was guilty of her great-aunt's murder, Mary was very short in her reply. The evidence shows that Leo M. Frank was guilty, she says. In the interview conducted in June, Ms Phagan said: a man once told me the names of all the lynch mob members. None are alive today, although members of their families are. She insists that no member of the Phagan family was in the Knights of Mary Phagan. Both she and Charles Wittenstein said that several lawyers are in the process of putting together a book on the Frank case and Mary hinted that two women are also writing a book.

The great grandson of Thomas Edward Watson challenged the new information supplied by Alonzo Mann. In his "Notes on the Case of Leo Max Frank and Its Aftermath," Tom Watson Brown said that Mann's affidavit lacks credibility. Mann's recitation of the scene in the factory that Saturday in 1913, said Brown, varies very little from the prosecution's assertion that Frank asked Jim Conley to carry Mary Phagan's body. Brown also concluded that "there was no mob influence on the trial or the jury."

So the controversy continues and will probably live on forever, along with the memories.

Endnotes

1. Alonzo McClendon Mann was born near Memphis, Tennessee on August 8, 1898. His father, also Alonzo Mann, was born in Germany. His mother, the former Hattie McClendon, was thirty years younger than his father. When Alonzo was only a small boy, his family moved to Atlanta where he spent most of his life. During the 1950s, he operated a restaurant there.

2. Born in 1927 in Nashville, Tennessee, John Lawrence Seigenthaler grew up Roman Catholic. As a child he remembers hearing "The Ballad of Mary Phagan." If you were born and raised in the South when I was, Seigenthaler says, you come to realize that you've been raised in a segregated society. Awareness of anti-Semitic attitudes soon follows. He joined *The Nashville Tennessean* as a staff correspondent in 1949, and over the years was assigned to investigate the periodic resurgences of the Ku Klux Klan. The Klan had originated in Tennessee near Pulaski in 1866. Seigenthaler became familiar with the Frank case through Harry Golden's *A Little Girl is Dead*. Leo Frank, Seigenthaler says, was an "American Dreyfus."

3. Seigenthaler says that initially, the *Tennessean*'s requests for information and material from Hebrew Union College in Cincinnati were met with hostility. The college was concered with newspaper sensationalism and anti-Semitic backlash.

4. In a March 14, 1982, *Washington Post* article about the Frank case, Haynes Johnson identified Alonzo Mann as a black man. This mistaken notion was picked up by other sources. There is a discrepancy in the Frank literature about Mann's race.

5. Jeffrey S. Ball of the Ball Investigative Agency conducted the voice stress and polygraph tests. He affirmed Alonzo Mann's truthfulness. The psychological stress evaluation measures voice stress, whereas the polygraph measures respiratory rate, pulse rate, blood pressure, and skin reaction.

6. About a week before the story ran in the *Tennessean,* Wayne Williams was convicted for the deaths of two young Atlanta blacks and suspected of being the mass murderer who terrorized Atlanta for months. His trial has been compared in terms of local public interest to the Frank case.

7. Thomas Bertram Lance is a comentator with station WXIA-TV in Atlanta. He is also a banker and former Director of the Office of Management and Budget in Washington.

8. Wittenstein was also assisted by Stuart Lewengrub in the area of Jewish community relations.

9. In a affidavit in the possession of the ADL in Atlanta, Annie Maud Carter gave this account of a conversation with Jim Conley: ". . . so during Christmas week I was talking with him in his cell and he said he would tell me the whole truth about it. I asked him why he waited so long. He said 'If I tell you will you marry me' and I told him yes. He then told me that he really did the murder of Mary Phagan, but that it was so plainly shown on Mr. Frank that he let it go that way."

10. The other board members were Mamie Reese, James Morris, Michael Wing, and Wayne Snow Jr.

11. In 1917, Mr. Smith left his law practice in Atlanta to become a carpenter in a shipyard in Charleston, South Carolina. Later he moved to Brooklyn, taking a job there as a security guard at another shipyard. Eventually he resumed his legal career, passing the New York bar exam and joining a Wall Street law firm. Following his retirement, William Smith settled in Dahlonega, Georgia. He died in 1949.

12. The involvement of the American Jewish Committee was also less at this stage. During this time, the charimanship of the Board had passed from Mobley Howell to Wayne Snow Jr. as part of a regular progression of leadership.

13. Mann passed away on March 18, 1985.

14. New York supported the Atlanta Office of ADL in whatever it decided to do, though certain decisions required justification to the main office.

Appendix 1
CHRONOLOGY

Mid–1840s:	First Jews come to Marthasville (later named Atlanta).
1862:	Attempt made to expel Jews from Thomasville, Georgia.
1864:	General William Sherman's Union troops burn Atlanta to the ground.
1880s:	Many Russian Jews immigrate to Atlanta. Until this time, most Jews in the city were of German origin. The German Jews had attempted to adopt the customs of the general public, whereas the Russian Jews do not.
April 17, 1884:	Leo Max Frank born to Rudolph and Rae Frank in Cuero, Texas. The Frank family moves to Brooklyn, New York, within a few months.
1894:	Captain Alfred Dreyfus, a Jewish officer, arrested on charges of treason in France.
June 1, 1900:	Mary Phagan born to John and Frances Phagan in Marietta, Georgia.

1901:	Tom Watson defends a Jew accused of murder in Georgia.
Spring 1906:	Leo Frank graduates with a degree in mechanical engineering from Cornell University.
September 1906:	Major racial riot in Atlanta; ten blacks and two whites killed.
December 1907:	Frank begins a nine-month apprenticeship in Europe under Eberhard Faber, world-renowned pencil manufacturer.
August 1908:	Leo Frank moves to Atlanta to learn and supervise National Pencil Company.
October 1910:	Leo Frank marries Lucille Selig of Atlanta. The couple resides with Lucille's parents.
July 21, 1911:	Menahem Mendel Beilis arrested in Kiev, Russia, on charges of ritual murder.
1913:	The Atlanta Jewish community becomes the largest in the South.
April 26, 1913:	Confederate Memorial Day in the South. Mary Phagan collects her pay at the National Pencil Factory where she is employed.
April 27, 1913:	Mary Phagan's body discovered in the basement of the National Pencil Factory by nightwatchman Newt Lee.
April 29, 1913:	Mary Phagan is buried at Marietta in Cobb County, Georgia. Leo Frank arrested as a material witness.
May 2, 1913:	Two suspects in the case, J. M. Gantt and Arthur Mullinax, released from police custody.
May 23, 1913:	Leo Frank formally indicted for the murder of Mary Phagan.

July 28, 1913:	Trial of Leo Frank begins at old city hall building in Atlanta.
August 25, 1913:	Jury of twelve white men returns a verdict of "guilty." Frank and his attorneys not present when the verdict is read.
August 26, 1913:	Frank sentenced to die October 10, 1913, by trial judge.
August 1913:	Newt Lee, the nightwatchman who found Mary Phagan's body, released from prison.
October 1913:	Anti-Defamation League chartered.
October 31, 1913:	Judge Leonard Roan denies motion for new trial for Leo Frank.
November 1913:	American Jewish Committee first considers the Frank case.
February 1914:	Jim Conley sentenced to one-year imprisonment as an accessory after the fact in the Phagan murder.
Summer 1914:	Hostilities in Europe intensify.
December 1914:	Writ of habeas corpus petition denied in U.S. District Court in Georgia.
March 1915:	Judge Leonard S. Roan, trial judge for Leo Frank, dies in New York.
April 19, 1915:	United States Supreme Court rejects Frank's last appeal.
June 1915:	Georgia Prison Commission rejects appeal for clemency.
June 20–21, 1915:	Governor John M. Slaton of Georgia commutes Frank's sentence to life imprisonment. Frank transferred from Fulton County prison to Milledgeville Penitentiary for his own safety.

June 1915:	Nathaniel E. Harris becomes governor of Georgia, replacing John Slaton.
Summer 1915:	Thomas E. Watson's *Jeffersonian* magazine vehemently urges that Frank not be allowed to escape justice.
July 1915:	Fellow convict J. William Creen slashes Frank's neck at Milledgeville prison farm.
August 16, 1915:	Leo Frank abducted from prison farm by a mob calling itself the Knights of Mary Phagan.
August 17, 1915:	Frank hanged in a tree in Frey's woods outside Marietta, Georgia.
August–September 1915:	Christian magazines respond to the lynching.
Autumn 1915:	Ku Klux Klan revitalized as an organization in a ceremony outside of Atlanta. The Knights of Mary Phagan formed the core of this group.
1917:	Hugh M. Dorsey, prosecutor in Frank case, becomes governor of Georgia.
1920:	Tom Watson becomes a U.S. Senator from Georgia.
March 1982:	Alonzo Mann, former office boy at the National Pencil Factory, swears he saw Jim Conley carrying Mary Phagan's body and that Jim Conley was the real murderer.
January 1983:	Anti-Defamation League submits application for Leo Frank's pardon to the Georgia Board of Pardons and Paroles.
December 1983:	Parole Board denies application.
March 18, 1985:	Alonzo Mann dies.
March 11, 1986:	Georgia State Board of Pardons and Paroles officially pardons Leo Frank.

Appendix 2

JUSTICE HOLMES' DISSENT

(*Frank* v. *Mangum* 237 U.S. 309)

Source: Oliver Wendell Holmes Jr. Papers
Harvard Law School Library

SUPREME COURT OF THE UNITED STATES

No. 775—OCTOBER TERM, 1914.

Leo M. Frank, Appellant,	Appeal from the District
vs.	Court of the United
C. Wheeler Mangum, Sheriff of	States for the Northern
Fulton County, Georgia.	District of Georgia.

[April 19, 1915.]

Mr. Justice HOLMES dissenting.

Mr. Justice Hughes and I are of opinion that the judgment should be reversed. The only question before us is whether the petition shows on its face that the writ of *habeas corpus* should be denied, or whether the District Court should have proceeded to try the facts. The allegations that appear to us material are these. The trial began on July 28, 1913, at Atlanta, and was carried on in a court packed with spectators and surrounded by a crowd outside, all strongly hostile to the petitioner. On Saturday, August

23, this hostility was sufficient to lead the judge to confer in the presence of the jury with the Chief of Police of Atlanta and the Colonel of the Fifth Georgia Regiment stationed in that city, both of whom were known to the jury. On the same day, the evidence seemingly having been closed, the public press, apprehending danger, united in a request to the Court that the proceedings should not continue on that evening. Thereupon the Court adjourned until Monday morning. On that morning when the Solicitor General entered the court he was greeted with applause, stamping of feet and clapping of hands, and the judge before beginning his charge had a private conversation with the petitioner's counsel in which he expressed the opinion that there would be 'probable danger of violence' if there should be an acquittal or a disagreement, and that it would be safer for not only the petitioner but his counsel to be absent from Court when the verdict was brought in. At the judge's request they agreed that the petitioner and they should be absent, and they kept their word. When the verdict was rendered, and before more than one of the jurymen had been polled there was such a roar of applause that the polling could not go on until order was restored. The noise outside was such that it was difficult for the Judge to hear the answers of the jurors although he was only ten feet from them. With these specifications of fact, the petitioner alleges that the trial was dominated by a hostile mob and was nothing but an empty form.

We lay on one side the question whether the petitioner could or did waive his right to be present at the polling of the jury. That question was apparent in the form of the trial and was raised by the application for a writ of error; and although after the application to the full Court we thought that the writ ought to be granted, we never have been impressed by the argument that the presence of the prisoner was required by the Constitution of the United States. But *habeas corpus* cuts through all forms and goes to the very tissue of the structure. It comes in from the outside, not in subordination to the proceedings, and although every form may have been preserved opens the inquiry whether they have been more than an empty shell.

The argument for the appellee in substance is that the trial was in a court of competent jurisdiction, that it retains jurisdiction although, in fact, it may be dominated by a mob, and that the rulings of the State Court as to the fact of such domination cannot be reviewed. But the argument seems to us inconclusive. Whatever disagreement there may be as to the scope of the phrase 'due process of law', there can be no doubt that it embraces the fundamental conception of a fair trial, with opportunity to be heard. Mob law does not become due process of law by securing the assent of a terrorized jury. We are not speaking of mere disorder, or mere irregularities in procedure, but of a case where the processes of justice are actually subverted. In such a case, the Federal Court has jurisdiction to issue the writ. The fact that the State Court still has its general jurisdiction and is otherwise a competent court does not make it impossible to find that a jury has been subjected to intimidation in a particular case. The loss of jurisdiction is not general but particular, and proceeds from the control of a hostile influence.

When such a case is presented it can not be said, in our view, that the State Court decision makes the matter *res judicata*. The State acts when by its agency it finds the prisoner guilty and condemns him. We have held in a civil case that it is no defense to the assertion of the Federal right in the Federal Court that the State has corrective procedure of its own—that still less does such procedure draw to itself the final determination of the Federal question. *Simon* v. *Southern Ry. Co.*, 236 U.S. 115, 122, 123. We see no reason for a less liberal rule in a matter of life and death. When the decision of the question of fact is so interwoven with the decision of the question of constitutional right that the one necessarily involves the other, the Federal Court must examine the facts. *Kansas City Southern*

Ry. Co. v. *C. H. Albers Commission Co.,* 223 U.S. 573, 591. *Norfolk & Western Ry. Co.* v. *Conley,* March 8, 1915. Otherwise, the right will be a barren one. It is significant that the argument for the State does not go so far as to say that in no case would it be permissible on application for *habeas corpus* to override the findings of fact by the state courts. It would indeed be a most serious thing if this Court were so bold, for we could not but regard it as a removal of what is perhaps the most important guaranty of the Federal Constitution. If, however, the argument stops short of this, the whole structure built upon the State procedure and decisions fall to the ground.

To put an extreme case and show what we mean, if the trial and the later hearing before the Supreme Court had taken place in the presence of an armed force known to be ready to shoot if the result was not the one desired, we do not suppose that this Court would allow itself to be silenced by the suggestion that the record showed no flaw. To go one step further, suppose that the trial had taken place under such intimidation and that the Supreme Court of the State on writ of error had discovered no error in the record, we still imagine that this Court would find a sufficient one outside of the record, and that it would not be disturbed in its conclusion by anything that the Supreme Court of the State might have said. We therefore lay the suggestion that the Supreme Court of the State has disposed of the present question of the appellant's right to be present. If the petition discloses facts that amount to a loss of jurisdiction in the trial court, jurisdiction could not be restored by any decision above. And notwithstanding the principle of comity and convenience, (for in our opinion it is nothing more, *United States* v. *Sing Tuck,* 194 U.S. 161, 168,) that calls for a resort to the local appellate tribunal before coming to the Courts of the United States for a writ of *habeas corpus,* when, as here, that resort has been had in vain, the power to secure fundamental rights that had existed at every stage becomes a duty and must be put forth.

The single question in our minds is whether a petition alleging that the trial took place in the midst of a mob savagely and manifestly intent on a single result, is shown on its face unwarranted, by the specifications, which may be presumed to set forth the strongest indications of the fact at the petitioner's command. This is not a matter for polite presumptions; we must look facts in the face. Any judge who has sat with juries knows that in spite of forms they are extremely likely to be impregnated by the environing atmosphere. And when we find the judgment of the expert on the spot, of the judge whose business it was to preserve not only form but substance, to have been that if one juryman yielded to the reasonable doubt that he himself later expressed in court as the result of most anxious deliberation, neither prisoner nor counsel would be safe from the rage of the crowd, we think the presumption overwhelming that the jury responded to the passions of the mob. Of course we are speaking only of the case made by the petition, and whether it ought to be heard. Upon allegations of this gravity in our opinion it ought to be heard, whatever the decision of the State Court may have been, and it did not need to set forth contradictory evidence, or matter of rebuttal, or to explain why the motions for a new trial and to set aside the verdict were overruled by the State Court. There is no reason to fear an impairment of the authority of the State to punish the guilty. We do not think it impracticable in any part of this country to have trials free from outside control. But to maintain this immunity it may be necessary that the supremacy of the law and of the Federal Constitution should be vindicated in a case like this. It may be that on a hearing a different complexion would be given to the judge's alleged request and expression of fear. But supposing the alleged facts to be true, we are of opinion that if they were before the Supreme Court it sanctioned a situation upon which the Courts of the United States should act, and if for any reason they were not before the Supreme Court, it is our duty to act upon them now and to declare lynch law as little valid when practiced by a regularly drawn jury as when administered by one elected by a mob intent on death.

True copy.
      Test: *Clerk Supreme Court, U.S.*

Appendix 3

THE CHRISTIAN RESPONSE

In addition to marking the time of increased Jewish immigration into the South, the American Civil War stands as a monumental dividing ridge in American religious experience[1]. From the beginning of colonial life in this country, religion served as a bond of unity, which helped overcome the effects of competing local interests and regional concerns. The Great Awakening of the 1740s, associated with theologians Jonathan Edwards and Gilbert Tennent, is a significant example of the cohesive value of religion in social terms.

The issue of slavery, however, produced such widespread social and theological dislocations that many churches were not able to stay united on the issue. As a result, many northern and southern Protestant denominations split. And relatively few southern denominations were able, or even found it desirable, to reunite with their northern counterparts after General Robert E. Lee surrendered to General Ulysses S. Grant on April 9, 1865, at Appomattox.

The three largest religious denominations in the South in the period after the war were the Methodists, Baptists, and Presbyterians. The Methodist Episcopal Church,

South, and the Southern Baptist Conference had emerged following the split in their respective national churches in 1845. The Presbyterians, as of 1870, were also split between North and South. The Protestant Episcopal Church stands as the one denomination which successfully merged northern and southern churches after 1865. Reverend Dr. C. B. Wilmer, one of the Christian leaders of Atlanta who spoke out on the Frank case, was the pastor of a Protestant Episcopal church.

The growing shift in ethnicity in the population of the United States after the Civil War was reflected in the proportionate strength of various religious groups. By 1900, at a national level, the Methodists and the Baptists were the largest American denominations, followed by the Lutherans and Presbyterians. The Roman Catholic Church grew dramatically after 1865. And with the great influx of Eastern European Jewish immigrants from 1880 to 1914, the American Jewish community also grew substantially. In addition, Buddhism became established on the West Coast with the arrival of Chinese and Japanese immigrants. America was becoming quite diverse religiously.

In Atlanta, Christian religious influence in the years immediately preceding the Frank case was devoted primarily to promoting orderliness, according to Harvey Knupp Newman. Revivalism succeeded in bringing in new members for the churches, but this increase in membership was accomplished at the expense of the orderliness they had been seeking for Atlanta.

From the last week of April 1913 until the first weeks of September 1915, the Atlanta newspapers were filled with articles about the Phagan murder. Leo Frank's trial and Governor John Slaton's dramatic decision to commute Frank's sentence on the day before Frank was to die and Slaton was to leave office grabbed the headlines of Fulton

County. The lynching in Marietta was a national story. In fact, the Frank case was given widespread national coverage beginning in the spring of 1914. From 1913 to 1915, more than a hundred articles appeared in the *New York Times* alone. Popular magazines such as *Everybody's*, *Collier's*, and *Outlook* also published pieces about the events in Atlanta.

With the exception of two small articles in *The Mennonite* (Berne, Indiana), the Christian press across the nation was essentially silent about the Frank case until after the lynching in August 1915. There is no record of ongoing Christian commentary on the trial, the judicial appeal process, nor the widespread petitioning for commutation of Frank's sentence, although there were a large number of general audience and academic Christian magazines and journals in existence at the time. When Christian views on the case did appear, they were limited in number; a survey of Christian magazines of the time revealed less than seventy-five articles on the entire Frank issue. Most Christian magazines offered no comment whatsoever.

The *Christian Century*, probably the most influential Protestant weekly journal of that era, provided no news coverage or discussion of the case. The only space in the *Christian Century* given to the issue was a poem by Mary White Ovington, "Mary Phagan Speaks." It was reprinted from the *New Republic*, a liberal popular magazine.

It is possible that much of the Christian response to the case was contained in sermons and homilies. However, most pastors' and priests' messages were never written down and collected, much less published. No well-known American theologians or clergymen commented on any aspect of Frank's fate in their recorded works.

Academic Christian journals of the early twentieth century did not, in general, deal with issues of the day. There was some discussion of the First World War and Woodrow Wilson's policies, but attention was more often focused on the distant past—Scriptural interpretation and archaeological discoveries in the Holy Land.

Many Christian denominational magazines of the time were limited to ecclesiastical or administrative affairs. The appointment of pastors, church conferences, and missionary activities were the usual subjects. Other magazines focused on devotional and liturgical concerns. Often, a denominational magazine served as a weekly guide to personal and family worship, providing Biblical references and short lessons.

Moreover, Christian magazines were a major source of news, particularly information about far off lands where missionaries were serving the church. Usually they carried a section in the front of their magazine devoted to "News of the Week," and when there was mention of the Frank case, it would often appear here.

In examining the responses of the Christian magazines it was necessary to consider whether the issue of Leo Frank's Jewishness was raised. Were specific statements made which denigrated Frank's character? Was the possibility of his being innocent considered? Was there a call for prosecution of the lynch mob?

Five articles referred to Frank's Jewishness or to anti-Jewish public sentiment. *The United Presbyterian* used "young Hebrew" in lieu of Frank's name. And this publication, along with *The Epworth Herald* and *Northern Christian Advocate* drew a direct correlation between Frank's being Jewish and the emotional public reaction to the Phagan murder. *The United Presbyterian* said that "there enters into the emotions which have been inflamed by local discussion not only sympathy with the girl but hatred of the man because he was a Jew." Similarly, *The Epworth Herald*, a magazine published by The Methodist Book Concern, noted that "because of his Jewish extraction, the mob spirit, which is easily aroused in Georgia, was swung against him, and his trial and conviction will remain a lasting disgrace to that state." "Much race feeling developed during the trial as Frank was a Jew," declared the *Northern Christian Advocate*.

The *Wesleyan Christian Advocate*, the principal news medium of the North Georgia Conference of the Methodist Episcopal Church, South, categorically rejected any link between Frank's Jewishness and the outcome of his trial.

> It was a most serious blunder from any and every standpoint for the counsel of Leo Frank in the trial to inject into the case the idea of racial prejudice. That Frank was a Jew had no more to do with the verdict of sworn jurors than it had to do with the tides of the sea. The Jews of this state have had every advantage accorded anybody else within the limits of the state. Our courts have been open to them for redress of their wrongs and the securement of their rights. They have been prominent in the industrial and commercial life of the commonwealth, and when they have chosen, they have had access to the best social circles of the state. They have come among us and a number of them have amassed fortunes. Their rights of person and property have been respected. That one of that race should have been charged with a crime and haled before the courts to establish his innocence or meet a verdict of guilt was no more than has been done time and again to Gentiles within the state. Most unfortunate is that the race sentiment has ever been brought into the case. And most regrettable will it be if this racial prejudice is to be fanned into flame now that Frank has gone to the bar of God.

Finally, the *Northern Christian Advocate* offered a brief report intended to demonstrate the influence of Jesus on the Jew, Leo Frank. When the mother of Frank was asked whether she could ever forgive her son's murderers, she is said to have replied that perhaps someday "I will be able to quote Leo's favorite passage from the Scriptures. It was: Father, forgive them, for they know not what they do." To this quotation, the editor of the *Northern Christian Advocate* added that "if this be as reported, it beautifully illustrates the influence of Jesus upon his brethren after the flesh." The Biblical passage had been taken from Luke 23:26 in the New Testament. "Brethren after the flesh" would refer to Jews. Christians would most likely have been referred to as Jesus' brethren after the spirit.

As for specific support of the jury's decision in the Christian press, *The Methodist*, a journal of the Methodist Episcopal Church, issued the most negative comment against Frank. For this magazine, a frenzied mob was "a worse menace to the state than such men as Frank, bad as their kind are." Most Christian journals, however, referred to Frank in neutral terms, although *The Herald and Presbyter*, a Presbyterian weekly journal, used "convicted murderer" to describe Frank. No magazine profiled Leo Frank, the man, beyond brief mention of his position at the National Pencil Factory and several other pallid facts.

The Reformed Church Messenger and *Lutheran Church Work* raised the possibility of Frank's innocence: "The people of the State [of Georgia] look on the lynching as criminal in the highest degree, especially in the face of the fact that there was and is much doubt as to Frank's guilt." In a brief outline of the main events in the case, *The Universalist Leader* mentioned that "there was a reasonable doubt of his innocence, and on this doubt the Governor commuted his sentence." The *Northern Christian Advocate* (August 19, 1915) also expressed doubt as to Frank's guilt for the murder.

"The question whether the man was guilty at all or not was too large for honest men to say that the crime had been fastened on him beyond reasonable doubt," *The Continent* asserted. And *The Epworth Herald* wrote: "The doubt of Frank's guilt was so strong in the minds of unprejudiced persons who reviewed the case that a national effort was made to save the condemned man."

Three different Christian magazines supported prosecuting the lynch mob. A national Baptist paper editorialized that "the mob must be individualized, and its individual members must be arrested and tried as murderers." Both *The Reformed Church Messenger* and *Lutheran Church Work* expressed hope that "the good name of Georgia and of the American public as a whole will be vindicated by a vigorous prosecution of the case until all that can be done will be done."

Not one of the Christian periodicals that devoted attention to the Frank case contained any overtly anti-Jewish commentary. And in summary, we have to conclude that the general tone of the articles appearing in Christian periodicals was neutral or favorable to Frank and sympathetic regarding to his fate. On the other hand, no Christian journal devoted ongoing coverage to the case from 1913 through 1915—although the *Wesleyan Christian Advocate* ran ten articles in 1915 relating to the case and its repercussions for the State of Georgia.

The overwhelming majority of Christian magazines of the time (which responded at all to the tragedy) found the Frank case as an excellent peg for discussing law and order, lynching, mob law, states' rights, sectional tensions and issues, the State of Georgia, and the South in general. The mob members involved in the lynching were described by the influential Roman Catholic magazine, *America*, as "armed cowards [who] flouted the law, trampled upon justice, [and] destroyed as far as they could the very foundations of civilization." In addition to denouncing the actions of the mob, *America* alleged that Thomas E. Watson was the "leader" of that group. It made it clear that Watson was not personally present at the hanging, but implied that because of the calumny disseminated in Watson's "abominable publication," *The Jeffersonian*, during the summer of 1915, he was the ideological force behind the lynch mob.

America also attacked Tom Watson for his anti-Catholicism. It called *The Jeffersonian*'s editor a "Georgia Pole-cat" and indicted him for stirring up "blind and unreasoning hatred of everything Catholic" and for launching a "campaign of hatred against the Catholic Church, decency and against civilization." The suffering of American Catholic men, women, and children at the hands of non-Catholic mobs, and the destruction of convents and churches were also noted. The magazine also said that Watson issued "threats of violence against any who might wish to show the innocence of this condemned and hated Jew," and discussed the American public's concern about Jew-baiting in Russia, suggesting that the United States had similar internal problems that warranted national attention.

Most of the Christian magazines that responded to the Frank case were published outside of Georgia—in New York, Chicago, Boston, Syracuse, Pittsburgh, Philadelphia, Harrisburg, and on the Pacific Coast. And Georgia was frequently indicted in their pages for its lawlessness, lack of justice, and the defense of the lynch mob by some prominent Georgian citizens. An editorial note in *The Presbyterian Banner* (and seconded by *The Christian Register*) asserted that "law and life are not regarded in Georgia as they are in Northern States," adding that for all the talk in Georgia of "chivalry" and "woman's honor," it does not protect its women and children with industrial legislation as most other states do.

The *Banner*'s editor considered the state of mind that encouraged lynchings as an "inheritance of slavery, in which a black man had no rights a white man was bound to respect, and the same spirit infected the whole social and political atmosphere and has poisoned the roots of justice and of civilization. . . . Only a change of mind, wrought by Christian education" would bring about a cure, the editor concluded. Georgia was also charged with failing in its responsibility for Frank's safekeeping at the penitentiary in Milledgeville. The prominent standing of the members of the lynch mob added to the gravity of the entire Frank affair, the editorial argued. Members of the mob included "solid businessmen and prominent church members;" criminals and "baser elements of the community" were purposely excluded.

In another *Presbyterian Banner* article on the Frank lynching the *Atlanta Constitution* was quoted as saying: "It is Georgia law and justice that was hanged upon that Cobb County tree." The article observed that despite rumors of an abduction attempt, the Milledgeville prison authorities took no special precautions, although this was not true for the early days of August 1915. But on the night Leo Frank was taken from the prison farm, the guard had been relaxed. *The Banner* also said large sums of money were being collected in the North to discover and punish the members of the lynch mob.

The State of Georgia was also criticized by *The Universalist Leader*:

> Georgia has made open confession that she can not, or will not, which is worse, command obedience to her own laws. She has disgraced not only herself but every state in the Union, and shamed our human nature. This latest crime of this nature startlingly illustrates how futile are laws which are not sustained by a public sentiment. . . .

The *Leader* contended that state or county officials in Georgia "apparently all propose to remain in ignorance" regarding the perpetrators of the crime. The "shadow of shame" shall be lifted from Georgia only when those people who consent to lynching "come to realize that crime can never cure crime."

Boston's *Congregationalist and Christian World* said the "murder of Frank has lowered the moral authority of the United States all over the world." Despite the resentment of many citizens of Georgia, in the editor's opinion the lynching of Leo Frank should be open to national scrutiny. An improvement in the laws of Georgia was obviously needed.

The *Congregationalist* also raised the same issue raised by *The Banner*: women and children. In Georgia at that time, children from ages eight to thirteen could work in factories, and the legal age of consent was ten. At the same time, the *Congregationalist* expressed hope that closer review of the evidence in the Phagan murder case might definitively resolve the question of Frank's guilt or innocence.

The lynching of Leo Frank was "but a culmination of

open defiance of the law which has been tolerated in the South," wrote the editor of the *Northern Christian Advocate*, which also said it was "one of the most law defying outrages ever committed and heaps more shame upon the state that has already been the scene of barbarous lynchings." It did note, however, that this deed did not have the approval and sanction of "the best South." Government officials were urged by the editorial to do something about lawlessness in the South.

An early September 1915 issue of *The Epworth Herald* declared that talk coming out of Georgia about the dignity of womanhood "has a strange sound" given that state's notoriously low standards in child and woman labor laws. However, the *Herald* did credit the newspapers of Atlanta with expressing outrage at Frank's lynching. And the magazine reprinted the statements of Atlanta's Mayor Woodward, who argued that the lynchers were "merely refusing to let justice be cheated by the governor's action in commuting Frank's sentence. . . . Censure of the act of the mob comes from every point save that in which the lynching occurred," the *Herald* wrote.

Urging contriteness and penance, *The Continent*, published in New York, suggested that

> Georgia must perform many an honest deed of expiation and many a bold and faithful act of justice before it can atone in its record for the superlative shame which attaches to the lynching of Leo M. Frank. . . . And Georgia can only confess with penitence the double dye of disgrace upon it for having been neither strong enough nor watchful enough to suppress the outbreak of such barbarism among its people.

By being condemned to life imprisonment by the judicial system of the State of Georgia, Frank was already subjected to much suffering. In the *Continent's* view the lynching was absolutely barbaric.

The editor of *The Pacific*, voice of the Congregational churches on the Pacific Coast, maintained that in the wake of Frank's lynching, "it begins to look as if the State of Georgia would have to alter her seal." The obverse side of the Seal of Georgia has the words "wisdom," "justice," and "moderation" adorning the banner which is draped about the columns.

Finally, *The Reformed Church Messenger* and *Lutheran Church Work*, from Pennsylvania, contended that "the good name of Georgia will swing in the balance until it is seen what will be done to punish the lawbreakers."

Two Christian magazines published outside Georgia extended support and sympathy to Georgia. The *Christian Advocate* in Nashville wrote that

> Governor Harris announces that no effort will be spared in the attempt to bring the guilty to justice, and a thorough investigation will be had to see whether any official failed in the discharge of his sworn duty. That this would be his attitude and his course of action, none who know Governor Harris have doubted. In this time of his State's humiliation and shame he and other officials can do much to prove to the world that the good citizenship of Georgia does not, in any measure, condone lawlessness. Georgia is on trial before the world, and those who believe in her and her people look with confidence to the day of the State's vindication.

In addition, the *Advocate* endorsed an article in the *Atlanta Journal* that referred to Georgia as a "law-abiding State."

The Watchman-Examiner, published in Massachusetts and New York, issued the caveat: "Let not venomous things be said about Georgia. Let the people everywhere sympathize with the State authorities as they strive to bring the evil-doers to justice, and thus to maintain the dignity of the law."

It is significant that this national Baptist paper urged that the lynch mob be "individualized" instead of including the lynch mob, the citizens of Cobb County, Georgians in general, and all the authorities of that state under the umbrella of lawlessness and anarchy.

Atlanta's *Wesleyan Christian Advocate* did not defend the lynching of Leo Frank. But it did suggest that some people outside the State of Georgia "have been too forward in their interference with the affairs of this state and far too bitter in their denunciation of our people as barbarians and our courts as swayed by the clamor of mobs." In the face of such external interference and meddling, "the people of Georgia have shown surprising self control." The sovereignty of Georgia's laws and its ability to administer justice according to duly enacted legislation were affirmed.

Another theme developed by the *Wesleyan Christian Advocate* was that "the lawless are everywhere and even the most shocking crimes are committed in all sections of the country." The *Advocate* resented the denigration of the good people of Georgia by *The Chicago Tribune*, the *Outlook* in New York, and the *Northwestern Christian Advocate* in Illinois. "Mobocracy cannot be tolerated" in Georgia, the *Advocate* wrote, but capturing "men who lynch other men" is a difficult task.

This Georgia Methodist magazine also discussed race prejudice and sectional animosities:

> The sensible people of this state condemn the horrible lynching of this prisoner, and it does no good but great harm to send out bitter denunciations that stir sectional and race hatred among the people of this country. Great harm will come of that, and the most harm will come to the people who foster and scatter such things. . . .

And in another article, "A Matter to Be Seriously Pondered." the *Advocate* issued this somber warning:

> Since the lynching of Frank there has been an effort, whether planned deliberately, or the result of intense and sudden passion, to keep alive racial animosity that can mean nothing but

evil alike for the Jews and the Gentiles. That way lie troubles not easily cured. Along that path is anarchy of the most awful sort. To blow on the embers of that heat is to kindle an unquenchable conflagration that will take in its consuming flames all the institutions we hold dear and count as worth while. That will not do. Those beyond the borders of this state who have made the impression that there is here at the base of this lynching of Leo Frank race prejudice are sowing the wind and they will sooner or later reap the whirlwind. Nor is that the way for the prosperity of those within the state for the Gentiles.

The reference to reaping the whirlwind was taken from Proverbs 11. The article would appear to contain a veiled threat to the Jews of Georgia.

W. C. Lovett, editor of the *Advocate*, argued that no mob kept Leo Frank from facing the jury at the time the verdict was rendered. "Mob business in this trial has been decidedly overdone," the editor concluded. Indeed, "if one is disposed to make much of the "mob spirit" during the trial, it should be remembered that the Supreme Court of this state and the Supreme Court of the United States were not under the remotest intimidation by a mob." This was true, but the Supreme Court of Georgia and the United States Supreme Court were not reviewing the facts and evidence of the case. Appellate consideration was confined to procedural points of the law.

Distinct from the majority of Christian magazines published outside of Georgia, the *Wesleyan Christian Advocate* strongly defended the juridical processes of the State of Georgia and the right of that state to manage its own affairs. But the journal did recognize a tendency within Georgia which, if left unchecked, might result in "mobocracy."

After studying the nationwide Christian response to the Frank case, the only conclusion that can be reached is that it was extremely meager.[2] And quite possibly Christian apathy and disinterest in the case could have contributed to the fact that this "Jewish issue" did not inspire widespread or prolonged discussion within Christian circles.

The record of individual Christian responses to the Frank case is quite diverse. Perhaps the most significant reaction, as we have seen, came from Mary Phagan's Bible School pastor, Dr. Luther O. Bricker. Before he died in 1942, Bricker wrote in *Shane Quarterly* that although the old Negro watchman, Newt Lee, would have been a poor atonement for the death of little Mary Phagan, Leo Frank was a "worthy victim to pay for the crime."

But he also said: "I went to see Leo M. Frank in jail many times thereafter. . . . I saw in his eyes all the long story of the sufferings of his race. He had no bitterness in his heart against anyone."

Bricker claimed that he "was the only minister in Atlanta who dared to go into his pulpit and demand that Mr. Frank be given a new trial. It nearly cost me my life. I was shot at twice, my home was set on fire. . . ." Whether Pastor Bricker's life was threatened is not known, but his statement that he was the only Atlanta pastor to demand a new trial for Frank is undermined by reports that appeared in the *New York Times, Washington Post, Louisville Courier-Journal,* and *Florida Times-Union.* And in light of the national outcry on Frank's behalf, Bricker's contention that "perhaps I alone am responsible for the act of Governor John M. Slaton's commuting his sentence to life imprisonment" is also questionable. The Reverend C. O. Brookshire of the Baptist Church in Lakemont, Georgia, had also written Governor Slaton asking that Frank's sentence be commuted. So had L. O. Miller, Treasurer of the Church of the United Brethren in Christ in Dayton, Ohio.

Dr. Bricker's assessment of his feelings at the time proved more valuable than his account of what transpired at the governor's mansion when a mob gathered there one June night in 1915. His feeling that Newt Lee "would be poor atonement for the life" of Little Mary Phagan was used forty years later by Charles Wittenstein and the Atlanta Office of the ADL.

Dr. Rembert G. Smith, pastor of the Methodist Episcopal Church in Marietta, Georgia, also "read a strong and positive denunciation of the crime which had been committed" on the Sunday after Leo Frank had been lynched. But, according to Atlanta's *Wesleyan Christian Advocate*, because of anti-Georgia sentiment, Dr. Smith's statement was denied publication in New York by some of the big daily newspapers. His congregation, the largest in Marietta, endorsed their pastor's denunciation.

In the course of discussing the Frank case and the lynching problem in the South, Reverend H. H. Proctor, D.D., a black Congregationalist minister in Atlanta, found some reason for positive comment.

> But dark as this case is, rays of light are seen bursting over the abyss. The very uniqueness of Atlanta vouchsafes a peculiar moral resiliency. Atlanta arose from the burning by Sherman's troops to face a new destiny. With the well-known Atlanta spirit, the city came out of the riot of 1906 a better city, . . .
>
> If this whole deplorable case shall result in the strengthening of public sentiment against this iniquity [lynching], in the enactment of a state law that will be effective as far as a state law can be, and, above all, in making lynching a Federal crime, our faith will be strengthened in the great truth that God causes the wrath of men to praise him.

Reverend Proctor noted that Jim Conley, after having served a year-long prison sentence for being an accomplice in the murder of Mary Phagan, "walked about in Atlanta and was not even threatened with violence."

Following a five-month visit to the South during 1915, the Reverend William Lindsay returned to the First Congregational Church in Milton, Massachusetts, and delivered a sermon titled "Self-Expression." The lynching of Leo Frank, said Reverend Lindsay, reminds us of "the dangers attending an outbreak of emotional egotism, and at the same time of the priceless worth of mental balance, correct thinking, and sound judgment." *The Christian Register* recorded much of Lindsay's sermon, which concluded: "Surely there must be . . . law-abiding citizens in Georgia who resent and condemn the murder of Leo Frank, and lynching in general."

Writing in *America* in 1915 Henry Woods of the Society of Jesus did not excuse the crime against Leo Frank. However, Father Woods argued that the courts and Executive Office of Georgia had been browbeaten by public pressure, and Governor Slaton's commutation of Frank's sentence to life imprisonment inspired the lynching, said the priest, who called this an outrage of "all our processes of justice . . . almost beyond expression."

Commenting on the widespread public reaction to the Frank case, Father Woods observed:

> From New York to San Francisco the newspapers retried and acquitted him. From San Francisco to New York ministers neglected the Gospel they are supposed to preach, to do the same in their pulpits; . . . .
>
> Such proceedings are a grievous injury to the courts of law.
>
> The editors, the ministers, the female agitators, the petitioners, the personal visitors, making up no small part of the people of the United States, unless they were moved by some hidden power, were convinced that the Courts of the State of Georgia, the Supreme Court of the United States, were resolved on a judicial murder, that the Governor of Georgia was consenting to it, and that the fact was so clear, as to justify an interference that otherwise would have to be judged as absolutely lawless. No worse insult can be imagined.

Father Woods seems to be suggesting that if the judicial decision to hang Frank on June 22, 1915, had not been altered by executive decision, the lynching would never have happened! And he appears to see the public outcry on Frank's behalf as an act more morally reprehensible than the lynching itself.

Father Woods did not mention the pressure editor Tom Watson applied on Governor Slaton, both in his magazines where he agitated vehemently against sparing Frank's life and by offering political rewards to Slaton if he denied commutation. "Authority without which no body politic can maintain itself is being brought into grave peril," Woods concluded, not by the actions of lynch mobs but by the actions of an outraged citizenry.

Reverend Alvan F. Sherrill, Dean of the Atlanta Theological Seminary, wrote a letter to the New York magazine *Outlook*, an excerpt of which was published a month after Frank was lynched.

> At some risk of your misunderstanding me, I will add, the men who hung Frank were not a 'mob' by any true sense of that word—they were a sifted band of men, sober, intelligent, of established good name and character—good American citizens. In all essentials of manhood and citizenship, they were your equals or mine. They believed it was a very exceptional exigency that demanded and justified the very exceptional act. Now, are you sure that your judgment one thousand miles away is better than theirs on the ground?

These words support the un-American doctrine of mob law, the *Outlook* declared. Despite several attempts to locate a reference to or history of the Atlanta Theological Seminary, none were found.

The Sunday following the lynching at Marietta, Reverend Alex Bealer of the Baptist Tabernacle in Valdosta, Georgia, delivered a sermon based on Matthew 22:31. And Jesus said, "Render therefore unto Caesar the things which are Caesar's and unto God the things that are God's." Pastor Bealer declared:

> Contempt for the laws led to the lynching of Jesus. The people hated Him, and despising the laws that protected Him, they ignored them and put Him to death as a criminal is lynched today. The spirit that animated these men is alive today. It lives in the hearts of the mobs of the country. . . .

Recorded Christian responses to the Frank case seem to support the theories of anti-Semitism which argue that American attitudes towards the Jew contain both positive and negative elements and the lack of any widespread Christian reaction could be the result of the negative elements, as well as apathy. The fact that some Christians supported Leo Frank and were disgusted over the anti-Jewish sentiment in Atlanta reflect the positive attitudes towards Jews. But the *Wesleyan Christian Advocate*'s sensitivity to allegations of anti-Jewish sentiment in Georgia suggests that anti-Semitism was not generally acceptable by American society as a whole at that time.

Throughout the two years of her husband's travails, Mrs. Frank received letters from many concerned Christians. "Knowing that you are Jewish," wrote one Seventh-Day Adventist from South Dakota, "I wondered if either of you have accepted Christ the Messiah as your Savior." Mrs. Hawley went on to say that "I have lived in the South a little and know just a bit of the mob spirit, also have no doubt that some of the jurors believe your husband innocent, yet are afraid to say so."

While serving time at the Tower and the prison farm, Frank received many letters from concerned Christians around the country. "I know that the mob spirit was responsible for your conviction," wrote Pastor J. C. Casaday of Birmingham. "But I have a very dear friend who is a jew by birth who is able to quiet the mob. His Name is JESUS CHRIST. And there is None other name given by which men can be saved." This Methodist minister hoped Mr. Frank would "not resent a word of kindness from a Gentile."

A woman from Nyack, New York, wrote that "if the blood of bulls and goats . . . were effectual in the days of Israel. How much more effectual would be the blood of the living Christ. Wont you accept this Savior?" She had written on behalf of the "Jewish Prayer Band." "We are sending you some tracts and papers," she continued, "and trust you will read them, and let Gods word become real to you and in them find Christ the Messiah."

"You cannot afford to not have me come and have a conference with the Gov.," said Reverend Thomas Foster in a letter dated June 10, 1914. Pastor Foster was an ordained evangelist from Columbus, Ohio, with "over 20 years experience as a detective in the slums and high places."

The wife of the manager of the Scott Telephone Company greeted Governor Slaton's decision to commute Frank's sentence with joy. "I am truly thankful that you were granted clemency and have thanked God many times for it." "Now Mr. Frank," she continued, "wont you consider giving your heart to Jesus?" Jesus' abiding presence "would make Heaven on earth, even tho' back of prison bars."

Endnotes

1. See Winthrop S. Hudson's *Religion in America*.

2. From 1916 to 1986, only two articles on the Frank case appeared in Christian magazines. One was published in the *Shane Quarterly* in 1943, the other in the *Christian Century* in 1985.

Appendix 4
CHRISTIAN PERIODICAL HISTORIES

America: A Catholic Review of the Week was published by the America Press in New York. The president of the America Press in 1915 was Richard H. Tierney. *America*, started in 1909, was an influential weekly of intellectual substance.

The *Christian Advocate* was the general organ of the Methodist Episcopal Church, South, and was published in Nashville. The Methodist Episcopal Church, South, had become an all-white religious body by 1870, though it had a black membership of over two hundred thousand in 1860. The majority of black Methodists in the South became part of the African Methodist Episcopal Church and the African Methodist Episcopal Zion Church.

The *Christian Century*, Chicago. This was perhaps the most influential Protestant weekly of the time. It was free from denominational ties by the time of the Frank case, and had begun life under that name early in 1900, as an organ of the Disciples of Christ.

The Disciples of Christ, or "Christians," combined a Presbyterian heritage with Methodist doctrines and Baptist polity and practice. Thomas Campbell (1763–1854) and his son Alexander (1788–1866) were instrumental in the founding and leadership of the Disciples of Christ.

The magazine itself accepted the date of its real beginning as 1908 when Charles Clayton Morrison purchased it. From the start, Morrison was guided by his conviction that the church was responsible for the character of society and tried to apply Christian principles to a broad range of contemporary concerns. He made the magazine a vigorous independent journal of intellectual stature and liberal outlook. Morrison was the editor during the period 1913–15.

The *Christian Century* continued the *Christian Century of the Disciples of Christ*, which began in 1884. It absorbed the *Christian Tribune* on June 7, 1900, and the *Christian Work* on April 1, 1926. Currently, the *Christian Century* is published by the Christian Century Foundation in Chicago.

The *Christian Observer*, founded in 1813, was a Presbyterian family newspaper. The journal was published by Converse & Co. in Louisville, Kentucky. Reverend David M. Sweets, D.D. was editor during the time of the Frank issue.

The classic form of Presbyterianism took shape in Scotland. Francis Makemie (1658?–1708) was the major figure associated with the growth of American Presbyterianism. The *Westminster Confession* (1729) serves as the doctrinal standard of American Presbyterianism.

The Christian Register was published by the Christian Register Association in Boston. The periodical was established in 1821.

The Congregationalist and Christian World succeeded *The Recorder* [founded in 1816] and *The Congregationalist* [founded in 1849]. It was published by the Pilgrim Press which was incorporated as The Congregational Sunday School and Publishing Society, Boston and Chicago.

The United Church of Christ was formed on June 25, 1957, following a merger of the Congregational-Christian Church and the Evangelical and Reformed Church. The

Congregational-Christian Church was the result of the uniting of the Congregational Church with the Christian Church in 1931.

The Continent was a Christian religious periodical, despite its non-theological name. It continued *The Interior* [established 1870] and *The Westminster* [established 1904]. Nolan R. Best was editor and Oliver R. Williamson was the publisher during the Frank period. The McCormick Publishing Company in New York was the proprietor.

The Epworth Herald was published by The Methodist Book Concern in Chicago and New York. The editor was Dan B. Brummitt during the time of the Frank case.

Herald and Presbyter: A Presbyterian Weekly Paper was published by Monfort and Co., Cincinnati and Saint Louis.

Lutheran Church Work was the official weekly paper of the General Synod of the Evangelical Lutheran Church in the United States of America. It continued *The Lutheran Missionary Journal* [1880–1908], *Lutheran Church Work* [1908–1912], and *The Lutheran World* [1908–1912]. It was published in Harrisburg and Philadelphia, Pennsylvania. The Reverend Frederick G. Gotwald, D.D. of York, Pennsylvania, was the editor during the Frank period.

The Mennonite: A religious weekly journal was the English organ of the Mennonite General Conference of North America. It was devoted to the interests of the Mennonite Church and to the cause of Christ in general. The journal was published by the Mennonite Book Concern in Berne, Indiana, and edited during the Frank period by Reverend C. Van der Smissen.

The Methodist was an inter-conference journal under the patronage of the Baltimore, Central Pennsylvania, and Wilmington Conferences of the Methodist Episcopal Church. This magazine was published in Baltimore. The publisher was W. V. Guthrie during the period 1913–15.

The *Northern Christian Advocate* was founded in 1841 and published in Syracuse, New York. H. E. Woolever was the editor during Frank period.

The Pacific was the spokes-vehicle for the Congregational Churches on the Pacific Coast. It was edited by W. W. Ferrin in 1915.

The Presbyterian Banner: An Illustrated Paper for the American Home was founded on July 5, 1814. The periodical was published by the Presbyterian Banner Publishing Co. in Pittsburgh, Pennsylvania. James H. Snowden was the editor during the Frank period.

Reformed Church Messenger was founded in November 1827 in Carlisle, Pennsylvania. It was the official organ of the Eastern, Potomac, and Pittsburgh Synods.

The United Presbyterian had as managing editor David Reed Miller, D.D. during the Frank period. The proprietors were Murdoch, Kerr & Co. of Pittsburgh, Pennsylvania.

The Universalist Leader: Our National Church Paper was edited by Frederick A. Bisbee, D.D. during the time of the Frank case. This journal continued *The Christian Leader*, *The Universalist*, and *The Gospel Banner*. It was published by the Universalist Publishing House, a religious corporation organized in April 1852 in Boston and Chicago.

Universalism was the counterpart of Unitarianism "among less urbane rural folk." The Universalist Profession of Faith and Conditions of Fellowship, which was adopted at Winchester, New Hampshire, has as two of its essential principles that there is "just retribution for sin" and "the final harmony of all souls with God." Universalism had been brought to America in 1770 by John Murray, and advanced under the leadership of Elhanan Winchester.

The Watchman-Examiner: A National Baptist Paper continued *The Watchman* [established 1819], *The Examiner* [established 1823], and *The Morning Star* [established 1826], in addition to *The National Baptist*, *The Christian Inquirer*, and *The Christian Secretary*. It was published in Worcester (Massachusetts), Boston, and New York.

The *Wesleyan Christian Advocate* was the principal news medium of the North Georgia Conference of the Methodist Episcopal Church, South, and later, as a result of denominational mergers, of the Methodist Church (U.S.) and the present United Methodist Church. It was published in Atlanta, Georgia, and edited by W. C. Lovett during the Frank period.

The Evangelical United Brethren [German Methodist] and Methodist Churches merged in 1968 to form the United Methodist Church.

Theodore Peterson's *Magazines of the Twentieth Century* was consulted for this appendix along with Winthrop S. Hudson's *Religion in America*.

Appendix 5

NON-RELIGIOUS PERIODICALS OF THE FRANK PERIOD

Century Magazine: The name of the earlier *Scribner's* magazine was changed to the *Century* in 1881.

Everybody's: This magazine has been grouped with *Collier's* as being engaged in muckraking. Muckraking refers to reporting unhappy conditions without advancing a program for correcting them.

Forum: A review founded in the hope that it would become a major influence in art, literature, politics, and science. The purpose of the *Forum*, according to Walter Hines Page, its editor until 1895, was "to provide discussions about subjects of contemporary interest, in which the magazine is not partisan, but merely the instrument."

The Literary Digest: This magazine was close to being a news magazine, but it was essentially a digest. As historian Calvin Ellsworth Chunn aptly described it in his doctoral dissertation "History of News Magazines" (1950), *Literary Digest* was more "a clipping service for public opinion" than a true news magazine.

The Literary Digest was founded in 1890 by Dr. Isaac K. Funk and Adam W. Wagnalls, former Lutheran ministers. These men were partners in the Funk and Wagnalls Company, a New York book publishing firm. In 1890, when *The Literary Digest* came out, it was intended to be especially helpful to educators and ministers. It was to be "a repository of contemporaneous thought and research as presented in the periodical literature of the world." The magazine extended its editorial scope in 1905 to cover general news and comment. That same year William Seaver Woods, a minister's son, became the editor. He held that post until 1933. The man who probably did most to guide *The Literary Digest* into becoming a national institution was Robert J. Cuddihy, its publisher from 1905 to 1937.

The masthead of the 1915 *Literary Digest* noted that *Public Opinion* [New York] was combined with *The Literary Digest*.

Nation: This magazine was born just after the Civil War ended and was the elder statesman among the journals of opinion in the twentieth century. Its founder was E. L. Godkin, a young journalist who had come to America from Ireland in 1856 to write about conditions in the South. Godkin's *Nation* denounced the Populists, railroad barons, Tammany, and currency inflation.

New Republic: This magazine was launched in the atmosphere of pre-World War I revolt and optimism. It stood alongside the *Nation* as an organ of liberalism, although the *New Republic* was younger by nearly half a century. In 1909, Herbert Croley was given money from Mr. and Mrs. Willard D. Straight for a magazine that would reflect Croley's liberal viewpoint. Croley was the author of *The Promise of American Life*, a book that became the creed of many liberals.

Outlook: This periodical first appeared in 1867 as a Baptist paper called the *Church Union*. Its name was changed to the *Christian Union*, which it held until 1893. The *Outlook* appeared in July 1893. The magazine attracted important contributors with important works. Theodore Roosevelt, after leaving the presidency, became a contributing editor for a time. There is discrepancy as to the origin of *Outlook*.

South Atlantic Quarterly: This journal was founded in 1902 in order to afford better opportunity in the South for discussion of literary, historical, economic, and social questions. It was published by the South Atlantic Publishing Co. at Trinity College in Durham, North Carolina.

Spectator: This magazine was published in London.

Theodore Peterson's *Magazines of the Twentieth Century* was consulted for this appendix.

ADDITIONAL READING

For readers interested in finding out more about certain aspects of the Frank case and its related issues, the following discussion provides some direction.

There are several sources that should be consulted for detailed study of the trial and lynching of Leo Frank. These include works by Leonard Dinnerstein, Comer Vann Woodward, and Clement Charlton Moseley. Leonard Dinnerstein's *The Leo Frank Case* stands as the authoritative scholarly book on the subject. Professor Dinnerstein had also done his doctoral dissertation on the Frank case at Columbia University in New York. In addition to being valuable for information on the Frank case itself, the writings of Dr. Vann Woodward and Dr. Charlton Moseley provide insight into the life of Thomas Watson and the activities of the Ku Klux Klan. Other works about the Klan include David Chalmers' *Hooded Americanism* and Kenneth T. Jackson's *The Ku Klux Klan in the City*. Fred Ragan's work on Tom Watson should also be consulted.

Christopher Connolly's pamphlet *The Truth About the Frank Case* [1915] stands as an excellent account of certain points of the trial testimony and the general atmosphere in Atlanta at the time. Franklin M. Garrett's *Atlanta and Its Environs (Vol. II)* along with Nathaniel Harris' *Autobiography* are also important sources of information on the case. Harris' writing is especially valuable because he was governor of Georgia during the time when Frank was lynched. Allen L. Henson's *Confessions of a Criminal Lawyer* is another important primary source.

The three major newspapers of Atlanta—the *Constitution*, *Journal*, and *Georgian*—are invaluable in providing firsthand insight into the murder of Mary Phagan and the trial and lynching of Leo Frank. The *New York Times* of that era is also a vital source of information. For an assessment of the coverage of the Frank case in major metropolitan papers, black papers, and the Jewish press, Eugene Levy's "Is the Jew a White Man?" should be consulted. Steven Hertzberg's *Strangers Within the Gate City* provides helpful background information on Jewish-black relations in Atlanta.

For readers interested in discussion and analysis of the phenomenon of anti-Semitism in America, the works of Oscar Handlin, John Higham, Richard Hofstadter, Leonard Dinnerstein, and Ernest Volkman should be reviewed. Steven Hertzberg's article in the *American Jewish Historical Quarterly* and his book, *Strangers Within the Gate City*, detail the Jewish experience in Atlanta, including the rise of Jewish discrimination in that city.

Books by Henry Feingold and Paul Mendes-Flohr/Jehuda Reinharz are two good sources for gaining historical appreciation for the Jewish experience in America and modern Western culture in general. Louis Schmeir has done some valuable work on specific Jewish experiences in Georgia.

Biographical information on the major political and judicial figures associated with the Frank case can be found in the *Biographical Directory of Governors of the United States* (Sobel/Raimo) and the *National Cyclopedia of American Biography*.

Statistics on lynching in America are included in Robert Moton's article, "The South and the Lynching Evil." The phenomenon of lynching is also addressed in "Lynching in the Southern States" [*Spectator*]; Winthrop Sheldon's "Shall Lynching Be Suppressed?"; and *Survey* [February, 1914]. The definitive work on lynching during the Frank era is

Thirty Years of Lynching in the United States 1889–1918 published by Negro Universities Press.

Insight into Atlanta history can be gotten from Walter G. Cooper's *Official History of Fulton County*; George J. Lankevich's *Atlanta*; and Thomas H. Martin's *Hand Book of the City of Atlanta*.

A good general overview of American religious experience is contained in Winthrop S. Hudson's *Religion in America*. For a detailed discussion of Christian responses to the Frank case, see Robert S. Frey's "The Case of Leo M. Frank in the Continuum of American History: An Assessment of Christian Responses" and also his article in the *Georgia Historical Quarterly*, Fall 1987.

All of the sources referenced above appear in the Bibliography.

BIBLIOGRAPHY

Books and Articles

"A. S. Colyar Makes Reply to Statement of Colonel Felder." *Atlanta Journal*, 24 May 1913, p. 3.

"Accuse Solicitor Dorsey." *New York Times*, 24 May 1916, p. 22.

"Acquits Burns Men in the Frank Case." *New York Times*, 1 February 1915.

"All Urged to Write Appeals for Frank." *New York Times*, 13 December 1914.

"Anti-Semitism and the Frank Case." *The Literary Digest* 50 (1915): 85–86.

"Appeal in the Frank Case." *Outlook* 109 (1915): 6–7.

Arnold, Reuben R. *The Trial of Leo Frank: Reuben R. Arnold's Address to the Court in His Behalf.* Baxley, Ga.: Classic Publishing Company, 1915. [Introduction by Alvin V. Sellers].

"Ask to Show Frank Films." *New York Times*, 14 September 1915, p. 7.

Atlanta City Directory. 1913, 1914, 1915.

"Atlanta Greeks Protest Against Headline Published in Extra of an Atlanta Afternoon Paper." *Atlanta Journal*, 8 May 1913.

"Attack Is Made on Child Labor." *Atlanta Constitution*, 28 April 1913, p. 1.

Baggott, James L. *History of the Atlanta Baptist Churches to 1964.* n.p., 1964.

Baker, Donald P. "Yes, Virginia, There Is a Movie Santa." *The Washington Post*, 4 July 1987.

Bauer, Esther M. "Frank Pardon Denied." *Atlanta Constitution*, 23 December 1983.

Bauman, Mark. "Role Theory and History: The Illustration of Ethnic Brokerage in the Atlanta Jewish Community in an Era of Transition and Conflict." *American Jewish History* 73 (1983): 71–95.

"Billy Sunday for Frank." *New York Times*, 12 May 1915.

"Bloody Thumb Print Is Found on Door." *Atlanta Journal*, 29 April 1913, p. 4.

"Both Sides Heard on Frank Appeal." *New York Times*, 15 June 1915, pp. 1,8.

Boylston, Elise Reid. *Atlanta: Its Lore, Legends, and Laughter.* Doraville, Ga.: Foote and Davis, 1968.

" 'Break' in the Frank Trial May Come with the Hearing of Jim Conley's Testimony." *Atlanta Constitution*, 3 August 1913, p. 3.

Bricker, L. O. "A Great American Tragedy." *Shane Quarterly* 4 (1943): 89–95.

Brown, Tom Watson. "Notes on the Case of Leo Max Frank and Its Aftermath." [Atlanta Miscellany File, # 572, Box 2; Emory University, Robert W. Woodruff Library, Special Collections Department]

"Burglars Try to Enter Home of Frank Juror." *Atlanta Constitution*, 29 July 1913, p. 1.

"Burns Confers with Leo M. Frank." *New York Times*, 18 March 1914.

"Burns Evidence for Frank." *New York Times*, 31 March 1914.

Burt, Olive Woolley., ed. *American Murder Ballads and Their Stories.* New York: Oxford University Press, 1958.

Busch, Francis X. *Guilty or Not Guilty? An Account of the Trials of the Leo Frank Case, the D. C. Stephenson Case, the Samuel Insull Case, the Alger Hiss Case*. Indianapolis: Bobbs-Merrill Co., Inc., 1952. [Part of the *Notable American Trials* series]

"Business Men Protest Sensational 'Extras'." *Atlanta Journal*, 30 April 1913, p. 1.

Cameron, Wilbert. "Anti-Semitism and the Frank Case." Master's thesis, University of Cincinnati, 1965.

"The Case of Leo M. Frank." *Outlook* 110 (1915): 166–68.

Chalmers, David M. *Hooded Americanism: The History of the Ku Klux Klan*. New York: Viewpoints, 1976.

"Character Witnesses Are Called in the Case by City Detectives." *Atlanta Journal*, 9 May 1913.

"Clash Comes Over Evidence of Detective John Starnes." *Atlanta Constitution*, 30 July 1913.

"Col. Thomas B. Felder Dictographed by City Detectives." *Atlanta Journal*, 23 May 1913, p. 1.

"Comment on Frank Case." *New York Times*, 13 December 1914.

"Commissioners at Prison When Mob Seized Frank." *Atlanta Journal*, 17 August 1915, p. 2.

"Complete Summary of Testimony of Witnesses at Inquest." *Atlanta Journal*, 30 April 1913, p. 6.

Concise Dictionary of American Biography. 3d ed. New York: Charles Scribner's Sons, 1980.

"Confidence Expressed in Leo M. Frank." *Atlanta Journal*, 2 May 1913.

"Confident Truth Will Out." *New York Times*, 5 March 1914.

"Conley, Not Frank, Called Slayer." *New York Times*, 4 October 1914, p. 13.

Connolly, Christopher Powell. "The Frank Case." *Collier's*, 26 December 1914, pp. 18–25. [Another article by C. P. Connolly appeared in the December 19, 1914 issue of *Collier's*.]

Connolly, Christopher Powell. *The Truth About the Frank Case*. New York: Vail-Bellou Company, 1915.

"*Constitution*'s Extra Tells Atlanta of the Verdict in Frank Case." *Atlanta Constitution*, 26 August 1913, p. 1.

"Contemptible Unfairness." *Wesleyan Christian Advocate*, 24 September 1915, p. 9.

Cooper, Walter Gerald. *Official History of Fulton County*. History Commission, 1934.

"Cornell Appeal for Frank." *New York Times*, 27 December 1914, p. 12.

"Coroner Donehoo Points Out the Law to the Jurors." *Atlanta Journal*, 9 May 1913.

"Coroner's Inquest Resumed 2:30 P.M.; Frank Will Testify." *Atlanta Journal*, 5 May 1913, p. 1.

"Coroner's Jury Visits Scene of Murder add [sic] Adjourns Without Rendering Verdict." *Atlanta Journal*, 28 April 1913, p. 2.

"Could Have Cleared Victim of 1915 Lynch Mob, Man Says." *The Washington Post*, 14 March 1982, p. A8.

"A Courageous Governor." *Outlook* 110 (1915): 492–93.

Davis, David. "The Leo Frank Case." *Jewish Digest*, December 1978, pp. 61–63. [Translated by Dorothy D. Sablosky and Annette Lashner.]

De Steffani, Azalia E. *Leo M. Frank: The Martyr Jew* (L.M.F. Love Mercy Faith) [Leo Frank File, MSS91, Box 6, Folder 10; Atlanta Historical Society]

"Defense Is Pleased." *Atlanta Constitution*, 29 July 1913, p. 1.

"Defense Riddles John Black's Testimony." *Atlanta Constitution*, 31 July 1913, p. 1.

Deitch, David. "Leo Frank: A Look at Georgia's Most Infamous Trial." Mimeographed. Westminster High School, 1984. ["Personality File"; Atlanta Historical Society]

"Denunciation of the South." *Wesleyan Christian Advocate*, 3 September 1915, pp. 3–4.

"Detective Harry Scott's Testimony as Given Before Coroner's Jury." *Atlanta Journal*, 9 May 1913.

"Detective John Black Tell [sic] the Jury His Views on the Phagan Case." *Atlanta Journal*, 9 May 1913.

"Detective Waggoner Describes Extreme Nervousness of Frank." *Atlanta Constitution*, 3 August 1913, p. 3.

"Detectives Confer with Coroner and Solicitor Dorsey." *Atlanta Journal*, 3 May 1913, p. 1.

"Detectives Eliminate Evidence in Conflict with Theory That Phagan Girl Never Left Factory." *Atlanta Journal*, 1 May 1913, p. 1.

"Did Murderer Seek to Burn Slain Girl's Body, and Did the Watchman Interrupt Him?" *Atlanta Journal*, 1 May 1913.

Dinnerstein, Leonard. *The Leo Frank Case*. New York: Columbia University Press, 1968. [This work is being reprinted for release in 1987 by the University of Georgia Press in Athens.]

Dinnerstein, Leonard. "The Leo Frank Case." Ph.D. dissertation, Columbia University, 1966.

Dinnerstein, Leonard. "Leo M. Frank and the American Jewish Community." *American Jewish Archives* 20 (1968): 107–26.

Dinnerstein, Leonard. "A Neglected Aspect of Southern Jewish History." *American Jewish Historical Quarterly* 61 (1971): 52–68.

" 'Dirty Gang' Filled Out Record or Else 'Fooled Dictograph'." *Atlanta Journal*, 24 May 1913, p. 1.

"Dorsey Accuses Frank Defense." *New York Times*, 30 April 1914.

"Dorsey Assails Slaton and Jews." *New York Times*, 12 September 1916.

"Dorsey Satisfied." *Atlanta Constitution*, 29 July 1913, p. 1.

"Dorsey Steers Clear of Felder Controversy." *Atlanta Journal*, 24 May 1913, p. 3.

Drachman, Bernard. "Anti-Jewish Prejudice in America." *The Forum* LII (1914): 31–40.

"Editorial." *The American Jewish Review*, July 1915, p. 1.

"Editorial Comment on Current Events." *The Watchman-Examiner*, 26 August 1915, p. 1903.

"Editor's Outlook." *Northern Christian Advocate*, 19 August 1915, p. 5.

"Editor's Outlook." *Northern Christian Advocate*, 26 August 1915, p. 5.

Eighmy, John Lee. *Churches in Cultural Captivity: A History of the Social Attitudes of Southern Baptists*. Knoxville: University of Tennessee Press, 1972.

Encyclopaedia Judaica. Jerusalem: Keter Publishing House, 1971.

"The End of the Frank Case." *Outlook* 111 (1915): 114–15.

"Evidence for Frank Ignored, She Says." *New York Times*, 14 March 1914.

"Factory Clock Not Punched for Hours on Night of Murder." *Atlanta Constitution*, 30 April 1913, p. 1.

Feingold, Henry L. *Zion in America: The Jewish Experience from Colonial Times to the Present*. rev. ed. New York: Hippocrene Books, Inc., 1981.

Ferrin, W. W. *The Pacific*, 1 September 1915.

"Finding of Dead Girl's Parasol Is Told by Policeman Lasseter." *Atlanta Constitution*, 3 August 1913, p. 3.

"Frank a Model Boy." *New York Times*, 14 March 1914.

"Frank Asks Six Questions." *New York Times*, 15 March 1914, p. 9.

"Frank Case." *Outlook* 108 (1914): 859–60.

The Frank Case. Atlanta: 1913.

"The Frank Case." *The Congregationalist and Christian World* C (1915): 314.

"The Frank Case." *New York Times*, 29 November 1914.

"Frank Case Damage Suit." *New York Times*, 21 January 1915.

"The Frank Case: Denying Posthumous Pardon." *Jewish Digest* 29 (1984): 56–57.

"Frank Case Soon Clear." *New York Times*, 4 October 1914, p. 13.

"Frank Case Yields New Bribe Charge." *New York Times*, 13 March 1914.

"Frank Convicted, Asserts Innocence." *Atlanta Constitution*, 26 August 1913, p. 1.

"Frank Goes to Prison for Life." *The Mennonite* XXX (1915): 7.

"Frank Is Innocent, Says George S. Dougherty." *New York Times*, 10 January 1915.

"Frank Jurors Did Not Even Know General Assembly Had Adjourned." *Atlanta Constitution*, 27 August 1913.

"Frank Lynchers Sought." *The Continent*, 26 August 1915, p. 1135.

"Frank Murderers to Go Unpunished." *The Herald and Presbyter*, 8 September 1915, p. 28.

"Frank Railroaded, E. V. Debs Asserts." *New York Times*, 28 December 1914, p. 4.

"Frank Rode to Macon on the Car 'Valdosta'." *Valdosta Daily Times*, 22 June 1915, p. 8.

"Frank Sentenced on Murder Charge to Hang Oct. 10." *Atlanta Constitution*, 27 August 1913, p. 1.

"Frank Sentenced to Die." *New York Times*, 27 August 1913, p. 3.

" 'Frank Tree' to Be Surrounded by Wall." *Macon Daily Telegraph*, 20 August 1915.

"Frank Trial Judge, L. S. Roan, Dies Here." *New York Times*, 24 March 1915, p. 11.

"Frank's Last Appeal." *New York Times*, 12 December 1914, p. 14.

"Frank's Last Letter to His Chief Attorney." *Atlanta Journal*, 17 August 1915, p. 1.

"Frank's Lawyers Amend Their Plea." *New York Times*, 29 April 1914.

"Frank's Mother Gives Last Letter He Wrote." *Macon Daily Telegraph*, 20 August 1915.

"Frank's Parents Learn of His Death by Mob." *Atlanta Journal*, 17 August 1915, p. 2.

"Frank's Statements." *New York Times*, 24 December 1914, p. 8.

"Frank's Wedding Ring Entrusted to Reporter." *Atlanta Journal*, 19 August 1915.

"Frequent Clashes Between Attorneys." *Atlanta Constitution*, 2 August 1913, p. 3.

Frey, Robert Seitz. "The Case of Leo M. Frank in the Continuum of American History: An Assessment of Christian Responses." Master's thesis, Baltimore Hebrew College, 1986.

Frey, Robert Seitz. "Christian Responses to the Trial and Lynching of Leo M. Frank: Ministers, Theologians, and Laymen." *Georgia Historical Quarterly* 71 (1987): 461–76.

"Friends Tell Frank in Tower of Jury's Verdict of Guilty; Prisoner Cheers Weeping Wife." *Atlanta Constitution*, 26 August 1913, p. 1.

"Gantt's Release Asked in Habeas Corpus Writ." *Atlanta Journal*, 29 April 1913, p. 1.

Garrett, Franklin Miller. *Atlanta and Its Environs: A Chronicle of Its People and Events.* New York: Lewis Historical Publishing Co., Inc., 1954. [3 vols.; Vol. II contains the material on the Frank case]

"Georgia Again." *The Congregationalist and Christian World* C (1915): 305.

Georgia, Governor, 1913–1915 [Slaton]: Supplement to message of the Governor to the General Assembly of Georgia, June 23, 1915, Atlanta, Ga.: C. P. Byrd, State Printer, 1915.

"The Georgia Mob." *Christian Advocate*, 27 August 1915, p. 1124.

"Georgia Stamped with Shame." *The Continent*, 26 August 1915, p. 1137.

"Georgia Tested and Found Wanting." *Wesleyan Christian Advocate*, 24 September 1915, p. 3.

"Georgia to Make Frank Investigation." *Christian Science Monitor*, 18 August 1915.

"A Ghastly Crime." *The Methodist*, 19 August 1915, p. 3.

"Girl Is Assualted and Murdered in Heart of Town." *Atlanta Constitution*, 28 April 1913, p. 1.

Glass, William R. "The Ministry of Leonard G. Broughton of Tabernacle Baptist Church 1898–1912: A Source of Southern Fundamentalism." *American Baptist Quarterly* 4 (1985): 35–60.

" 'God's Vengeance Will Strike Brute Who Killed Her,' Says Grandfather of Mary Phagan." *Atlanta Journal*, 28 April 1913, p. 2.

Goldberg, Boris. "Mendel Beilis: A Russian Counterpart." *Jewish Monthly*, October 1982, p. 23.

Golden, Harry Lewis. *A Little Girl Is Dead*. Cleveland: World Publishing Company, 1965.

Goldgar, Vida. "The Story Behind the Story." *The Southwest Israelite*, 12 March 1982.

"Governor Asks All to Read Statement on the Frank Case." *Atlanta Journal*, 21 June 1915, p. 1.

"Governor Is Notified of Frank Lynching." *Atlanta Journal*, 17 August 1915, p. 2.

"Governor Shocked." *Atlanta Constitution*, 17 August 1915, p. 1.

"Governor Slaton on the Frank Case." *The Jewish Times (and Observer)*, 13 August 1915.

"Governor Slaton Shocked by News of Lynching." *Atlanta Journal*, 17 August 1915, p. 2.

"Gov. Slaton's Courageous Act." *Atlanta Journal*, 21 June 1915.

Gralnick, W. R. "Leo Frank Pardon Denied." *Reform Judaism* 12 (1984): 6–7.

Grapho. "Just from Georgia: The Atlanta Spirit and the Upward Movement." *The Congregationalist and Christian World* CI (1916): 633,642.

Greene, Ward. *Death in the Deep South: A Novel About Murder.* New York: Stackpole, 1936.

Guide to the U.S. Supreme Court. Washington, D.C.: Congressional Quarterly, Inc., 1979.

"Had Not Given Up Hope." *Atlanta Constitution*, 18 August 1915, p. 3.

Hahn, Steven. *The Roots of Southern Populism: Yeoman Farmers and the Transformation of the Georgia Upcountry, 1850–1890.* New York: Oxford University Press, 1983.

Hammond, Edmund Jordan. *The Methodist Episcopal Church in Georgia.* Atlanta: n.p., 1935.

Hammond, John W. "Leo Frank's Dying Statement Given in Missing Chapter of Milledgeville-Marietta Story." *Athens Banner* (Ga.), 24 August 1915.

Handlin, Oscar. "American Views of the Jew at the Opening of the Twentieth Century." *American Jewish Historical Quarterly* 40 (1951): 323–44.

Harris, Art. "Frank Case Still Painful for Atlanta's Jews." *The Washington Post*, 14 March 1982, p. A12.

Harris, Nathaniel Edwin. *Autobiography: The Story of an Old Man's*

Life with Reminiscences of Seventy-Five Years. Macon, Ga.: J. W. Burke Co., 1925.

"Harris to Probe Frank Lynching." *Atlanta Constitution*, 18 August 1915, p. 1.

Henig, Gerald S. "California Progressives React to the Leo Frank Case." *California History* 58 (1979): 166–78.

Henson, Allen Lumpkin. *Confessions of a Crminal Lawyer.* New York: Vantage Press, 1959.

The Herald and Presbyter, 25 August 1915, p. 28.

"Here Is Testimony of Witnesses Given at the Final Session of Coroner's Jury in Phagan Case." *Atlanta Journal*, 9 May 1913.

Hertzberg, Steven. "The Jewish Community of Atlanta from the End of the Civil War Until the Eve of the Frank Case." *American Jewish Historical Quarterly* 62 (1973): 250–85.

Hertzberg, Steven. *Strangers Within the Gate City: The Jews of Atlanta 1845–1915.* Philadelphia: Jewish Publication Society, 1978.

Higham, John. "Anti-Semitism in the Gilded Age: A Reinterpretation." *Mississippi Valley Historical Review* 43 (1957): 559–78.

Higham, John. "Social Discrimination Against Jews in America, 1830–1930." *American Jewish Historical Quarterly* 47 (1957): 1–33.

Hill, Samuel S., ed. *Encyclopedia of Religion in the South.* Macon, Ga.: Mercer University Press, 1984.

Hofstadter, Richard. *The Age of Reform: From Bryan to F.D.R.* New York: Alfred A. Knopf, 1955.

"Holloway Denies Affidavit He Signed for Solicitor." *Atlanta Constitution*, 1 August 1913, p. 1.

"How Mob Carried Out Its Attack on Prison Buildings." *Atlanta Journal*, 17 August 1915, p. 3.

Howe, Mark DeWolfe, ed. *Holmes-Laski Letters: The Correspondence of Mr. Justice Holmes and Harold J. Laski.* Cambridge: Harvard University Press, 1953.

Howe, Mark DeWolfe, ed. *Holmes-Pollock Letters: The Corres-pondence of Mr. Justice Holmes and Sir Frederick Pollock 1874–1932*. Cambridge: Harvard University Press, 1941.

Hudson, Winthrop S. *Religion in America: An Historical Account of the Development of American Religious Life*. 2d ed. New York: Charles Scribner's Sons, 1965.

Hurtel, Gordon Noel. "Mystery of 14–Year-Old Mary Phagan's Tragic End Adds One to Long List of Atlanta's Unsolved Crimes." *Atlanta Constitution*, 10 May 1913, p. 2G.

Information Please Almanac Atlas & Yearbook 1985. 38th ed. Boston: Houghton Mifflin Co., 1985.

"Inquest This Morning." *Atlanta Constitution*, 30 April 1913.

"Is a Dreyfus Case Possible in America?" *The Independent* LXI (1906): 166–68.

"J. L. Watkins Says He Did Not See Phagan Child on Day of Tragedy." *Atlanta Journal*, 8 May 1913, p. 8.

"J. M. Gantt Is Arrested on His Arrival in Marietta; He Visited Factory Saturday." *Atlanta Journal*, 28 April 1913, p. 1.

Jackson, Kenneth T. *The Ku Klux Klan in the City 1915–1930*. New York: Oxford University Press, 1967.

"Jews for Preparedness." *New York Times*, 5 May 1916.

Johnson, Haynes. "Those Were the Bad Old Days; It Couldn't Happen Now." *The Washington Post*, 14 March 1982, p. A3.

"The Journal's Big Story of Dictograph and Alleged Bribe Has Stirred the Whole City." *Atlanta Journal*, 24 May 1913, p. 3.

Joyce, Fay S. "Pardon Denied for Leo Frank in 1913 Slaying." *New York Times*, 23 December 1983, p. A10.

"Judge Roan's Charge to Jury; Deals with Reasonable Doubt." *Atlanta Constitution*, 26 August 1913, p. 4.

"Jury Selected to Try Frank. " *Atlanta Constitution*, 29 July 1913, p. 1.

Katz, Jacob. *Exclusiveness and Tolerance: Studies in Jewish-Gentile*

Relations in Medieval and Modern Times. New York: Behrman House, 1983.

Keppel, David. "Editor's Outlook." *Northern Christian Advocate*, 26 August 1915, p. 5.

"Klan Fights Plan to Pardon Frank." *Atlanta Constitution and Journal*, 4 September 1983.

Kohl, Manfred Waldemar. *Congregationalism in America*. Oak Creek, Wisc.: Congregational Press, 1977.

"L. M. Frank, Factory Superintendent, Detained by Police." *Atlanta Journal*, 29 April 1913, p. 1.

"Lanford Is the Controlling Genius of Conspiracy to Protect the Murder of Little Mary Phagan." *Atlanta Journal*, 25 May 1913, p. 5.

Lankevich, George J., comp. and ed. *Atlanta: A Chronological and Documentary History 1813–1976*. Dobbs Ferry, N.Y.: Oceana Publications, Inc., 1978.

"Last Legal Stage of the Frank Case." *Outlook* 109 (1915): 958–59.

"Leaders Needed by Jews Says Gov. Alexander." *Christian Science Monitor*, 25 August 1915, p. 1.

"Lee, Dull and Ignorant, Calm Under Gruelling [sic] Cross Fire." *Atlanta Constitution*, 30 July 1913.

"Lemmie Quinn Grilled by Coroner But He Sticks to His Statement." *Atlanta Journal*, 8 May 1913, p. 8.

"Leo Frank." *New Republic* 3 (1915): 300.

"Leo Frank and the Liberty of the Press." *America* XIII (1915): 494.

"The Leo Frank Case." *ADL Bulletin*, February 1984, p.7.

"Leo Frank Expressed Hope of Vindication in Letter July 4." *Atlanta Journal*, 17 August 1915, p. 3.

"Leo Frank Forcibly Taken from Prison; He Is Hanged to a Tree

Near Marietta; His Body Has Been Brought to Atlanta."
Atlanta Journal, 17 August 1915, p. 1.

"Leo Frank Hanged by Mob." *Christian Observer*, 25 August
1915, p. 839.

"Leo Frank Lynched." *The United Presbyterian*, 26 August 1915,
p. 7.

"Leo Frank Pardoned." *ADL Bulletin*, April 1986, p. 3.

"Leo Frank Pardoned." *The National Jewish Post & Opinion*, 19
March 1986, p. 2.

"Leo Frank Taken from Prison by Armed Men; Vow to Put His
Body on Mary Phagan's Grave." *The Washington Post*, 17 August 1915, p. 1.

"Leo Frank's Accuser Shot." *New York Times*, 18 January 1919.

"Leo M. Frank Holds Conference with Lee." *Atlanta Constitution*, 30 April 1913, p. 1.

"Leo M. Frank Indicted for Murder of Girl, No Action Against
Lee; Negro Swears Frank Asked Him to Write Certain Notes
on Friday; Woodward Sought Evidence Against Both Chiefs,
Says Dictograph." *Atlanta Journal*, 24 May 1913, p. 1.

"Leo M. Frank Kidnapped." *Christian Science Monitor*, 17 August
1915, p. 4.

"Leo M. Frank Kidnapped at Night from Georgia State Prison
Farm by Armed Men in an Automobile." *New York Times*, 17
August 1915, p. 1.

"Leon [sic] Frank Pardoned by Georgia Board." *Baltimore Jewish
Times*, 21 March 1986, p. 5.

"Lesson from Frank Case." *New York Times*, 28 December 1914,
p. 4.

"A Letter on the Frank Case and a Reply to It." *New York Times*,
10 January 1915.

"Letters by Frank Are Made Public." *Atlanta Constitution*, 18
August 1915, p. 3.

Levy, Eugene. " 'Is the Jew a White Man?': Press Reaction to the Leo Frank Case, 1913–1915." *Phylon* 35 (1974): 212–22.

Lhamon, W. J. "Why Does the Jew Remain?" *Christian Century*, 2 October 1913, p. 8.

"Lied Against Frank, A Newsboy Swears." *New York Times*, 5 March 1914.

"Likens Frank to Beilis." *New York Times*, 22 March 1914, p. 1.

Lippy, Charles H. *Bibliography of Religion in the South*. Macon, Ga.: Mercer University Press, 1985.

"Local Ministers Preach Very Strong Sermons." *Valdosta Daily Times*, 24 August 1915, p. 3.

"Lots of Easier Ways to Earn $2 a Day Than Being a Juror." *Atlanta Constitution*, 3 August 1913, p. 3.

"Loyal Wife of Leo Frank, Condemned to Die Begs Americans to Believe Him Innocent." *Southwest American* [Fort Smith, Ark.], 4 May 1915.

Lucchese, Sam F. "Leo Frank Case One of Notable Eight in Busch's Notable American Trials."

"Lynching in the Southern States." *Spectator*, 5 February 1921, pp. 166–67.

"The Lynching of Frank." *The Epworth Herald*, 4 September 1915, p. 862.

"The Lynching of Frank." *Lutheran Church Work*, 2 September 1915, p. 2.

"The Lynching of Frank." *The Reformed Church Messenger* LXXXIV (1915): 22.

"The Lynching of Leo Frank." *The Christian Register*, 9 September 1915, p. 861.

"The Lynching of Leo Frank." *The Presbyterian Banner*, 26 August 1915, p. 6.

"Lynching of Leo Frank Denounced by Daniels." *Atlanta Constitution*, 18 August 1915, p. 3.

Malone, Henry T. *The Episcopal Church in Georgia, 1733–1957.* Atlanta: Protestant Episcopal Church in the Diocese of Atlanta, 1960.

"Man Held for Girl's Murder Avows He Was with Another When Witness Saw Him Last." *Atlanta Journal,* 28 April 1913, p. 2.

"Marietta Officials Didn't Know of Mob." *Atlanta Journal,* 17 August 1915, p. 3.

Marrus, Michael R. *The Politics of Assimilation: The French Jewish Community at the Time of the Dreyfus Affair.* Oxford: Clarendon Press, 1980.

"Marshall Denies Dorsey's Charges." *New York Times,* 13 September 1916.

Marshall, Edward. " 'Frank Is Innocent'—Burns." *New York Times,* 20 December 1914, p. 9.

Martin, Thomas H., comp. *Hand Book of the City of Atlanta: A Comprehensive Review of the City's Commercial Industrial and Residential Conditions.* Southern Industrial Publishing Co., 1908(?). [Atlanta City Council and Atlanta Chamber of Commerce]

Martz, Ron. "The Mary Phagan Legacy." *Atlanta Constitution,* 22 September 1983.

Martz, Ron. "Pardon Asked 70 Years Later for Leo Frank." *Atlanta Journal and Constitution,* 22 March 1987.

"Mary Phagan at Home Last Friday, Says Mother." *Atlanta Journal,* 30 April 1913, p. 7.

"Mary Phagan Speaks." *Christian Century,* 2 September 1915, p. 8.

"A Matter to Be Seriously Pondered." *Wesleyan Christian Advocate,* 27 August 1915, pp. 3–4.

Melton, R. H. "A Virginia Ham." *The Washington Post,* 5 June 1987.

Mendes-Flohr, Paul R., and Reinharz, Jehuda., eds. *The Jew in the*

Modern World: A Documentary History. New York: Oxford University Press, 1980.

"Ministers Ask for New Trial." *Florida Times-Union*, 16 March 1914.

"Ministers in Pulpits Urge New Trial for Frank." *Louisville Courier-Journal*, 16 March 1914.

"Miss Daisy Jones Convinces Jury She Was Mistaken for Mary Phagan." *Atlanta Journal*, 8 May 1913, p. 8.

"Miss Hattie Hall, Stenographer, Left Pencil Factory at Noon." *Atlanta Journal*, 8 May 1913, p. 8.

"Mississippi Mob Lynches a Negro." *New York Times*, 21 January 1915.

"Mob Hanging Better Than Judicial Murder Says John M. Slaton." *Atlanta Constitution*, 18 August 1915, p. 1.

"Mob's Own Story in Detail." *Atlanta Constitution*, 18 August 1915, p. 1.

Montgomery, Bill. "Accuser's Lawyer Risked Safety After Taking Up Frank's Cause." *Atlanta Journal and Constitution*, 4 May 1982.

"More Pastors Urge Retrial for Frank." *New York Times*, 23 March 1914.

"More Than 6000 Frank Petitions Are Received." *The Daily News* [San Francisco], 13 May 1915.

Moseley, Charlton. "Latent Klanism in Georgia, 1890–1915." *Georgia Historical Quarterly* 56 (1972): 365–86.

Moseley, Clement Charlton. "The Case of Leo M. Frank, 1913–1915." *Georgia Historical Quarterly* 51 (1967): 42–62.

Moton, Robert R. "The South and the Lynching Evil." *South Atlantic Quarterly* 18 (1919): 191–96.

Mott, Frank Luther. *American Journalism A History: 1690–1960*. 3d ed. New York: MacMillan, 1962.

"Movies Not Permitted to Use Frank Pictures." *Macon Daily Telegraph*, 20 August 1915.

"Mr. Frank's Treatment of Girls Unimpeachable, Says Miss Hall." *Atlanta Journal*, 8 May 1913, p. 8.

"Mrs. Frank Goes to Relatives in Athens." *Atlanta Journal*, 17 August 1915, p. 2.

"Mrs. Frank on Verge of Collapse on Train." *Macon Daily Telegraph*, 20 August 1915.

"Mullinax Held in Phagan Case." *Atlanta Constitution*, 28 April 1913, p. 1.

"The Murder of Frank." *The Congregationalist and Christian World* C (1915): 275.

Nashville Tennessean. Special News Section. 7 March 1982. [Contributions by Frank Ritter, Jerry Thompson, Bob Sherborne, Sandra Roberts, and John Seigenthaler.]

National Cyclopedia of American Biography. New York: James T. White & Co. Volumes III, XVIII, 26, and 52. [Year varies with volume]

"Negro Lurking in Factory Seen by Wife of Employee." *Atlanta Constitution*, 2 August 1913, p. 3.

"Negro Shot to Death by 'Tarheel' Mob." *Atlanta Constitution*, 26 August 1913, p. 1.

"Negro Watchman Tells Story of Finding Girl's Body and Questions Fail to Shake Him." *Atlanta Journal*, 30 April 1913, p. 1.

"Negro Watchman Wrote Note Found Beside Dead Girl, Experts Declare, After Seeing Frank's Handwrighting [sic]." *Atlanta Journal*, 30 April 1913, p. 1.

Newman, Harvey Knupp. "The Vision of Order: White Protestant Christianity in Atlanta, 1865–1906." Ph.D. dissertation, Emory University, 1977.

"Newt Lee Tells of the Talk He Had in the Popice [sic] Station." *Atlanta Journal*, 9 May 1913.

Night Witch. [a play]

"No Active Pursuit by Frank Family." *New York Times*, 22 August 1915, p. 11.

"No Lamar Decision Yet." *New York Times*, 27 December 1914, p. 12.

"Officer Tells About Discovery of Body of Girl in Basement." *Atlanta Constitution*, 30 July 1913.

"The Official Record in the Case of Leo Frank, a Jew Pervert." *Watson's Magazine*, September 1915, pp. 251–97.

"One Frank Lyncher Said to Be Known." *New York Times*, 22 August 1915, p. 11.

Oney, Steve. "The Lynching of Leo Frank." *Esquire*, September 1985, pp. 90–104.

Ostash, Aaron. "The Leo Frank Case: 1982 Update." *Jewish Digest*, October 1982, pp. 55–57.

"Other Tragedies Near Phagan Murder Scene." *Atlanta Journal*, 30 April 1913.

"An Outlaw State." *Outlook* 110 (1915): 945–47.

" 'An Outlaw State'. " *Wesleyan Christian Advocate*, 3 September 1915, pp. 1–2.

Oxman, Daniel K. "California Reactions to the Leo Frank Case." *Western States Jewish Historical Quarterly* 10 (1978): 216–24.

"Pardon Held Unlikely for Leo Frank." *The Washington Post*, 14 March 1982, p. A2.

Parker, D. M. "A Georgian on Justice." *New Republic* 4 (1915): 23.

Peterson, Theodore. *Magazines in the Twentieth Century*. Urbana: University of Illinois Press, 1956.

"Petition for Frank Signed by 15,000." *New York Times*, 12 May 1915.

"Phagan Inquest in Session; Six Witnesses Are Examined Before Adjournment to 2:30." *Atlanta Journal*, 8 May 1913, p. 1.

"Phagan Trial Will Be Great Legal Battle." *Atlanta Constitution,* 27 July 1913, p. 3.

"Pictures of Fifty Girls Found in Search of Bowen's Trunk." *Atlanta Journal,* 6 May 1913.

"Pinkertons Hired to Assist Police Probe the Murder of Mary Phagan." *Atlanta Constitution,* 29 April 1913.

"Plan to Pursue Frank." *New York Times,* 1 February 1915.

Plotte, Monte. "NBC Plans Leo Frank Miniseries." *Atlanta Journal and Constitution,* 22 March 1987.

"Police Think Negro Watchman Can Clear Murder Mystery; Four Are Now Under Arrest." *Atlanta Journal,* 28 April 1913, p. 1.

"Policeman W. F. Anderson Tells of Newt Lee's Telephone Call." *Atlanta Constitution,* 2 August 1913, p. 3.

"Posses Chase Frank Mob." *Atlanta Constitution,* 17 August 1915, p. 1.

Powell, Arthur Gray. *I Can Go Home Again.* Chapel Hill: University of North Carolina Press, 1943.

"Prison Officers Tell Graphic Stories of Seizure of Frank." *Atlanta Journal,* 17 August 1915, p. 2.

"Prison Officials Held Blameless." *Atlanta Constitution,* 18 August 1915, p. 3.

Proctor, H. H. "An Uncovering of the South: Local Sidelights on the Frank Case." *The Congregationalist and Christian World* C (1915): 364.

"Pulpit Appeal for Frank." *New York Times,* 26 April 1915.

"Pulpit for Frank." *The Washington Post,* 16 March 1914, p. 3.

Ragan, Fred. "Obscenity or Politics?: Tom Watson, Anti-Catholicism, and the Department of Justice." *Georgia Historical Quarterly* 70 (1986): 17–46.

"Ragsdale Swears to Perjury Plot." *New York Times,* 29 January 1915.

Ready, Milton L. "Georgia's Entry Into World War I." *Georgia Historical Quarterly* 52 (1968): 256–64.

"Recalls the Frank Case." *New York Times*, 11 June 1919, p. 9.

"The Remedy for Lynching." *The Christian Register*, 19 August 1915, p. 771.

"Replies to Attorney Rosser." *New York Times*, 5 March 1914.

"Reward of $1,000 Is Appropriated by City." *Atlanta Journal*, 30 April 1913, p. 7.

Richardson, Ernest Cushing. *Religious Periodicals Currently Taken–1934*. Washington, D.C.: Library of Congress, 1934.

"Rogers Describes Mr. Frank's Manner When Told of Tragedy." *Atlanta Journal*, 8 May 1913, p. 1.

Rosenbaum, Stanley N. " 'Our Willie' and the Leo Frank Case." *Christian Century*, 9 October 1985, pp. 887–88.

Ross, Edward Alsworth. "The Hebrews of Eastern Europe in America." *The Century Magazine*, 1914, pp. 785–92.

Rothschild, Janice O. *As But a Day: The First Hundred Years, 1867–1967*. Atlanta: Hebrew Benevolent Congregation, The Temple, 1967.

Rudavsky, Shari. "Senior's Thesis Contributes to Pardon in 70-Year-Old Georgia Murder Case." *The Harvard Crimson*, 1 April 1986.

"Rumor That Frank Married in Brooklyn Not True, Says Eagle." *Atlanta Journal*, 12 May 1913.

Samuels, Charles., and Samuels, Louise. *Night Fell on Georgia*. New York: Dell Publishing Company, 1956.

"Says His Analysis Vindicates Frank." *New York Times*, 27 December 1914, p. 12.

"Says State Is on Trial." *Atlanta Constitution*, 18 August 1915, p. 3.

Schmeir, Louis E. " 'No Jew Can Murder': Memories of Tom

Watson and the Lichtenstein Murder Case of 1901." *Georgia Historical Quarterly* 70 (1986): 433–55.

Schmeir, Louis E. "Notes and Documents on the 1862 Expulsion of Jews from Thomasville, Georgia." *American Jewish Archives* 32 (1980): 9–22.

Seigenthaler, John. "New Light Shed on Old Murder." *Nashville Tennessean*, 7 March 1982.

"Sentenced to Death for Killing Employee." *The Mennonite* XXVIII (1913): 7.

"Sergeant Dobbs Resumes Stand At Tuesday Afternoon Session." *Atlanta Constitution*, 30 July 1913.

"The Shame of Georgia." *The Presbyterian Banner*, 26 August 1915, p. 8.

"The Shame of It." *The Universalist Leader*, 28 August 1915, p. 819.

Shankman, Arnold. "Atlanta Jewry 1900–1930." *American Jewish Archives* 25(2): 131–55.

Sheldon, Winthrop D. "Shall Lynching Be Suppressed?" *Outlook* 111 (1915): 152.

Shewmaker, W. O. "A Kentucky Lynching That Didn't Occur." *The Continent*, 19 August 1915, p. 1106.

Shipp, Bill. *Murder at Broad River Bridge: The Slaying of Lemuel Penn by Members of the Ku Klux Klan.* Atlanta: Peachtree Publishers, 1981.

Sibley, Celestine. "Players Gone, Not Forgotten." *Atlanta Constitution*, 3 March 1978, pp. 1–A, 30–A.

"Slaton Gives Reasons For Commuting Frank." *Atlanta Journal*, 21 June 1915, p. 1.

Smith, Charles Henry. *The Story of the Mennonites.* 3d ed., rev. Enl by Cornelius Krahn. Newton, Kan.: Mennonite Publication Office, 1950.

Smith, Hilrie Shelton. *In His Image, But . . . : Racism in Southern*

Religion, 1780–1910. Durham, N.C.: Duke University Press, 1972.

Smith, R. G. "Some Lurid Lessons from the Frank Case." *Public* 18 (1915): 952–53.

Smith, W. M. "Discussion of the 'Murder Notes'." [John Marshall Slaton Collection, AC# 00-070; Georgia Department of Archives and History]

"Smith's Change Voluntary." *New York Times*, 4 October 1914, p. 13.

Snyder, F. B., ed. "Leo Frank and Mary Phagan." *Journal of American Folklore* 31 (1918): 264–66.

Snyder, Gerald. "Leo Frank: 'An Innocent Man Was Lynched'." *Jewish Monthly*, October 1982, pp. 22–24.

Sobel, Robert., and John Raimo., eds. *Biographical Directory of the Governors of the United States 1789–1978.* Westport, Conn.: Meckler Books, 1978.

"Solicitor Dorsey Is Making Independent Probe of Phagan Case." *Atlanta Journal*, 2 May 1913, p. 1.

"Souvenirs of Frank Lynching Were Sought." *Valdosta Daily Times*, 18 August 1915, p. 1.

Speer, Robert Elliott. "Inadequate Religions: How the Religion of Jesus Christ Fares Amid the Wreckage of Ancient Faiths." *Christian Century*, 29 October 1914. [unpaged]

Stacey, James. *A History of the Presbyterian Church in Georgia.* Atlanta: Westminster Co., 1912. "Stains on Shirt Were Not Made While Shirt Was Being Worn." *Atlanta Journal*, 8 May 1913, p. 8.

"Stepfather Thinks Negro Is Murderer." *Atlanta Journal*, 29 April 1913.

"Story of Paul Bowen's Arrest As Told by Associated Press." *Atlanta Journal*, 6 May 1913.

"Strand of Hair in Machine on Second Floor May Be Clew [sic] Left by Mary Phagan." *Atlanta Journal*, 28 April 1913, p. 2.

Straus, Hal., and O'Shea, Brian. "Lynched Factory Manager Vindicated, Jewish Groups Say." *Atlanta Constitution*, 12 March 1986.

"Superintendent Frank Is Once More Put on Witness Stand." *Atlanta Journal*, 9 May 1913.

Survey, 14 February 1914, p. 625.

Taylor, Ron. "Digging Into Case Uncovered Ugly Chapter of City's History." *Atlanta Constitution*, 12 March 1986.

"There Is Another Side." *Wesleyan Christian Advocate*, 10 September 1915, pp. 3–4.

They Don't Forget. [motion picture] 1937.

Thirty Years of Lynching in the United States 1889–1918. New York: Negro Universities Press, 1969. [Originally published in 1919 by the National Association for the Advancement of Colored People.]

Thompson, Ernest Trice. *Presbyterians in the South*. Richmond: John Knox Press, 1963–1973. [3 vols.]

Thompson, Wytt Ephraim. *A Short Review of the Frank Case*. Atlanta: 1914.

"$1,000 Bribe Offer to Implicate Frank." *New York Times*, 15 March 1914, p. 9.

"$1,000 Reward." *Atlanta Constitution*, 29 April 1913.

"Three Witnesses Describe Finding Mary Phagan's Body." *Atlanta Constitution*, 30 July 1913, p. 1.

Trachtenberg, Joshua. *The Devil and the Jews: The Medieval Conception of the Jew and Its Relation to Modern Antisemitism*. Philadelphia: Jewish Publication Society, 1983.

Train, Arthur. "Did Leo Frank Get Justice?" *Everybody's* 32 (1915): 314–17.

"Trial of Leo M. Frank on Charge of Murder Begins; Mrs. Coleman, George Eeps and Newt Lee on Stand." *Atlanta Constitution*, 29 July 1913, p. 1.

"20 Year Jail Sentence for Connally [sic]." *New York Times*, 25 February 1919, p. 5.

"Two Murdering Notes Add Mystery to Crime." *Atlanta Journal*, 28 April 1913, p. 2.

"Two New Witnesses in Phagan Mystery to Testify Thursday." *Atlanta Journal*, 7 May 1913, p. 1.

"$2,200 Reward!" *Atlanta Constitution*, 30 April 1913.

"A Typical Eastern Comment on the Lynching of Leo Frank." *Atlanta Journal*, 19 August 1915.

"Unusual Interest Centers in Mrs. Frank's Appearance." *Atlanta Constitution*, 29 July 1913.

"Use of Dictaphone on Frank and Negro Is Denied by Police." *Atlanta Journal*, 30 April 1913, 1.

" 'Vilifying a State.' " *Nation* 101 (1915): 251–52.

Volkman, Ernest. *A Legacy of Hate: Anti-Semitism in America.* New York: Franklin Watts, 1982.

"A Warning to Be Heeded." *Wesleyan Christian Advocate*, 15 October 1915, pp. 4–5.

" 'We Have Enough Votes If We Get the Evidence,' The Mayor Is Quoted by the Dictograph." *Atlanta Journal*, 24 May 1913, p. 1.

Wesleyan Christian Advocate, 27 August 1915, p. 6.

Wesleyan Christian Advocate, 10 September 1915, p. 9.

Wesleyan Christian Advocate, 17 September 1915, p. 6.

"Where Was Mary Phagan on Saturday Afternoon?" *Atlanta Journal*, 29 April 1913, p. 4.

"While Hundreds Sob Body of Mary Phagan Lowered into Grave." *Atlanta Constitution*, 30 April 1913.

"Who Saw Pretty Mary Phagan After 12 O'Clock on Saturday?" *Atlanta Constitution*, 29 April 1913.

Who's Who in America. 44th ed. Wilmette, Ill.: Macmillan Directory Division, 1986–1987. [Marquis Who's Who]

"Why Was Frank Lynched?" *Forum* 56 (1916): 677–92.

"Will Leo Frank's Lawyers Put Any Evidence Before the Jury?" *Atlanta Constitution,* 29 July 1913.

"Witnesses Positive Murdered Girl Was Same Who Created Scene at the Terminal Station on Friday." *Atlanta Journal,* 29 April 1913, p. 1.

"Woman's Assailant Lynched in Decatur." *Atlanta Constitution,* 18 August 1915, p. 1.

Woods, Henry. "The Crime at Marietta." *America* XIII (1915): 535–37.

Woodward, Comer Vann. *Tom Watson: Agrarian Rebel.* 2d ed. Savannah, Ga.: Beehive Press, 1973.

"Wouldn't Trust Ragsdale on Oath." *New York Times,* 30 January 1915, p. 8.

Yates, Bowling C. *Historic Highlights in Cobb County.* Marietta, Ga.: Cobb Exchange Bank, 1973.

Yoemans, Manning Jasper. "Some Facts About the Frank Case." [Atlanta Miscellany File, # 572, Box 2; Emory University, Robert W. Woodruff Library, Special Collections Department]

Zoren, Neal. "Virginia a Stand-in for Georgia in 'The Ballad of Mary Phagan'." *Atlanta Constitution,* 25 June 1987.

Legal Sources

Affidavit in the State of Tennessee, County of Sullivan. [Alonzo McClendon Mann; Gore & Hillman Attorneys, Bristol, Tennessee; March 4, 1982.] (Anti-Defamation League of B'nai B'rith in Atlanta)

Annie Maud Carter Affidavit. (Anti-Defamation League of B'nai B'rith in Atlanta)

Decision in Response to Application for Posthumous Pardon for Leo M.

Frank. [State Board of Pardons and Paroles, 1983.] (Personality File; Atlanta Historical Society)

Frank v. *The State.* [Supreme Court of Georgia, October Term, 1913.] (Microfilm 260/56 & 57 6–3911 & 6–3912; Georgia Department of Archives and History)

Leo M. Frank, Appellant v. *C. Wheeler Mangum, Sheriff of Fulton County, Georgia Apellee.* [Supreme Court of the United States, October Term, 1914, No. 775.] (John Marshall Slaton Collection, AC# 00-070; Georgia Department of Archives and History)

Pardon. [Signed by Wayne Snow Jr., March 11, 1986.] (Anti-Defamation League of B'nai B'rith in Atlanta)

Petition for Writ of Habeas Corpus. [District Court of the United States for the Northern District of Georgia, October Term, 1914.] (Leo Frank File, MSS91, Box 6, Folder 16; Atlanta Historical Society)

Personal Interviews

Charles Wittenstein: Southern counsel for the Anti-Defamation League of B'nai B'rith, at his home in Atlanta. May 27, 1987.

Special Collections and Archives

Atlanta Historical Society
Leo Frank File MSS91
"Personality File"

Emory University
Robert W. Woodruff Library, Special Collections Department
Atlanta Miscellany File # 572, Box 2

Georgia Department of Archives and History
John Marshall Slaton Collection 2094–01, 51–60 (restricted)
Materials in the John Marshall Slaton Collection (AC# 00–070) survived two fires before being housed in the Department of Archives. The full collection went to the Archives in 1979.

Harvard Law School Library
Oliver Wendell Holmes Jr. Papers: containers 4, 12, 34, and
Paige Box

Telephone Conversations

Janice Rothschild Blumberg: Author of *As But a Day*, board
member of the American Jewish Historical Society. June 2,
1987.

Mary Phagan: Great-niece of the murdered girl. June 13, 1987
and June 14, 1987 (Nancy Thompson-Frey).

Dale Schwartz: Attorney with Troutman, Sanders, Lockerman &
Ashmore. June 1, 1987.

John Seigenthaler: Publisher of *Nashville Tennessean* and Editorial
Director of *USA Today*. July 22, 1987 and July 30, 1987 (Nancy
Thompson-Frey).

Jerry Thompson: Reporter for the *Nashville Tennessean*. August 4,
1987 (Nancy Thompson-Frey).

INDEX

M